NICOMEDES GUZMÁN

NICOMEDES GUZMÁN

PROLETARIAN AUTHOR IN CHILE'S

LITERARY GENERATION OF 1938

LON PEARSON

University of Missouri Press, 1976

ISBN 0–8262–0178–4
Library of Congress Catalog Card Number 75–19334
Copyright © 1976 by The Curators of the University of Missouri
Printed and bound in the United States of America

Library of Congress Cataloging in Publication Data

Pearson, Lon, 1939–
    Nicomedes Guzmán, proletarian author in Chile's
literary generation of 1938.

    Bibliography: p.
    Includes index.
    1. Guzmán, Nicomedes, 1914–   I. Title.
PQ8097.G85Z8   863 [B]   75–19334
ISBN 0–8262–0178–4

TO MY MOTHER AND MY WIFE

Acknowledgments

For their assistance and consideration in my research on Nicomedes Guzmán, I am indebted to many people in Chile. Letters, articles, and books were sent me by Marcial Tamayo, the late Padre Alfonso Escudero, and Professor Eduardo Godoy Gallardo of the University of Chile, who also extended his hospitality to me during my stays in Valparaíso. I am indebted to Lucía Salazar, Ester Panay, and other members of Guzmán's family for their hospitality and for allowing me to see books, manuscripts, articles, letters, and pictures during my visits. To Homero Bascuñán and other members of Guzmán's generation I am indebted for books, articles, and much kindness. In addition to the ideas and criticism offered by countless professors in Chile, the following administrators of the University of Chile made suggestions and provided facilities: Professor Juan Uribe Echevarría, Department of Extension and Social Action; Professor Carlos Santander, Chairman, Department of Spanish, East Campus; Professor Hernán Loyola, Director, Institute of Chilean Literature; and Dean Armando Cassígoli, School of Philosophy and Letters, East Campus, who as President of the Sociedad de Escritores Chilenos invited me to visit sessions of that group where I was introduced to several of Guzmán's colleagues.

Summer Fellowships in 1971 and 1973 that permitted me to go to Chile to obtain research materials were provided by the Office of the Dean of the Graduate School, University of Missouri—Rolla. Smaller subsequent grants from that office were extended for photocopying and for travel. I owe much to my colleagues at the University of Missouri for helpful suggestions, books, and research facilities.

I would also like to give special thanks to the Dean of Arts and Sciences of The Johns Hopkins University for making available a grant to computerize the index, and to Professor William W. Huggins and Paul S. Hartman who worked with me on the project.

Permission to quote from Guzmán's *Una moneda al río y otros cuentos* has been granted by Paul J. Cooke of the Monticello College Press. Jean Franco has allowed me to quote from *An Introduction to Spanish-American Literature*, as has Russell Owen Salmon from his dissertation, "The *Roto* in Chilean Prose Fiction." A personal note of thanks is due to Thomas Edgar (Ted) Lyon for his permission to quote from *Juan Godoy* and for his warm and inspiring counsel.

I am especially happy to thank the following people who have assisted directly in this study. Professors John A. Crow and John E. Englekirk of the University of California, Los Angeles, gave me guidance, counsel, encouragement, and constructive criticism. Professors Donald F. Fogelquist and J. Donald Bowen, University of California, Los Angeles, Juan Loveluck, University of South Carolina, and Guzmán's widow, Ester Panay, also read the manuscript and suggested improvements. I thank most sincerely Professor Fernando Alegría, Stanford University, for offering to read the manuscript in its final form. His perceptive comments on the study allowed me to correct some inadvertant exaggerations that made Guzmán look less humble than he actually was. Professor Alegría extended permission to quote from *Literatura chilena del siglo XX*. Last, I wish to express my gratitude to my wife, Janet, for typing, editing, and countless other tasks that she shared with me.

Contents

I

Nicomedes Guzmán:
An Obscure Proletarian Existence

1

Youth and Formative Years

All the words ever recorded about Nicomedes Guzmán's life, whether biographies, autobiographies, or merely anecdotes, reflect a unanimous opinion: he was extremely modest. His life and his personality revealed a tremendous humility and cordiality, which stemmed in part from his lower-class birth.

His inherent humility and his humble origins led him to identify deeply with the Chilean masses. His life, his writings, and his philosophy purposefully accentuate the exceptional fact that he was totally proletarian, both in origin and philosophy.

The second of twelve children born to Rosa Guzmán Acevedo and Nicomedes Vásquez Arzola, Nicomedes Guzmán bore the full name of Oscar Nicomedes Vásquez Guzmán. He was born on June 25, 1914, on Rondizzoni Street in "Club Hípico," an extremely poor section near the old Parque Cousiño on the southern outskirts of Santiago, Chile. He placed particular importance on the year of his birth, for he felt that his psychological development was affected by the debacle of World War I and that crucial factors in his career and personal philosophy were determined by the era in which he was born. Guzmán died in Santiago, on June 26, 1964, the day after his fiftieth birthday.

When he was four or five years old, his family moved, and Nicomedes grew up in a different area of the city, near the streetcar depot, a place he called Barrio Mapocho, which was a slum district contiguous to the Mapocho River—a "squalid stream" full of garbage, filth, and disease. This neighborhood attracted the dregs of society: vagabonds and other poverty-stricken persons who subsisted through their half-hearted efforts as rag pickers and rubbish or tin collectors.

It was in these slums that the young Nicomedes saw and experienced the great contrasts that were later incorporated into his writing and view of life. In spite of the poverty, squalor, and tragedy he witnessed in his barrio, Guzmán was able to discover and portray surprising elements of beauty, especially in his poetic descriptions of nature.

The details of his boyhood experiences in these neighborhoods are sketchy. A childhood friend of Guzmán's, Marcial Tamayo, has nevertheless taken advantage of the author's fame to publish newspaper articles on their relationship.

The Vásquez family moved several times during these years, generally remaining within the Quinta Normal district of Santiago. When Nicomedes entered school at five years of age, he wore thick eyeglasses to correct a congenital cross-eyed condition. Children singled out his defect and taunted him, calling him "Mampara" (glass doors) until his mother insisted that doctors correct his condition through surgery. She also put him into a new school at this time, perhaps to give him a fresh start with new friends. The child soon proved himself to be extremely talented, with a special gift for drawing and sketching. Throughout his educational career, short as it was, he always excelled in his studies.

Guzmán seldom wrote about his personal life, but when he did he often repeated the same essential details, as if he were cautiously avoiding any possible contradictions. His reticence may be due simply to the fact that, until 1953, no one requested intimate autobiographical data from Guzmán and that Guzmán answered subsequent requests for information with copies of the manuscript he had sent Paul J. Cooke of the Monticello College Press in 1953.[1] Perhaps it is for this reason that Fernando Santiván feels that there is no intentional contradiction when Guzmán writes in one place that his father is a streetcar mechanic (*maquinista tranviario*) and in another—the dedication to his first novel—that he is an ice cream peddler:

A MI PADRE,   heladero ambulante;
Y A MI MADRE,   obrera doméstica.

The mother had to help supplement the family's income by caring for upper-class homes on occasion, and the father, a typical unskilled laborer who had to earn money wherever he could, changed jobs often. Recently some of the previously obscure elements of the novelist's life have been made public by his son, the journalist

---

1. The rough draft of Guzmán's autobiography is entitled "Pequeñas notas autobiográficas" (Santiago, November 21, 1953). Portions of this document are reproduced in two Guzmán anthologies: "Notas del autor al lector," *Una moneda al río y otros cuentos* (Godfrey, Illinois: Monticello College Press, 1954), and Fernando Santiván, "Algunas palabras sobre Nicomedes Guzmán," *El pan bajo la bota* (Santiago: Empresa Editora Zig-Zag, 1960). Further citations from these three works will be noted in the text.

Oscar Vásquez Salazar, with the result that one can more vividly comprehend just how humble Guzmán's existence was. One article, for example, recalls how Guzmán's father had to get up early to go out in the cold and sell his basket of pastries; it also elaborates on the difficulties of his life as an ice cream peddler.

Guzmán deliberately emphasized his upbringing in an extremely humble home. Moreover, he constantly asserted that virtue and goodness can be found at any level of society, but especially in the proletarian class. In order to strengthen this thesis, he stressed the best qualities of his father and mother, both in his autobiography and in his novels. Certainly the theory of proletarian integrity is not original with Guzmán, but his unique use of it as a literary theme is important in Spanish American literature and will be studied further in later chapters.

Guzmán's writings also presented work as an element of hope and salvation for all proletarians, as it had been in his own life. The development of this political theory as a literary theme will be studied in Chapter 9, but for the moment it is important to see how it applied to Guzmán's life. The proletarian's constant need to work is mentioned in his autobiography in a moment of reflection on his youth as a precocious laborer: he worked from early childhood, and he was grateful for the maturing effects of work, which broadened his view of the world (*Una moneda al río*, 7). Gone too soon were the carefree days that he portrayed autobiographically in his novel *La sangre y la esperanza* (*Blood and Hope*, 1943). He was forced out into life so young that by his adolescence, an age when many Chileans are working for the first time, Nicomedes Guzmán had already endured many difficult trials in the competitive job market. When he was eleven, he was a typesetter and bookbinder's assistant; later, he was a truck driver's helper and an errand boy; he also carried boxes in a cardboard factory. Finally, when he was about sixteen, he obtained what he termed "a humble position in a modest office of a real estate brokerage." He later confessed that it was in this place of business that he began to be curious about writing, the arts, and humanities. Surprisingly enough, he placed the responsibility for this new curiosity on two typewriters:

Aquí comienza tal vez mi formación intelectual. Y en este lugar conquisté algunos de mis más caros afectos ajenos al hogar. Entre estos afectos se destacaban dos máquinas de escribir, dos aparatos, el uno viejo como una locomotora derrengada, y el otro más joven, brioso, si así puede decirse; pero ambos materia dispuesta a mi curiosidad y a mis afanes de echar a perder carillas. (*Una moneda al río,* 7)

Fortunately, the hopeful young author was endowed with great perseverance, for he describes his first vignettes, sent to a "revista infantil," as inferior, and they were never published. But when he needed family support more than ever, his mother seems to have opposed his efforts to write, telling him to forget about writing if he was being ignored: "Writing is for people with money" (*Una moneda al río,* 7).

But Guzmán never gave up. Perhaps he had been indirectly goaded on by his mother, who frequently reminded him of his proletarian status. In spite of initial defeats, he took advantage of a relatively prosperous period at the real estate office where he was employed and evaded the tasks expected of him there so that he might cultivate his literary and artistic talents.

His artistic talents were developed when he took an evening art course from the Chilean painter Nicanor González Méndez. Ironically, when Guzmán sent some of his drawings to the same juvenile magazine that had rejected his anecdotes, the drawings were published. Later he added short literary captions to his pictures. A twist of fate reversed the situation, however, for he next wrote brief stories that he illustrated himself, and ultimately the magazine published only what he wrote and not his sketches ("Pequeñas notas autobiográficas").

As a teenager, Guzmán organized clubs with other youths interested in developing their talents. One of the societies they created was the Centro Cultural y Deportivo (Cultural and Sport Center); another was called Loyola, after the street and neighborhood where the Vásquez family later moved.

Striving to improve their talents, the members of these groups sang, recited poetry, staged plays, ran track, drank malts, and even had boxing matches with other groups of young men in Santiago. In addition, they published magazines or reviews such as *El Peneca* (metathesis of *pequeña,* "small"), a children's magazine that dates from 1908. Guzmán had been a member of the *Peneca* group for several years and had contributed many pages when, at the age of twenty-one, he was elected vice president of the Centro Artístico y Literario de *El Peneca*.

Young Nicomedes published a good deal of material in other journals. During his formative years he used the pen name Ovaguz, short for his legal name, Oscar Vásquez Guzmán; later his pseudonym was Darío Octay. He wrote articles about the meaning of the Chilean flag and about the nineteenth century in Chile; he also composed many poems, and he published several short stories. Between 1933 and 1935 a film review, *Ecrán*, published works by Guzmán and other young poets of his generation.

Many of the writers whom the author knew intimately in later years as members of the Generation of 1938 lived at one time or another in the Quinta Normal area, and several attended the Liceo Federico Hanssen night school with Guzmán. No matter where he lived or studied, he was active in artistic groups, and his talents made him a leader wherever he went. In his high school, according to his mother, "he became the soul of a leftist magazine" (*La Espiga*).[2] Guzmán also helped form an important and sophisticated literary society, Los Inútiles, organized in Rancagua.

Although we do not know what political activities took place in these groups or in Guzmán's home, we do know that some of the members of the mature groups (such as Los Inútiles) were Communists, which suggests that the author's initiation to Marxism came through his literary contacts. For example, an athlete friend, Victoriano Vicario, introduced Guzmán to the Chilean writer Jacobo Danke (pseudonym for Juan Cabrera), a well-known Communist who later became one of Guzmán's closest comrades and his compadre. While attending the Liceo Federico Hanssen they lived together, and Danke soon became Guzmán's spiritual counselor, motivating the promising young novelist and guiding his reading of good literature. Guzmán dedicated a poem to Danke; later Danke wrote the preface to Guzmán's first novel, *Los hombres obscuros* (*Obscure Men*, 1939) and a new preface for the third edition in 1943.

Among this circle of the author's youthful friends, several besides Danke later attained renown in Chilean literature. Most of them became leftists and worked with the Popular Front. The condemnation of social injustice was their philosophy, and literature was the element that united and inspired them. From the many reunions of these groups of budding young writers emerged the nucleus of the Generation of 1938, which will be discussed in Part II.

Though he was greatly motivated by the challenge of his new

2. Oscar Vásquez Salazar, "Niñez y adolescencia de un gran novelista," *El Siglo* (Santiago), July 9, 1967; reprinted as "Niñez y adolescencia de Nicomedes Guzmán," in *PLAN: Política Latinoamericana Nueva* (Santiago), July 31, 1969.

friendships, Guzmán discovered that in order to achieve his goals he had to compete with his colleagues. This posed a problem for him, because his limited income compelled him to work during the day. Only at night could he attend classes, write, read, and participate in extracurricular activities. Despite his youthful energy and enthusiasm, Guzmán was often faced with disheartening criticism. His mother's disappointing counsel to leave writing to the rich was echoed in the advice of his employer, who was willing to help him with anything but literature:

> Mi jefe por ese tiempo—cuenta Nicomedes—, había sorprendido mis aficiones literarias, y un día me llamó para decirme:
> —Mira hombre, ten la seguridad de que yo te ayudaré en todo, porque he observado que tienes talento. ¡En todo, menos en literatura! (*El pan bajo la bota*, 10)

Further discouragement confronted Guzmán when he asked Manuel Rojas, one of his favorite authors, for his opinion of a novel that Guzmán had written. Rojas commented that although his book was not mediocre, it was too long: "Your book is not publishable, believe me . . . try to forget about reading pirate novels. Look at life" (*El pan bajo la bota*, 11).

Several stories have circulated concerning Guzmán's reaction to this suggestion. Fernando Santiván and Oreste Plath wrote that Guzmán immediately burned the manuscript.[3] Hugo Goldsack stated that in a rage Guzmán tore the huge bound folder into pieces; but at that moment Jacobo Danke happened along, calmed Nicomedes down, and helped him tape the manuscript together and edit it into the shorter work that was eventually published. Guzmán's wife, Lucy, admitted that when Nicomedes came home angry because of his seeming failure as a novelist, she hid the manuscript to keep him from burning it.[4] This long work, entitled "Un hombre, unos

3. Santiván, "Algunas palabras sobre Nicomedes Guzmán," p. 11; and Oreste Plath, "Quién es quién en la literatura chilena: Nicomedes Guzmán," *La Nación* (Santiago), August 6, 1939.

4. It is most probable that a total of six copies (two different versions of the manuscript) existed and Guzmán destroyed four of them. In 1971 it was claimed that two people had copies of the manuscript, but I was never able to examine it in order to observe Guzmán's narrative development. When I returned to Chile in 1973, having developed a stronger rapport with the family, I became the first critic in thirty-five years to be allowed to examine the original. Reports have circulated that the original manuscript was 600 pages

ojos negros y una perra lanuda," was later restructured, with the help of Danke, into Guzmán's first novel.

Granted, these contradictory anecdotes are interesting, but—much more important—they show that Guzmán's obscure life took on a fictitious, almost mythical, aspect at times. Another point to be observed is that, like Juan Godoy, whose *Angurrientos* had circulated widely in manuscript, Guzmán sought help and constructive criticism during his formative years from established writers.[5] He constantly attempted to improve his work stylistically and to polish his narrative. This humility about his work remained with him throughout his life, for even in 1960, when he was a seasoned author, he amazed the other participants at the First Workshop of Writers of the University of Concepción with his humble attitude and willingness to accept criticism of what he had written.[6]

In spite of their negative criticisms, Guzmán felt that his most helpful associations were with Jacobo Danke, Manuel Rojas, and Domingo Melfi, who taught him through their sincere friendship how a writer might gain self-discipline and success. Guzmán, in turn, exhibited a similar fraternal attitude in guiding less-known writers of his own generation as we will see in later chapters.

Fortunately, harsh evaluations of his work did not discourage him for long. In July 1938, at the age of twenty-four, Guzmán published his first book, a small volume consisting of nine poems, entitled *La ceniza y el sueño: Poemas (Ashes and Dreams: Poems.)* This book was soon out of print; undoubtedly the edition was very small. A second edition, with two added poems and drawings by Aníbal Alvial, was printed in 1960 by the National School of Graphic Arts and published by the Ediciones del Grupo Fuego de la Poesía. Today it is nearly impossible to locate copies of either edition.

If Guzmán was pleased to have his poems published, he was soon

---

long and that Guzmán eventually adapted only the last 200 pages into final form; nevertheless, neither of the two existing versions is more than 300 pages long.

5. Thomas Edgar Lyon, Jr., *Juan Godoy* (New York: Twayne Publishers, 1972), p. 17. Guzmán's manuscript was read by Juan Godoy, Manuel Rojas, Jacobo Danke, Luis Enrique Délano, and Juan Modesto Castro.

6. Braulio Arenas, "El taller de escritores," *Atenea*, 394 (1961), 133–37; Mario Ferrero, "Cincuenta años y un día," *La Nación* (Santiago), July 11, 1965; Fernando Alegría, "Historia de un Taller de Escritores," *Nueva Narrativa Hispanoamericana*, 1 (1971), 10.

disappointed, for the Chilean public did not receive them as favorably as had Guzmán's radical colleagues.[7] Apparently Guzmán himself grew to share this sentiment, for in later years he seldom referred to *La ceniza y el sueño* either publicly or privately. He described the poems simply as creations of his adolescence, written "when he was fifteen, more or less."[8] Optimistically, the aspiring young poet presented a copy of the first edition of the book to Pablo Neruda. Neruda's thoughtful reply is more benevolent than critical, tactfully avoiding any offense: "Es una hermosa edición" (*El pan bajo la bota*, 11). Nevertheless Guzmán found Neruda's comment inspiring: "His words were the encouragement that true talent knows how to give. Since then we have been friends" ("Pequeñas notas autobiográficas").

Even though little public mention has been made of *La ceniza y el sueño* because of its limited stylistic importance, it has some historical value—the principal reason, undoubtedly, that a second edition was printed.

This book was Guzmán's first attempt to convey his personal vision of the world. His principal theme and stylistic device is contrast. Contrasted to the "ashes"—*la ceniza* of the title—are "dreams," *el sueño*. Other shades of meaning of the words *ceniza* and *sueño* are reality (*lo real*), which opposes idealism (*lo ideal*), or past (ashes), which is the antithesis of future (dreams). In a sensual connotation, disillusion (*desengaño*) is the opposite of desire (*deseo*).

In Guzmán's later works this *claroscuro* develops into a socially oriented antithesis between despair and hope. Ultimately these opposites take on a revolutionary cast, and violence is pitted against Marxist hope; or human incomprehension thwarts proletarian tenderness (*ternura*). Eventually *destruction* of human dignity is contrasted to action through *revolution*. The contrast of violence to hope is shown in both the title and the structure of *La sangre y la esperanza*, Guzmán's second novel, published in 1943. The baroque *claroscuro* characteristic of all his work, was also adopted by the

7. Milton Rossel, "*Hombres obscuros*, por Nicomedes Guzmán," *Atenea*, 180 (1940), 443: "Nicomedes is a young writer who had previously published books of little literary merit." Rossel faithfully represents the feeling of the critics; at this time, however, Guzmán had published only one other book, *La ceniza y el sueño*.

8. Orlando Cabrera Leyva, "Nicomedes Guzmán: 'Se nace escribiendo porque sí,'" *Zig-Zag*, April 10, 1964, p. 14.

writers of his generation. The idealism in Guzmán leads him to evoke a distant glow that he sees in humanity—an eternal light which Marxists have called hope. Its antithesis is the overpowering darkness of corruption—a gloom that is produced by social inequalities and the tyranny of an oppressive government.

The publication of *La ceniza y el sueño* led in time to a close friendship between Guzmán and Neruda both of whom became well-known Chilean Communists. In 1948, when the president of Chile, González Videla, was attacking both men for their Marxist leanings, they sometimes traveled together over northern Chile, getting to know the dry, desolate region and the people who lived there. Later Neruda wrote a prologue to the 1960 edition of *La ceniza y el sueño*.

This book of poetry was inspired by Lucía Salazar, whom Guzmán had met when he was fourteen. Born in Chillán on December 17, 1917, Lucía was nearly three-and-one-half years younger than Nicomedes. The couple was married on June 7, 1936, in the Iglesia de Lourdes by the well-known Padre Marchant; their marriage was also recorded in the civil registry of Quinta Normal. Guzmán was not yet twenty-two at the time of his marriage.

One of the nine poems, the "Romance Marino de Lucy," is a metaphorical description of his sweetheart. The dedication, "A Lucía a través de mi mamá," is ambiguous in its mention of two women. The dedication of the second edition reflects a similar ambiguity: "Hazte cargo, perpetua luz de estas pequeñas páginas, que son tuyas desde tiempo inmemorial." Lucía and others assumed that the book was dedicated to her, but Ester Panay assured me that Guzmán dedicated it to her.

Guzmán has stated that these poems were written when he was fifteen but published later, after he had attempted to write a novel and some short stories. It is hard to say whether the author is exaggerating, trying to make himself appear to have been a child prodigy and at the same time suggesting that he failed at poetry only because he was so young. Possibly he really did write the poems at the age of fifteen. Most of the images, however, are more mature than those a fifteen-year-old boy would ordinarily employ. For example, there is the recurring symbol of the author's pipe, its smoke, and its ashes —both realistic ashes and ashes of time. The pipe, Guzmán's constant companion, appears in five of the nine poems; ashes and smoke are predominant elements as well. Other mature images are erotic metaphorical comparisons of a woman with the sea.

Furthermore, Danke's book of verse *Las barcarolas de Ulises* (Santiago: Ercilla, 1934) seemingly inspired Guzmán, who in turn, wrote a poem on the theme of Ulysses entitled " 'Titania' o la leyenda de Orfeo y Vilma," dedicating it "Para Jacobo Danke, Camarada," in *La ceniza y el sueño.* The fact that Guzmán dedicated this poem to Danke, whom he did not know until he was about twenty, leads one to suspect that this particular poem, at least, was not written when Guzmán was fifteen. Certain other poems that Guzmán is known to have written when he was younger are obviously different from *La ceniza y el sueño.* For instance, an unpublished book of poetry entitled *Croquis del corazón: Poemas*, dedicated to Lucy and still in her care, includes pictures the young poet drew in October of 1933 and in 1934, and it is signed Darío Octay. The India ink sketches and the romantic verse take up seventy-eight pages, divided into the following sections: "Crepuscular—Los poemas tristes," "Sonrisas—Los poemas alegres," and "Primicias de campestre (poemitas dedicados a mi madre)."

In retrospect, then, Guzmán's early poetry is very important as a lyrical foundation for his later prose works. If *La ceniza y el sueño* is evaluated in historical terms, it is far from a failure, for these poems help to complete the total vision of Guzmán the stylist, who like so many of his colleagues, started as a poet. The book attains even greater significance if it is regarded as a tool with which the writer learned to express himself. In other words, through his first publication Nicomedes Guzmán gained some confidence in himself and in his writing; it enabled him finally to enter the world of accomplished artists. Guzmán was one of the first successful writers from the Chilean proletarian class, and he was the first to identity himself as proletarian:

> El caso no es único en Chile: hay actualmente dos escritores conocidísimos, de los mejores y más finos, que provienen también del pueblo bajo. No hay para qué nombrarlos: con todo el auge y hasta la insolencia de la "rebelión de las masas" los viejos prejuicios de situación y de sangre conservan todavía prestigio suficiente para que, aun en son de elogio, esa circunstancia pueda no resultar agradable a personas dignas de respeto.[9]

Guzmán and his generation were the first Chilean writers willing to acknowledge their lower-class origins; before their time, writing

9. Alone [Hernán Díaz Arrieta], "Crónica literaria: *Los hombres obscuros*," *El Mercurio* (Santiago), August 27, 1939.

in Chile was the metier solely of members of the middle or upper classes.

As he discovered a way to express his feelings as a lyric poet and a revolutionary, Guzmán eventually realized that his best mode of expression was not poetry:

> A fin de cuentas, no era el verso lo más valedero para mí. En un país de grandes poetas como Chile—Neruda, Cruchaga Santa María, Huidobro, la Mistral, de Rokha, Juvencio Valle, Jacobo Danke y tantos otros—mis afanes líricos no iban a prosperar.
> Y seguí trabajando. (*Una moneda al río*, 8)

As Raúl Silva Castro points out, communication is the basic purpose of radical or revolutionary literature. Hence poetry is not the genre most suitable to the radical writer, for it does not reach the largest public possible. Narration—especially the short story—was to become the best method for the Generation of 1938 to reveal Chilean social injustice.[10]

As Guzmán "kept working," he wisely confined himself to prose while still retaining the symbols, the metaphors, and much of the lyricism that characterized his poetry. In this manner, he created a narrative form that is surprisingly poetic although it incorporates elements of social protest that might seem to belong only in essays.

As he matured, Guzmán became actively involved in leftist political activities. His close friend and compadre Homero Bascuñán recalls Guzmán's militant role in the Partido Nacional Revolucionario (National Revolutionary Party) during the few months prior to the important presidential elections of 1938:

> De ese naciente P.N.R. era secretario de Prensa y Propaganda Nicomedes Guzmán, entonces poeta (*La ceniza y el sueño*) y gran promesa como novelista. Allí nos conocimos. El permaneció muy poco en ese partido y luego emigró a otra tienda. Mas, nuestra amistad quedó sellada para siempre.[11]

Like other writers of his generation, Guzmán left the PNR, a synthetic, insignificant party, to join the Popular Front coalition, which seemed to embody the revolutionary movement that the young writers were seeking.

During the early 1930s Chilean Communists suffered many defeats

10. Raúl Silva Castro, *Panorama literario de Chile* (Santiago: Editorial Universitaria, 1961), p. 334.

11. Homero Bascuñán, "Recuerdos de una vieja amistad," *Cultura*, 96 (1964), 20.

and remained political underdogs. By the middle of the decade, however, they were beginning to attract supporters. In a move to gain strength for the 1938 elections, they joined forces with the Socialists and segments of other parties, including the majority of Chile's Radical Party,[12] and created an alliance called the Frente Popular. Because of the global depression of the thirties, a leftist movement was created by many middle-of-the-road Chileans and even some conservatives. The younger generation was especially influenced, and many middle-class young people adopted socialist ideals.

The time was ripe for the Frente Popular, a coalition that also included many small leftist and middle-of-the-road parties, such as the Falange Nacional, headed by Eduardo Frei Montalva, who later became president of Chile (1964–70). The Popular Front has enjoyed some success in several countries; in France and Spain it was extremely popular, but it was ultimately defeated in both countries. In Chile the front won an astounding victory during the elections of 1938, and even though it remained in power only two years and twenty-one days, falling mainly because of the death of President Aguirre Cerda, it had not lasted this long in either France or Spain. Like many young people, Guzmán was drawn to the appealing ideology of the Frente Popular and its demands for social reform in Chile.

When Guzmán left the PNR for the Frente he actually moved to the left, to the Communist Party and a commitment to socialist literature. The Popular Front inspired him with idealistic anticipations of proletarian equality, and it gave him an additional impetus to create a new style of revolutionary literature. The socialist ideals of the Popular Front were foremost in Guzmán's mind and in his plans, as has been shown by Homero Bascuñán. Guzmán transformed many of the social injustices that he had experienced into a litera-

12. The word *radical* in this study is intended to have a leftist connotation but should not be confused with the Chilean Radical Party, which consists of both right and leftist factions. The party itself was established during the nineteenth century by the middle-class descendants of Juan Godoy, the woodcutter who discovered silver at Chañarcillo in Chile in 1832. The Radical Party was much more socialistic at its inception than it has been since the founding of the Chilean Communist and Socialist parties, also organized in mining regions. At the time of the Popular Front coalition, the Radical Party was a middle-of-the-road body with left, right, and center factions. It was the majority party of the popular alliance and had the most voice and control. The Radical Party has become more reactionary through the years; today it is considered to be one of the more conservative political forces.

ture of social protest, and although his style often obscures his method of attack, he became Chile's most representative Marxist novelist.

Guzmán's interpretation of Marxism was somewhat unorthodox, however, in that he was also a man of sincere religious conviction. Nevertheless, it is not uncommon to find Chileans who are active Marxists in their political lives but fervent Christians in their religious beliefs.

Guzmán constantly emphasized the humanist qualities of early Marxism and, as he matured, he abandoned the hard party line the Russians had imparted to communism. Though he had been a militant Marxist in his youth, living and exalting socialist ideals, in his later life Guzmán turned to the Bible and read it regularly. He and Lucy had been married in the Catholic Church, and he made an offering each month to San Pancracio.[13] He saw that each of his children was baptized shortly after birth, although his own "fe de bautismo" is dated 1916, when he was two years old.

The change toward humanism is important in Guzmán's writings, and it places him in a unique position. In fact, this evolution from Marxism tempered his outward life to such an extent that colleagues considered him only a passive communist.

Not at all passive, however, is Guzmán's first novel, *Los hombres obscuros* (sometimes spelled *oscuros*), written in the early months of 1938 and published July 15, 1939, a year after *La ceniza y el sueño*. It is a first-person narration of a series of episodes in the life of a young bootblack. Although first novels are often autobiographical, little of the author's actual life appears in *Los hombres obscuros*. Yet the character Inés bears a slight resemblance to Guzmán's wife. Guzmán's devotion to Lucía is reflected in the novel through the love of the protagonist, Pablo, for the frail and timid Inés, who, unlike Guzmán's wife, dies, as did many a romantic protagonist, of tuberculosis.

Lucía was an attractive woman with striking blue eyes, a young mother burdened by the responsibilities of a large family. She and

---

13. The *Enciclopedia universal ilustrada europea-americana* (Madrid: Espasa-Calpe, 1920), vol. 41, lists two obscure saints by this name, both martyrs. The first, a young man who knew Christ, was a bishop when he was killed. His day is April 3. The other, whose memory is celebrated May 12, was beheaded at the age of fourteen in A.D. 304. Neither saint is familiar to English-speaking Catholics.

Guzmán had five children. The oldest, Oscar Eduardo Vásquez Salazar, was born October 29, 1936. He chose the career of journalist much against his father's wishes, for Guzmán did not want his children to write for a living. Oscar has also published poems and short stories, including the book *Chacharacha y otros relatos* (*Tatterdemalion and other stories*, 1972).

Ximena Lucía was born on February 16, 1939. She married the Chilean composed Carlos González Torres, who has also directed the annual Festival de la Canción de Viña popular music competition.

Florencia Marcia, whom Guzmán preferred to call Florencia Adriana, was born on August 31, 1940. She developed her talents as an artist and sculptress for a time at the University of Chile, but later abandoned a potential career in art to marry Carlos Gustavo Encinas González and become a housewife.

Darío Nicomedes was born on August 4, 1945. He taught in an elementary school for several years but has recently begun to study the teaching of mathematics at the Universidad Técnica de Estado.

Pablo Lautaro (named after Pablo Neruda) was born on February 22, 1950. He is currently studying chemical engineering at the University of Chile and is a mathematics teacher in the Escuela Industrial de Puente Alto. The boys have married—or have "compañeras," as Darío and Pablo prefer to put it—and each of the children has pursued a meaningful career with their father's encouragement. In fact, the lives of the children show that Guzmán helped mobilize his offspring economically and socially, though not necessarily politically, so that they might rise above the misery of a proletarian existence.

There was also a humorous and warm side to the novelist of the slums; Guzmán was a great one for nicknames. The family and friends call Oscar "Oscarín," to distinguish him from his father, who is also known as Oscar; but Guzmán called his oldest son "Corozo," or when he was a child he was "El Rey Corozo." Ximena was simply Ximenilla; Florencia was Belenda or Belenchita. The two youngest boys had the most inventive names: Darío was Dariolín Cacao Deo Lao, and Pablo was Pernil Chico. Guzmán even addressed their letters with these names when he traveled.[14]

During the first three or four years of their marriage, both Lucía

---

14. Oscar Vásquez Salazar, "¡Así era mi padre!" *El Siglo*, June 26, 1966.

and Nicomedes attended evening classes held in the Liceo Federico Hanssen. Nicomedes finished the second year of courses in humanities and started the third year, but he failed to finish.

These years of study and fellowship with his many schoolmates and their social, cultural, and political activities were of primary importance in the formation of Guzmán's character. In 1940, working with his colleagues, among them Manuel Guerrero, Guzmán organized homages to several deceased Chilean writers who had bequeathed Guzmán's generation a heritage of socially oriented literature: Carlos Pezoa Véliz, Carlos Sepúlveda Leyton, and Chile's great realist short-story writer Baldomero Lillo. In the public assemblage on Lillo, the most successful and the most heralded of the series, Guzmán gave the keynote address of homage, followed by the poet and professor Samuel A. Lillo (Baldomero's brother), Januario Espinosa, and Augusto D'Halmar. Guzmán took the responsibility of writing newspaper articles both anticipating and summarizing each event. The affairs were held in the Salón de Honor of the University of Chile. Sponsors were the Santiago Local of the School Teachers' Union of Chile and the Popular Front's Alianza de Intelectuales de Chile (Alliance of Chilean Intellectuals), a group organized at the outset of the Spanish Civil War. This segment of the Popular Front promoted socialist literature, fine art, and music, and it furnished a common ground for young men to continue the cultural revolution they had set in motion in their neighborhood societies. Such group activities signaled the beginnings of Guzmán's "fraternity," and they were also final evidence of his national repute as a writer.

2

Toward a Mature Expression

First Novels

Since the typewritten manuscript of Guzmán's first novel, originally entitled "Un hombre, unos ojos negros y una perra lanuda," had circulated among his friends, he was indebted to them for many suggestions for improving it. Ultimately, he decided to utilize only the last 100 pages of the 300-page manuscript. He was able to publish it only at a great economic sacrifice, but he was able to offset some of the expense by helping the printer set the type:

> Mi primera novela, *Los hombres obscuros*, 1939, se escribió con sacrificio y se editó con un sacrificio mayor aún. Don Alberto Lagos, propietario de una pequeña imprenta cercana a mi barrio, hizo componer la obra a "tipo parado" y la imprimió personalmente en una prensita a pedal. Las tapas—lo recuerdo bien, porque el canto de los gallos nos sorprendió dándole término—se hicieron a la luz de una vela, puesto que a mi editor le habían suspendido el suministro de energía eléctrica, compréndase bien por qué. (*Una moneda al río*, 8)

The entire book was set letter by letter, and it took six months to finish the printing. The plate from which the cover of this first edition was printed is in my possession.

This small edition appeared in July 1939, was rapidly distributed, and soon went out of print. On December 20, 1939, a second printing was issued by the same obscure publisher, Editorial Yunque (anvil).

Unlike his book of poetry, *La ceniza y el sueño*, Guzmán's novel was widely read and immediately became a popular—and sometimes controversial—topic of discussion. During the first ten months after its publication, *Los hombres obscuros* received the phenomenal number of six reviews in *Atenea* alone.

It was to be expected that some readers would be shocked by the novel's harsh realism and extremely vulgar language, especially in the speech of one of the characters. Some of the *Atenea* reviewers attempted to prepare their public by pointing out that the vulgarities employed by Guzmán faithfully reflected the *conventillo*, or slum, where Guzmán was reared. The most conservative critic, Milton Rossel, suggested that the novel would have been better without this language and these descriptions, which he claimed, bordered on pornography or coprolalia.[1]

One or two of the *Atenea* reviewers were anxious to point out structural errors and problems with imagery, but they all expressed amazement at the young novelist's narrative ability. Although not all the critics sympathized with the underlying Marxist philosophy of the novel, they all agreed that Guzmán was the first writer able to describe convincingly and compassionately the abject poverty of the Santiago slums. They also noted that Guzmán wrote not from the point of view of an outsider but as a son of the slums.

Up to this time, *criollista* novels, which dealt with problems of man confronted by an enormous and hostile land, had been popular in Chile. *Los hombres obscuros* promised a change. This new kind of narrative was fascinating, especially in light of the political success of the Popular Front, with its promised social reforms. As a novel of sociological and stylistic importance, the book also offered hope that Chile might finally achieve major literary status among Spanish American nations; *Los hombres obscuros* might rank with *Doña Barbara* (Venezuela), *La vorágine* (Colombia), and *Los de abajo* (Mexico).[2]

The success of *Los hombres obscuros* caused Guzmán at least one personal setback. This was the loss of his job at the real estate office, where he had enjoyed some freedom to write, at the risk of slighting his work. When his employer realized the success of Guzmán's novel, he dismissed him after nine consecutive years of employment. Whether it was for personal or political motives was never clarified.

Fortunately for Guzmán, a close relative helped him find employment as a carpenter's apprentice on a construction site. He was later promoted to the position of *alistador*, the person who keeps the time cards, the books, and a record of all the men and materials that go in and out of the project. This new type of work allowed Guzmán to associate closely with unions and other labor groups, so for many years he was involved in labor activities, always championing the proletarian cause.

The next phase of Guzmán's progress has remained obscure. His plight as a promising novelist nearly starving to death, forced to labor as a carpenter to support his family, apparently came to the

---

1. Milton Rossel, "*Hombres obscuros*, por Nicomedes Guzmán," *Atenea*, 180 (1940).

2. *Ilustrado*, June 20, 1943.

attention of the Popular Front president of Chile, Pedro Aguirre Cerda, who obtained a position for Guzmán in his government. Guzmán is vague, almost mysterious, about this appointment:

> Y más tarde, mediante pormenores novelescos, por lo dramáticos, obtuve un puesto en el Departamento de Extensión Cultural del Ministerio de Trabajo. (*Pan bajo la bota*, 12)

As to Guzmán's literary achievements, the immediate success of his first novel had already singled him out, among his group, as a writer of outstanding artistic capabilities and great promise. His next move brought him a still broader reputation as a leader of his generation, and it was a giant stride toward the definition of the Generation of 1938. In 1941, the Editorial Cultura published Guzmán's first anthology of Chilean short-story writers, *Nuevos cuentistas chilenos*. Included in this anthology were stories written by most of the leaders of the new generation, as well as stories by other close friends, for Guzmán felt that most of his colleagues showed considerable promise.

Critics disagree as to Guzmán's ability to discern promising talent. One writer calls the anthology a failure because only three of the twenty-four writers eventually achieved fame, but others acclaim the book because eleven or twelve of the twenty-four have become well known in Chile.[3] Though he wrote the introduction, Guzmán did not include any of his own short stories in his anthology.

This collection is important not for the quality of the selections but as the herald of a new generation. It is mainly because of this work that Nicomedes Guzmán is usually considered a leader in the Generation of 1938.

Continuing his creative writing, Guzmán moved with his young family from the area of Población Lautaro back to his childhood district in the Barrio Mapocho, across from the trolley terminal. Here, living in a *cité* or a *conventillo*,[4] he began working on his

---

3. Antonio de Undurraga, *28 cuentistas chilenos del siglo XX, Antología* (Santiago: Empresa Editora Zig-Zag, 1963), p. 237; and Luis González Zenteno, "Nicomedes Guzmán, figura representativa de la generación del 38," *Atenea*, 392 (1961), 126.

4. Both *cité* and *conventillo* are proletarian multiple dwellings. In the *conventillo* all of the rooms are situated around the patio, with a family crowded into a small room having to share toilet facilities and water faucets

second novel, *La sangre y la esperanza*. In 1940 the first chapter was published as a short story in *Atenea*. After the novel was completed, sometime in 1941, the author entered it in a national contest judged by Eduardo Barrios, Rubén Azocar, and Ricardo A. Latcham.[5] While Guzmán's novel did not win, the work held its own in competition with those by several of his colleagues, many of whom had been included in his anthology. According to Fernando Uriarte, the judges of the contest failed to recognize the merit of Guzmán's novel and rejected it without comment.[6] Yet the modest Guzmán was extremely magnanimous and gave high praise to the prize winners, his companions in the Generation of 1938.[7] Latcham helped Guzmán find a publisher, Orbe; after the book was published, it enjoyed considerable success and won the 1944 Santiago Municipal Prize in literature, Chile's most distinguished honor for a single work. Within a year, a second printing appeared. The book was received favorably by the critics, and the reading public kept the copy at the National Library well worn.[8] Nevertheless, this novel was also controversial.

Guzmán's fame eventually reached Europe. Juan Urribe Echevarría mentioned that when the Spanish novelist Camilo José Cela arrived in Chile, he stated he wanted to meet the author of *La sangre y la esperanza*, so Guzmán went to meet him.

In his second work Guzmán retains the first-person point of view used in his first novel. Unlike *Los hombres obscuros*, however, *La sangre y la esperanza* is so autobiographical that it is impossible even for Guzmán's family to distinguish the factual elements in it from the pure invention.[9] The narrator relates his experiences as a young boy between the ages of four and eight growing up in the

---

which are located centrally in the patio. The *cité* is somewhat less plebeian; the family has a suite of rooms, not just one small room, but, like the apartment rooms of the conventillo, they are located along a passage or patio.

5. Ricardo A. Latcham, "Nicomedes Guzmán," *La Nación* (Santiago), July 5, 1964; reprinted in *Cultura*, 96 (1964), 24–28 with the title "El escritor en su universo."

6. Fernando Uriarte, "*La sangre y la esperanza* (Orbe), por Nicomedes Guzmán," *Atenea*, 223 (June 1944), 92.

7. Nicomedes Guzmán, *Nuevos cuentistas chilenos. Antología* (Santiago: Editorial Cultura, 1941), p. 235, n.

8. Francisco Santana, "*La sangre y la esperanza*," *Atenea*, 225 (1944), 282.

9. Oscar Vásquez Salazar, "Niñez y adolescencia de un gran novelista," *El*

slums of Santiago in the 1920s. Because of his innocence, this youth is an unbiased witness to all sorts of atrocities perpetrated on various working-class personages by strike-breaking police, bullies, and fellow slum dwellers, such as deviates or alcoholics, whose actions are predetermined by the oppressive environment in which they live. As always, a striking element in Guzmán's narrative is the description of the conventillo.

The boy narrator, Enrique Quilodrán, is a potential vagrant who wanders through the slums, forced to play in unwholesome areas; yet he is an obedient child. He admires his hard-working parents and decides on his own to go to work to support them when his father is injured by a policeman during a strike. To some extent, the novel is the story of a family's struggle to overcome setbacks from every side: accidents, strikes, robbery, poverty, illegitimacy, and death. The work is not entirely pessimistic, however; the word *blood* (*sangre*) in the title is only half of an antithesis. The other half is *hope* (*esperanza*) and optimism, although these qualities are often disguised as Marxist values: work, children (even if illegitimate), and revolution.

During this creative period of Guzmán's life, he formed a most fortunate relationship with Francisco Javier Fuentes, the publisher of his *Nuevos cuentistas chilenos* (1941). Fuentes published a new edition of *Los hombres obscuros* in 1943, and Guzmán's fame after having been awarded the Municipal Prize for *La sangre y la esperanza* caused both books to sell well.[10] The relationship was further solidified when Guzmán collaborated with Fuentes as consulting editor of the Editorial Cultura. Besides being the highly respected editor of Cultura, Fuentes is the proprietor of the Cultura bookstore in Santiago. During their association Guzmán worked closely with Fuentes on commercial details. For example, Guzmán wrote and published for Cultura a book catalogue that also contains a short, popular critical history of Chilean literature.

To attain the editorial position, Guzmán had proposed to organize and direct the publication of a collection of twelve novels, to be sold only as a set, and to be named "La Colección 'La Honda.' " It would

Siglo, July 9, 1967. See also Nicomedes Guzmán, "Plan de una novela," *Cultura,* 96 (1964), 44.

10. Francisco Javier Fuentes, "En las tareas editoriales," *Cultura,* 96 (1964), 36–37.

consist, he had suggested, of new novels by several of the well-known authors of the Generation of 1938, such as Francisco Coloane, Reinaldo Lomboy, Gonzalo Drago, and Oscar Castro.[11] The novels would be published in an attractive edition available to book collectors and the general public on a subscription basis. When the twelve proposed volumes were delivered, however, the subscribers failed to make the payments they had promised. The publisher then had to make up the deficit, which put Guzmán in a bad light: "De alma limpia y diáfana, jamás creyó que quienes le habían prometido ayuda para tan bella idea le iban a pagar en esa forma."[12]

This incident is typical of Guzmán's trust in his associates. Lucía relates another story that illustrates Guzmán's total trust in his fellow man. One night he found a stranger sleeping on the ground in the patio of the apartment complex across the street from 730 Pezoa Véliz. Guzmán invited this complete stranger into their home to sleep on the floor and lent him a few blankets and a charcoal burner to lessen the winter chill. Fearing for their safety, Lucy was frightened and did not sleep well all night long; but in the morning the man had slipped out quietly and nothing was missing from the house.

Guzmán's generosity was surpassed only by his idealism. When acquaintances describe these two characteristics of Nicomedes Guzmán, they inevitably employ superlatives.[13] One aspect of this idealism is seen in his wish to promulgate socialism over the entire world and aid his comrades to do the same. Thus it was through his efforts and especially his anthology that a generation of writers was established. His friends have stated that he attempted to carry other artists to fame on his coattails.

In spite of all Guzmán's success, little by little his world began to crumble:

> Lo que a otros mueve apenas, en él es catástrofe. Conflictos emocionales, pesadumbres, hechos, palabras, intenciones le afectan tremendamente. Acusa hondo el doloroso efecto, en una suerte de hematidrosis, en que la faz apenas pulsa en rictus. Pero en sus ojos está la verdad: una melancolía de toda la vida trata de agazaparse en lo profundo,

11. Refer to the Bibliography for the complete series of "La Honda" novels.
12. Fuentes, p. 37.
13. Edmundo Concha, "Responso por el compañero," *Cultura*, 96 (1964), 18–19; Francisco Coloane, "Palabras de Francisco Coloane (Discurso fúnebre)," *Cultura*, 96 (1964), 14.

detrás de las retinas, melancolía de ver y de ver sintiendo tanto y tan acendradamente.[14]

He had many serious personal problems. As a boy, he had been excessively affected by the deaths of some of his brothers and sisters and by a mother who often whipped him soundly with a belt; as a result, he suffered in his youth from nightmares and "terrores nocturnos," fear of the night when one is awake (all the family slept in the same room). This led eventually to a neurotic malady called "angustia vital" ("agony of life"). As Guzmán matured, he became noticeably hypersensitive. He was also greatly concerned about the welfare of his family—a concern that was complicated by his relationships with other women.

In 1943 Guzmán met a strikingly attractive, intelligent woman at a party. She was introduced to him by Juan de Luigi, literary critic of La Hora. Art history professor Leopoldo Castedo also introduced them on another occasion. Later, on a streetcar, Guzmán approached her and began to talk to her as though he knew her. She replied, "I don't know you."

"Sure you do," he insisted. "We have been introduced three times, previously."

This woman who ignored Guzmán because she thought him petulant was Ester Panay. Their relationship caused an additional conflict in Guzmán's personal life. She was beautiful, intelligent, and well educated, and although they became lovers, in some ways she was a middle-class antagonist to Guzmán's proletarian ideology. She had a degree in psychology and worked as a social worker in Santiago. On March 25, 1945, a son, Rodrigo Nicomedes, was born to Ester and Nicomedes.

Before meeting Ester, Guzmán had an affair with a nurse. When their liaison ended she married an American and moved to Los Angeles, California, to avoid further involvement with the married novelist. Guzmán could not forget her, however, and named his third daughter, Florencia Adriana, after her (and Florence Nightingale). Lucy knew of the illicit intrigue and insisted on calling her Florencia Marcia.

Lucy also knew about Ester. Guzmán confided to his novelist friend Juan Donoso that on one occasion, when Ester became ill

14. Reinaldo Lomboy, "Nicomedes Guzmán y el claroscuro," Zig-Zag, September 15, 1956.

and could not nurse Rodrigo, Lucy took the infant and nursed him with her own Darío. Guzmán attempted to portray her abstract love and "tenderness" in "Rapsodia en luz mayor" ("Rhapsody in Light Major"), a short story depicting a similar situation.

These domestic complications troubled Guzmán deeply, and he began drinking. Soon, alcohol became a serious problem. Other problems began mounting up as well. The Colección "La Honda" speculation failed. The Frente Popular had officially broken up in 1941; after the 1944 elections, it fell from popularity and completely disintegrated, threatening, theoretically at least, the very existence of the Generation of 1938, which had been nurtured by its success and its ideals. The victory of Pedro Aguirre Cerda, the Popular Front candidate, had raised the poor people's hopes in 1938, but Aguirre Cerda met an untimely death on November 25, 1941. Called "Don Tinto" because of his swarthy complexion and his extensive vineyards which produced "vino tinto," Aguirre Cerda had achieved many successful economical and cultural reforms. His death was mysterious. Some thought he died of drink, but according to popular legend he was poisoned. This assassination theory appealed to Aguirre Cerda's followers, the masses, who identified strongly with the obscure popular hero. A frail, sickly man, Aguirre Cerda actually died of tuberculosis.[15] Juan Antonio Ríos was elected to finish his term, which was concluded rather ineffectually in 1946.

With the fall of most leftist groups, people like Guzmán at first tried desperately to stay on top and remain useful to the liberals. During Aguirre Cerda's regime, the Communists had not taken any ministerial posts, apparently preferring to maintain control from backstage. Today it appears that they were engaging in obstructionist tactics which eventually led to the downfall of the Popular Front. Later, during Gabriel González Videla's term as president of Chile (1946–52), three cabinet posts were given to Communists in return for party support during the elections. This was the first time Communists occupied high government positions in South America. Because they proved troublesome, González Videla dismissed the three Communist members of his cabinet after five months; then, to receive United States aid and cooperate with capitalist interests, he expelled the Communist deputies and senators from the Chilean Congress and broke off diplomatic relations with Russia. González

15. Interview with Claudio Solar, Viña del Mar, Chile, July 21, 1971.

Videla kept a notorious "blue book," a list of all suspected Communists. These persons, considered threats to Chilean democracy, were under police scrutiny. Though he was in the notorious blue book as a Communist, Guzmán was never seriously threatened with incarceration until once in the North he was informed that if he attempted to go to a certain mine to visit some friends he would be jailed immediately. Needless to say, this warning, given in confidence by a government agent, was sufficient for Guzmán.

It was during this stormy political period that Pablo Neruda was expelled as a senator and pursued as a pariah in his own fatherland, and Nicomedes Guzmán was ousted from the bureaucracy in the Extensión Cultural del Ministerio del Trabajo because of his ties with the Communists.

The Mature Years

After the fall of the Popular Front, times became difficult for Nicomedes Guzmán. Having been dismissed from the Ministry of Labor, he was virtually unemployed from 1945 to 1949 except for his work as a writer and lecturer. He planned many novels; one was to be a collaboration with his close friend, the folklore journalist Homero Bascuñán. But first because of lack of time and later because of lack of motivation, he failed to get a single one of these projected novels under way, so from 1943 on, most of his efforts were turned to writing short stories.

His days were empty after 1945, so he accompanied Ester Panay on her confidential visits as a social worker and psychologist. Doors were thereby opened to Guzmán that he could never have entered otherwise. He witnessed tragic conditions, received insight into intimate emotional situations, and gathered material for many plots. He discussed psychological problems with Ester and began to penetrate an expanded and personal proletarian world that he had never known.

In 1944 Editorial Orbe published a collection of seven of his short stories, which Guzmán preferred to call "novelas breves." The title of the book, *Donde nace el alba* (*Where Dawn Is Born*), is subtly symbolic, referring to the glimmering lights that glow in each soul —especially in children—in spite of the world's extreme darkness.[16]

16. Lautaro Yankas, "*Donde nace el alba*, de Nicomedes Guzmán," *Atenea*, 238 (1945), 76.

Once again, Guzmán employs the device of antithesis that he has used in other works. Here good is contrasted to bad, dawn to darkness. In comparison with his earlier antitheses, this one is quite abstract.

Most of the stories in the book are like snapshots of the intimate life of a proletarian protagonist. To my mind, one story stands out far above the others: "Extramuros" ("Outskirts"), a story about four vagabonds and a cat huddled around a fire on a cold rainy night.[17] Though John Dyson has a different opinion (" 'Extramuros' is a very slow moving story that reveals the life these men lead"),[18] I feel that in style, structure, and images it is one of Guzmán's finest short stories.

The next year, 1945, Ediciones Amura, a subsidiary of Editorial Cultura, published *La carne iluminada* (*Pequeñas narraciones*). As the words of the title *The Illuminated Flesh* (*Short Narrations*) imply, the author is portraying once again that inner light of humanity, a particular tenderness, sincerity, or sensibility that continues to glow in a humble soul in spite of the world's imposing darkness. Or, in a more Marxist interpretation: if ways of the flesh and carnality, as imposed on the poor by the world, lead to darkness, there is an internal light of truth in the proletarian soul that brightens and shows a more exalted way.

La carne iluminada contains only two short stories: "Rapsodia en luz major," in which a wife whose rival has died in childbirth nurses her husband's newborn illegitimate child, and "Una perra y algunos vagabundos" ("A Bitch and Some Vagabonds"), which culminates with vagabond children watching an abandoned bitch give birth to her pups. The theme of vagrant children, which appears often in twentieth-century Chilean fiction, will be examined at some length in Chapter 12.

As Guzmán's narrative abilities increased, more writing opportunities became available to him, but some of these took precious time away from his artistic endeavors. From 1944 to 1946 he wrote a column called "Cosas y tipos populares de Chile" ("Chilean popular types and things"), which appeared in *El Siglo* of Santiago. He

17. "Extramuros" appeared originally in *El Mercurio* (Santiago). "Destello en la bruma" originally appeared in *El Siglo* (January 26, 1941), with the title "Mujeres."

18. John P. Dyson, "Los cuentos de Nicomedes Guzmán," *Atenea*, 404 (1964), 236.

also wrote a column in Santiago's *La Nación* on new Chilean authors, and he was on the editorial staff of *Las Noticias de Última Hora* (Santiago). The first issue of the Popular Front journal *Voz de América* (May 1944) lists Guzmán as one of the secretaries of the editorial board, and Arturo Torres-Ríoseco mentions still another obscure literary position: secretary of public relations of the review *Otoño.*[19]

In 1946 Guzmán traveled to Montevideo, Uruguay, and to Argentina, where the Buenos Aires publishing firm Siglo Veinte arranged to publish *La sangre y la esperanza.* This transaction brought Guzmán some international fame, and it increased his reputation in Chile as well. An Argentine newspaper, *Clarín,* ran an article about him which expressed great admiration for him as a person and as an ambassador of proletarian good will. Praising him highly for his concern about social problems, the newspaper's editors also held him in high esteem as a novelist, rating him equal to José Eustasio Rivera or Jorge Icaza.[20]

As a result of his travels to Argentina, in 1947 he was invited to return to teach a course on Chilean literature at the Colegio Libre de Estudios Superiores de Buenos Aires.[21] According to Ester Panay, it was mainly through such lectures that Guzmán supported his children during these years of irregular employment. While lectures paid poorly and obliged him to travel constantly, what little money they earned was better than no income at all, and they brought Guzmán some fame as he came into contact with people throughout the continent. He spoke on the radio and in schools and packed city auditoriums from Punto Arenas to Arica; people wanted to hear the author of *La sangre y la esperanza.* If his delivery had been more conventional, he might have been even more popular as a speaker, but his friends claim that his addresses were peculiar, even ludicrous, as he would murmur, then growl out his comments, emphasizing the wrong words, twisting erratically, and gesticulating awkwardly. Though he was extremely well prepared, his delivery was not effective because of his mannerisms, and his personal style

19. Arturo Torres-Ríoseco, *Breve historia de la literatura chilena* (Mexico City: Ediciones de Andrea, 1965), p. 164.

20. J. P., "Nicomedes Guzmán en Buenos Aires," *Clarín,* July 22, 1946.

21. Necrology of Nicomedes Guzmán in the *Boletín del Instituto de Literatura Chilena,* 7–8 (1964), 57.

probably tended to give the impression that he was uncultured. The truth was that Guzmán was one of the best-read writers of his generation, and he aspired to create a proletarian culture in Chile. It is unfortunate that in his lectures his personal idiosyncrasies tended to detract from his charisma as a potential proletarian leader.

Because Guzmán was so well read in Chilean and western-world proletarian literature (through Spanish translations), Mariano Latorre, the Chilean novelist, professor, and leader of the criollista school, aware of his economic situation, tried to obtain a permanent position for him as a lecturer at the Instituto Pedagógico of the University of Chile. Despite Latorre's efforts and Guzmán's qualifications, however, the University of Chile could not hire a man who had no formal degree.

Although Guzmán and his colleagues had achieved considerable renown and had published several books, it was not until 1948 that the new generation of Chilean writers—especially the short-story writers—were finally acknowledged as important contributors to the national literature. Ten years had passed since a debate over the short story in Chile had begun. Guzmán's generation had first attacked the criollistas and then disputed among themselves whether the short story should be socially compromised or surrealistically structured (see Chapter 5 for the history of this polemic). Guzmán had played a major role in the dialogue through his *Nuevos cuentistas chilenos*, in which he emphasized the importance of social fiction. In 1948 the most representative of the young writers, Guzmán among them, were recognized as important Chilean writers by their inclusion in the comprehensive anthology *El cuento chileno* (*The Chilean Short Story*) published in *Atenea*, no. 279–80.

Guzmán's "Una moneda al río" was included in the anthology.[22] It is the story of an hour in the life of a poor Chilean laborer who meets a poor widow in a used clothing shop, where he ends up buying her dead husband's suit. Then she kindly offers him a gift of the shoes worn by her deceased husband. At the pivotal point of the story, to suggest the possibility of optimism even amid pessimism, Guzmán introduces the popular folk superstition of throwing a coin in the Mapocho River whenever one crosses the Pío

22. The story was later translated into English as "A Coin in the River" and published in *Amigos*, 3, No. 2 (Spring, 1950), a review published at Monticello College, Godfrey, Illinois.

Nono Bridge. Guzmán himself followed this practice: "It was his habit. His custom, his superstition."[23]

Although the subject matter may seem banal, "Una moneda al río" is a fairly well-written story. The author's psychological development of the protagonist is excellent, nearly existentialist in its execution.

In 1948 Guzmán traveled to northern Chile. At times he accompanied Pablo Neruda; at other times he was with Ester Panay, who was born in the North, and he was introduced to her family and her childhood surroundings there. The history of Guzmán's affair with Ester was well known to friends, but neither Ester nor Lucy has volunteered any information about the situation that came about when Rodrigo was born to Ester in 1945. It is not known whether Lucy found out about Ester before Rodrigo's birth, but this year seemed to bring a culmination of the author's problems; after the loss of his government position (also in 1945), Guzmán's attitude seemed to change—even in his writings. It is not accurate to say that he and Lucy separated, for even after she found out about the other woman in her husband's life, she was forgiving and still accepted him. He obtained an apartment for Ester at 865A Pedro Leon Ugalde Street—on the opposite side of the block from Lucy's small house, which he had purchased during his more prosperous years, at 730 Pezoa Véliz in the "Polígono" sector of Quinta Normal.

Though Guzmán spent time with Ester in her visits to poorer districts, he lived with Lucy and did much of his writing in her house. He also maintained a workshop or writing office in downtown Santiago and often slept there. Eventually, because of pressure from Ester, Nicomedes formally separated from Lucy, but he continued to accept the responsibilities of both households. The author's friends emphasize his conscientiousness in seeing that his family was cared for. Guzmán would leave Ester's apartment early in the morning and walk around the block to Lucy's, where he would get his children up and off to school; then he would sit down in Lucy's house at his typewriter and write the rest of the day. Lucy, who was heartbroken by this kind of separation, especially because Guzmán still remained so close to her and his children, finally confronted him one day in tears: "Oscar, why did you go off and leave

23. Oscar Vásquez Salazar, "Y me has dejado tu sangre y tu esperanza en mi hombro, Padre," *Cultura*, 96 (1964), 41.

us?" His reply surprised her. He had felt that the noisy children and crowded conditions did not afford him the peace and quiet to write.[24]

Undoubtedly the separation was partly brought about by Guzmán's travels during the latter half of the 1940s, yet only through such trips could he eke out an existence. Even during his long absences he was constantly preoccupied with Lucía and the many obligations to his family. In a public address, Homero Bascuñán declared that when Guzmán was visiting somewhere and liked the food, he would ask for some to take home for his wife and children. Once he returned home from the North with his suitcase full of food and books for Bascuñán. On another occasion he wrote Bascuñán about fees from lectures he had given which he was sending Lucy, concerned about her financial situation and her poor letter-writing habits. "He could forget himself," said Bascuñán, "but he would never forget others, especially his friends and 'his clan.' "[25]

Since the lack of money for his family was a constant problem, Guzmán helped defray some of his travel expenses by writing endorsements for LAN-Chile, the national airline. An example is the brochure "Camino de alas: Sobre el norte de Chile (a bordo de una aeronave de la Línea Aérea Nacional)," designed and written by Guzmán. On each page is a picture together with Guzmán's impressions of each city on the airline's northern route. For such efforts he often received free passage. He flew so often that he knew the flight crews and spent hours in the cockpit conversing with the pilots learning how the plane operated. He set his heart so much on having a son become a pilot that Rodrigo eventually became a pilot in the Chilean Air Force Reserve. During his travels Guzmán also gathered materials for his next novel.

Immediately after his return to Santiago from a trip of many months the North, Guzmán traveled to the southern tip of Chile, writing the novel he had begun in the North as he visited new cities. This extended travel made Guzmán aware of social problems in other regions of Chile, and his Marxist-humanist philosophy expanded beyond the slums of Santiago. But because of this broadening of his horizons, something was lost to him as a writer. Prior to this period of travel his works and anthologies had been struc-

24. Interview with Lucía Salazar, Santiago, Chile, August 7, 1971.
25. Homero Bascuñán, "Sueños, cenizas y recuerdos," speech delivered at the Santiago Jewish Center, Jehuda Ha-Levy, during the latter part of 1964.

tured from a point of view of time—biographical and interior—and the authors in his anthology had been listed according to their birth dates. After his trip to the North, however, his concept of literature evolved toward a spatial structure. For example, his later anthologies interpreted the different areas of Chile region by region, or custom by custom, attempting to discover the essence of the national culture through a meticulous examination of the people and the different environments found in every corner of the country. Guzmán began to talk of the novel as a great social epic, and he was undoubtedly influenced by Neruda, who was emphasizing space over time in his *Canto General*, composed during this period. This evolution in Guzmán's approach to novelistic structure will be discussed further in Part III.

Between July 1948 and January 1949 Guzmán continued working on his new novel as he traveled the twenty-six-hundred-mile length of Chile. Not until 1951, two and a half years later, was the book, *La luz viene del mar* (*The Light Comes from the Sea*), published.

Though a second edition was printed in 1963, his last work has not enjoyed great popularity. Ricardo Latcham's criticism offers succinct and reliable explanations of the lack of popularity of *La luz viene del mar*. Latcham feels that, although certain chapters are outstanding, the plot and structure are difficult to follow, and lyricism and sex detract from the development of the characters and the unity of the book.[26] Guzmán had been able to describe faithfully the Santiago slums, but the critics felt that he had not spent enough time in the North to be able to depict it as capably as several writers in the Generation of 1938—Andrés Sabella, Mario Bahamonde, Luis González Zenteno, Homero Bascuñán, and Gonzalo Drago, all very close friends of Guzmán. Guzmán was emulating these authors when he produced his interpretation of the vast North in the hope that it would be one of the great novels of that region.

Chileans often tend to place an exaggerated emphasis on regionalistic development in a novel, including a faithful interpretation of the types or characters of the area. Individual reviewers often disregard psychological interpretations or the humanistic value of an outsider's point of view, and with some critics, this concern has become so narrow that it is somewhat picayune. For example, one critic demanded a faithful description not only of Santiago but of

26. Latcham, "Nicomedes Guzmán."

a certain barrio, or even a neighborhood. Reflecting this attitude, Homero Bascuñán insisted that Guzmán could not comprehend the pampas or desert in a trip of a few days, "see it completely, penetrate it, know it with the eyes of a *pampino* . . . and love it like a dreamer would who was born and bred in the nitrate zone. Guzmán confessed it to me in a letter: 'The pampas is difficult, old friend, it escapes me; I swear it escapes me. . . .' "[27] Ultimately, however, such regionalistic criticisms are insignificant, for, as Latcham points out, the areas of weakness in *La luz viene del mar* are in characterization and structure. The cyclical pattern of the plot recalls the style of William Faulkner. The greatest defect in the novel's whorl-like structure is a lack of psychological development. The episodic rotating of the plot and the shifting of the setting cause the unskilled reader to lose sight of the theme and to miss both the climax and final development. When I discussed the problems of the novel's structure and the abstract ending with Ester Panay, whose childhood was the model for that of Virginia, the protagonist, she replied that my interpretation was closest to Guzmán's. In Part IIII, I shall attempt to reevaluate *La luz viene del mar* in these terms.

After the period of Guzmán's travels throughout Chile, the government relaxed its vigilant anti-Communist activities, and in 1949 the writer was given a position with the Departamento de Cultura y Publicaciones del Ministerio de Educación Pública. He accumulated more than twelve years of service in this capacity before he was retired because of ill health. At his death in 1964, issue no. 96 of the ministry's review, *Cultura*, was dedicated to his memory. Edited by Guzmán's successor, Luis Sánchez Latorre, this issue of *Cultura* contained twelve articles and eulogies by Guzmán's closest friends, many of them famous in Chilean letters. It also included three works by Guzmán, two of them previously unpublished, as well as eighteen photographs of Guzmán during various periods in his life, of his family, and of the neighborhood setting of *La sangre y la esperanza*.

In 1953 Guzmán's *Leche de burra*, subtitled "novela," but actually a short story, was published in a tiny two-by-three-inch shirt-pocket edition of fifty-five pages by Ediciones Renovación. When this story appeared in *El pan bajo la bota* in 1960, it required only fifteen pages.

---

27. Bascuñán, "Sueños, cenizas y recuerdos."

The next year, 1954, Paul J. Cooke, language professor and director of the Monticello College Press, Godfrey, Illinois, published eight short stories by Guzmán.[28] Cooke had taken an interest in Guzmán after translating "A Coin in the River," which he had discovered in *El cuento chileno*. After several years of correspondence with Guzmán, he published a collection of the writer's stories in Spanish—*Una moneda al río y otros cuentos*. This anthology contains only two short stories not previously published in Guzmán's books: "El pan bajo la bota" and "La jauría." However, the volume is most important for its inclusion of Guzmán's only autobiography, the brief "Notas del autor al lector," which were cautiously compiled by Guzmán so they would not contradict his explicit lifelong philosophy. Only a few writers and critics, among them Fernando Santiván in his prologue to *El pan bajo la bota*, have had reference to a copy of Guzmán's entire original draft called "Pequeñas notas autobiográficas."

Cooke describes an interesting incident concerning his communications with Guzmán. After *Una moneda al río* was ready to go to press, Guzmán sent his previously published story "Sólo unas cuántas lágrimas" ("Only a Few Tears") to Cooke, hoping to have it included in the anthology.[29] Cooke rejected it, but instead of stating that it had arrived late and could not be included, he impetuously replied that he felt that the subject matter made the story too controversial for him to include it in an American edition. The protagonist of the story had been a prostitute but had left that life when she married. In the story, she is seated in a café with her husband and two children when two men who knew her before she was married come into the café. They make obscene gestures and insult her, but when her strong laborer husband stands up to them, they slink out, ashamed and embarrassed at their actions. Guzmán conceived this story from his experience working with the anarchist publisher of *Los hombres obscuros*, Alberto Lagos, who had married a prostitute.

Extremely offended at the answer he received from Cooke, Guzmán took the rejection of the story as a personal affront; it was not the first time that he had felt the sting of rebuff from a publisher. Ten years earlier, in his short story "La angustia" ("Anguish," in *Donde nace el alba*), he had written about the problem of edi-

28. Following a merger in 1971, the school was named Lewis and Clark College. It is now a part of the Illinois state college system.

29. It had appeared in *Donde nace el alba* (1944), pp. 131–52.

torial rejection. In the story the protagonist becomes enraged and is driven to the verge of suicide when his publisher rejects a manuscript because the author refuses to change two inappropriate words —"piojoso" ("lousy," "louse-infested") and "parir" ("to give birth")—and their respective sentences to satisfy the editor. "La angustia" appears to have several autobiographical elements. The young author-protagonist works in an office of the government dealing with cultural affairs; he has a meager income; he is separated from his wife; and poverty seems nearly to have overcome him. In the story the author is contemplating suicide when notice reaches him of the death of his child, shocking him back to his senses. This short story became a prophecy, in part, of what was to befall Guzmán at a later date, and it may have been based on his dealings with publishers, for he had very strong feelings about editorial rejections.

Notwithstanding the publication of three novels and more than a dozen stories, this most promising and fertile period of Guzmán's career produced less literature than one would have predicted at the outset, for the prolific production and the mature expression that his earlier novels promised never became a reality. He had little time to write, and his personal conflicts around the year 1945 compounded the crisis brought about when he became a political outcast in his own country. After several difficult years of unemployment and political harassment, he found himself back in the bureaucracy confronted with a new task: to disseminate Chilean culture to each of the hidden corners of his nation without using leftist ideas. The revolution continued in his heart, but his heart was not in his writing.

3

The Declining Years

During the last ten years of his life, while his creative writing showed a decline in quality and quantity, Guzmán collected and edited material for at least four anthologies.

The first, a collection of short stories, *Antología de Baldomero Lillo* (*Anthology of Baldomero Lillo*), was published in 1955 to commemorate the fiftieth anniversary of *Sub terra* (*Underground*, 1904), Lillo's book of stories about miners. Guzmán's anthology, emphasizing those of Lillo's stories that focus on Chile's social problems, proved quite popular and was reprinted in 1965, 1969, and 1970.

A second collection, *Antología de Carlos Pezoa Véliz: Poesía y prosa* (*Anthology of Carlos Pezoa Véliz: Poetry and Prose*), was published in 1957. Pezoa Véliz was a member of Chile's second group of *modernistas* (those who wrote around 1900, following the departure of Rubén Darío from Chile). Guzmán considered Pezoa Véliz to be a member of the Generation of 1900 along with Lillo, and he especially admired and praised Pezoa Véliz's socially oriented writings.

The *Antología de cuentos de Marta Brunet* (*Anthology of Short Stories by Marta Brunet*) appeared in 1962. Marta Brunet frequently brought out essential elements of Chile's social conflicts, so Guzmán selected the most socially important stories, hoping to make them accessible to public, especially young people. (This had also been his goal with the anthology of Baldomero Lillo.) The Brunet anthology has been reprinted twice in recent years.

A fourth collection, the high-priced *Autorretrato de Chile* (*Self-Portrait of Chile*, 1957), was of a far different nature. Seemingly inspired by Mariano Latorre's criollista concept of Chile as expressed in the title of one of Latorre's personal anthologies, *Chile, país de rincones* (*Chile, Country of Corners*), Guzmán included articles or essays on his nation by nearly fifty of Chile's leading contemporary literary figures. All but one or two of the selections had been written specifically for this work, whose purpose is to present the varied regions and climates of the country that are unified by a common history and culture, and to emphasize national types such as the *roto*.

There was some negative reaction to Guzmán's criollista idea of a volume on regions and customs of Chile. Such a philosophy seemed to negate efforts of members of the Generation of '38 who aspired to supersede the criollistas and implant a new type of literature in Chile. Representative of the attitude of the Generation of '38, once championed by Guzmán, is a letter from Luis González Zenteno I found among Guzmán's personal papers in 1973. González Zenteno refused to be included in *Autorretrato de Chile*, preferring to collaborate in a work that might be "efectivamente social."

These four anthologies were issued by the well-known Santiago publishing firm Empresa Editora Zig-Zag, which in 1960 also published Guzmán's last personal collection of short stories, *El pan bajo la bota (Bread under the Boot)*. This book was a compilation of seven previously published stories and five new ones. The author had stated that the work was almost ready for publication in 1954 in *Una moneda al río*; yet nearly six years passed before it was published. A second printing followed in 1963.

The prologue to *El pan bajo la bota* was written by Fernando Santiván, an early nonviolent socialist writer whom some critics associate with Chile's Generation of 1900 and who, along with D'Halmar, was one of the founders of the famous Tolstoy Colony. Santiván wrote a short biography paraphrasing Guzmán's "Pequeñas notas autobiográficas," since the only published account of the author's life was in *Una moneda al río*, which had not been easily accessible to the Chilean public. In his preface, "Algunas palabras sobre Nicomedes Guzmán" ("A few words about Nicomedes Guzmán"), Santiván also included reviews, published originally in obscure southern Chilean newspapers, of each of Guzmán's major works as they had appeared through the years.

Guzmán had also been working for several years on an anthology of Chilean short stories by various authors which he had planned to call "Chile en las manos" ("Chile in One's Hands"). This title, which had been promised in the second edition of *La ceniza y el sueño* (1960, p. 4), became the title for the first pamphlet in a series that Guzmán published in the Ministry of Education dealing with geography, history, literature, culture, archaeology, and art.

This same anthology, which Guzmán renamed "Cuentistas ci-

meros de Chile" ("Top Short Story Writers of Chile") in the manuscript stage, did not appear until 1969, when Nascimento published
it with the new title *Antología de cuentos chilenos* (*Anthology of
Chilean Short Stories*). In his final attempt to interpret Chile through
its contemporary prose fiction, Guzmán grouped well-known short
stories under seven headings: six geographical (North, South, and
so forth) and one of folk culture—"Cuentos humorísticos, mágicos
y de leyendas" ("Humoristic, Magic, and Legendary Stories").

During most of the 1950s Guzmán continued his relationship
with Ester, but this strong and intelligent woman wanted Guzmán
to marry her and legitimize their son. Guzmán was constantly torn
in his allegiance and responsibilities between the two households
he had created. Pressures from Ester finally became so great that he
persuaded Lucy to concede him an annulment on August 27, 1957,
since there is no divorce in Chile.

Nicomedes and Ester were married shortly thereafter, and on
April 30, 1959, a second child, Olaya Vásquez Panay, was born.
Olaya has written short stories and has entered several of them in
contests; at the age of eleven, she won third prize in a contest sponsored by the Federación de Estudiantes of the Universidad Técnica
Federico Santa María. Ester has also tried her hand at writing and
has won at least one prize. Nicomedes' and Ester's oldest son, Rodrigo, graduated as a mechanical engineer from the Universidad
Técnica Federico Santa María and works in the Chilean automotive
industry but has always aspired to achieve his father's dream and
become a full-time pilot.

While Lucy knew Guzmán as Oscar, Ester always called him
Nicomedes. There is no obvious hostility between the two wives in
spite of popular myth to the contrary. At Guzmán's death in 1964,
they were rumored to be at odds, like the two women in Gabriel
García Márquez's *Cien años de soledad* who fight over the body of
their deceased mate. Though several professors at the University of
Chile argued that such a conflict did occur at Guzmán's funeral, all
members of the family flatly deny such talk as slanderous and malicious. Each of the two branches of the family seems to be aware and
proud of the accomplishments of the other; in 1971 Lucy and Ester
both boasted that Guzmán's heirs totaled seven children and fourteen grandchildren including a set of twins.

Ester Panay now resides in El Sol, a section of Quilpué near

Viña del Mar. She has recently retired from her professional position as a psychologist and is pursuing a small private practice. She obtained through marriage the publishing rights to all of Guzmán's works, including any royalties that his ever-popular works may produce.

Lucía was left only the house on Pezoa Véliz and a pension of sixty *escudos* a month, an insignificant amount, since under Chile's high rate of inflation sixty *escudos* is now worth only a few pennies.[1]

Nicomedes Guzmán was well known and liked in his neighborhood. The people referred to him as "Don Oscar" and were extremely proud of his contributions to Chilean culture. In his honor and memory several neighborhood centers have been founded. First, because Guzmán organized teams for young people during his more successful years and held athletic tournaments, paying for the prizes and trophies out of his own pocket, the Nicomedes Guzmán Sports Club was established in his name. Also carrying the Guzmán name are a cultural center and the Centro de Madres, Nicomedes Guzmán, a neighborhood home economics training center where Lucía has worked.

In spite of his fame as a political writer, Guzmán did not have a reputation as an active Communist. A resolution offered in the Chilean Chamber of Deputies (Congress) on July 7, 1964, by a Popular Front colleague of 1938, the Communist deputy César Godoy Urrutia, rationalizes Guzmán's passive role:

> Nicomedes, durante unos años, militó en el Partido Comunista, si bien, su trabajo, sus viajes, sus dificultades materiales, su salud, impidieron que hiciera una militancia regular y continua.[2]

Marcial Tamayo adds that there was only one time during his life that Guzmán was publicly recognized as a Communist:

> Cuando se le rindió un homenaje a España en el Teatro Caupolicán, el año 1952, se le hizo entrega simbólicamente a Nicomedes, a Pablo Neruda . . . de un carnet como militantes del partido comunista. Y ese fue el único acto público que se le conoció a Nicomedes como comunista.[3]

1. Lucy's unfortunate economic plight was pointed out by Marcial Tamayo, "Nicomedes Guzmán y su herencia literaria," *El Siglo*, June 26, 1971.

2. Cited from a two-part letter from Marcial Tamayo to me, dated October 21–22, 1970, Santiago.

3. Letter from Tamayo, October 21–22, 1970.

It should also be pointed out, however, that a group of Communist youths paid their last respects to the great proletarian author by marching at his funeral.

By the 1950s, although no mention of it had yet been made in print, it was widely known that Guzmán had a serious problem with drinking.[4] Several of his friends, wanting to acknowledge the seriousness of his illnesses without publicly linking his maladies to a liquor problem, have often referred to his pitiable incapacitation. A most pathetic description of his mental and physical deterioration and loss of weight is Luis Sánchez Latorre's introduction to *Cultura*'s number in homage to Guzmán, which mentions how the winter cold penetrated his body, threatening his health and causing him to find a stove to warm himself:

> ¡Qué impresión desoladora nos produjo el estado de flaqueza en que había vuelto al mundo! Parecía sobreviviente de un viaje milenario. Yo, que lo concocí hace veinticuatro años y que me asombré de comprobar que "ese muchacho" era el autor de *Los hombres obscuros*, no lograba explicarme cómo la enfermedad había podido descomponer, hasta provocar la sensación del arrasamiento, aquel rostro de niño grande y bueno.[5]

Somewhat more obvious is Daniel Belmar's reference to his "lack of care for his health around 1954 in spite of the counsel and warning given by his closest friends."[6] Similar references to his ailments are abundant, but perhaps the most shocking is Edmundo Concha's, still without mention of alcoholism. Disquieted that Guzmán hardly recognized him from less than two meters away, Concha realizes the severity of his illness: "La enfermedad ya había hecho presa de casi todo su organismo."[7] At an informal meeting at the Sociedad de Escritores Chilenos in July 1973, Guzmán's son Oscarín divulged what others in the family have never made public: Guzmán suffered from diabetes, which compounded his other problems.

Just what may cause disillusion in a socialist writer of Guzmán's stature is difficult to ascertain. Occasionally a Marxist, upon suffering a betrayal of his political ideals, will turn to writing a very personal

---

4. None of the articles about Guzmán published to date have mentioned alcoholism; they have only hinted at it.

5. L.S.L. [Luis Sánchez Latorre], "Nicomedes Guzmán," *Cultura*, 96 (1964), 11.

6. Daniel Belmar, "Presencia de Nicomedes Guzmán," *El Siglo*, July 19, 1964.

7. Edmundo Concha, "Responso por el compañero," *Cultura*, 96 (1964), 18–19.

kind of literature, as did the Argentine novelist Ernesto Sábato, who embraced Marxism at one time but turned from its collective utopianism to a more personal expression. Other authors may try simply to shock their readers with raw realism, some critics see Guzmán's entire production in this vein. Yet Guzmán and others have felt that socialist realism employs shock as a means of exposing social inequalities.

Evidently Guzmán sought to escape his disillusion through heavy drinking. He seems to have begun to drink while he was still quite young, and, like most Chileans, he drank wine and occasionally beer. Ester Panay asserts that she saw Guzmán drunk three times in 1943, but never saw him drunk after that. He tended to drink continually without appearing obviously drunk. He did not stagger or seem to lose the use of his faculties. When Guzmán was at his worst, if he was out of the house on an errand, he would stop at a bar in every block to have a drink. On one occasion when he was drinking with friends, he was observed going around the room after everyone-had left, draining their partly filled glasses.

During my stay in Chile in 1971, I asked every close acquaintance of Guzmán's, "When did drinking become a problem for Guzmán?" The purpose of this question was to attempt to pinpoint when his literary output began to decline and what relation alcohol had to this decline. The answers varied greatly. Many people were inclined to think that Guzmán had begun heavy drinking early in life, as a child or adolescent. Ester Panay and some of his closest friends felt that he had always had a problem with alcohol and that his weakness for it was brought on by a neurosis. Lucía, however, did not agree. She stated that her husband's drinking problems began when he became involved with Ester, because the birth of his illegitimate son brought on family entanglements that he could not cope with. It should be noted also that 1945 was not only the year of Rodrigo's and Darío's births, but also the year that Guzmán's most serious political and economical conflicts began.

Guzmán was by no means the only member of the Generation of '38 to have a drinking problem. His comrade from the north of Chile, Luis (Lucho) González Zenteno, died an alcoholic, and several others of his generation are suffering from or have succumbed to alcoholism. A notorious alcoholic member of the generation is the novelist and former leader of the group, Juan Godoy, a good friend of Guzmán's who has suffered a similar decline in his artistic abilities because of alcoholism.[8] Unlike Guzmán, however, Godoy has been known to be extremely offensive and unpleasant when intoxicated. Both writers had shown great promise as leaders of the Generation of 1938, but their weakness for intoxicants slowly destroyed their talents.

In later years, Juan Godoy had two or three plots for novels formulated in his mind, but he seldom, if ever, enjoyed the tranquility to be able to set them down in writing.[9] At various times, Guzmán announced novels that he had outlined and was writing, but undoubtedly many of his aspirations were limited by his alcoholism. Some of the books he projected were promised repeatedly as early as 1944. The titles are as follows: *Las manos rudas* (*Rough hands*);[10] *Papá fisco* (*Father Fiscus*); *El gran Pilatos* (*The Great Pilate*); *Tiempo de la bruma* (*Time of Fog*); *Por esta luz que me alumbra* (*Through This Light Which Illuminates Me*), a projected novel in collaboration with Homero Bascuñán; *El fuego sempiterno, novela cíclica*: 1. *Sudor contra lágrimas*, 2. *Tranquila está la tarde*, also announced by Guzmán as a separate novel, and 3. *De polvo eres . . .* (*The Everlasting Fire, Cyclical Novel*: 1. *Sweat Against Tears*, 2. *Tranquil is the Afternoon*, 3. *From Dust Thou Art . . .*).[11] Homero Bascuñán stated that Guzmán wanted him to write the novel they were going to do together and Guzmán would edit it. Bascuñán always put Guzmán off, because he did not like the arrangement. What he did appreciate were Guzmán's efforts to help him publish. A book of a different nature was one that Luis Sánchez Latorre saw Guzmán writing on don Francisco Encina. Though the work was never mentioned in writing, it was to be an essay on heroes in Chilean history.

A final novel, mentioned only in the "Pequeñas notas autobiográficas," is *Las buenas historias de Pellín Queltehue*. Although it is unlikely that Guzmán did much work on any of these projects, he did write a portion of his final novel, *Los trece meses del año*, before

8. Thomas Edgar Lyon, Jr., *Juan Godoy* (New York: Twayne Publishers, 1972), p. 18.

9. Lyon, p. 25.

10. This is a novel that was listed as "in preparation" in the first edition of *Los hombres obscuros*, but we may speculate that it became *La sangre y la esperanza*, as it was never mentioned again.

11. These are notations from several of Guzmán's books, including *La sangre y la esperanza* (1943), *Donde nace el alba* (1944), *Una moneda al río* (1954), and the 1960 edition of *La ceniza y el sueño*.

he was hospitalized because of serious complications due to alcoholism.

People who were close to Guzmán unanimously echo the words of Marcial Tamayo about Guzmán's appalling mistreatment of his body and carelessness in his personal affairs: "Nicomedes neglected himself greatly during his last years. After having worked hard he couldn't prevent wine and good or bad food from destroying him from within. . . . He drank like a condemned man and died like one."[12] He would go for days without proper food or sleep; then he would veer to the other extreme and overeat or consume greasy and starchy foods only. His poor diet combined with alcoholism brought on physical deterioration and finally led to a psychological obsession that was irritating and embarrassing to him. After losing so much weight, Guzmán had the weird sensation of constantly losing his pants and shoes—he felt that they were actually growing larger on him.[13] He also lost his balance. In the final months of the disease he had to think out methodically each step he took, with the result that he walked slowly and mechanically, like a robot.

Ester Panay was a professional psychologist and should have been able to help her husband, but her efforts were futile. A specialist advised her that any motivation toward change in Guzmán would have to come from outside the family.

Apparently more than once Guzmán showed signs of recovery from alcoholism, for in 1958 Juan Loveluck invited him to participate in the Primer Encuentro de Escritores Chilenos and Gonzalo Rojas Pizarro offered him the opportunity to present ten lectures, both events to take place concurrently at the University of Concepción in January 1958. This meeting of writers of the Generation of 1938 was so successful that a second convention, El Segundo Encuentro de Escritores Chilenos, involving mainly the Generation of 1950, took place in Chillán six months later, July 19–24, 1958.

In the Primer Encuentro Guzmán presented a paper later published in *Atenea*, which treats the novel and short story in Chile from a proletarian point of view.[14] This issue of *Atenea* also included bio-

---

12. Letter from Tamayo, October 21–22, 1970.

13. "Filebo" [Luis Sánchez Latorre], "Nicomaco," *Revista de los Sábados, Las Últimas Noticias*, June 26, 1971.

14. "Encuentro emocional con Chile," *Atenea*, 380–81 (1958), 77–78. Paulo de Carvalho-Neto, attending correspondent from Brazil, stated that Guzmán

graphical notes on Guzmán and the other participants in the Encuentros. The article mentions that Guzmán's *La sangre y la esperanza* was translated into Czechoslovakian, but it is the only source to state this fact.

The rector and other directors of the University of Concepción must have been impressed with Guzmán's participation in the first *encuentro*, for Fernando Alegría invited Guzmán to return to Concepción for a writers' workshop which he directed, the Taller de Escritores, which lasted four months, from October 1960 to January 1961. Guzmán was highly honored by winning the grant as writer-in-residence, which allowed him time and means to work further on his novel.

The authors participating in the workshop were to produce publishable works during the sessions, and they were required to read aloud the manuscripts of the novels they had been drafting. The works were then discussed openly and criticized by the other writers and visiting critics.

The novel Guzmán had decided to write, a reflection of many disappointing years in bureaucratic posts, was to attack the evils of bureaucracy. The manuscript, written in the first person, was entitled "Los trece meses del año" ("The Thirteen Months of the Year"), and was to be a sequel to *La sangre y la esperanza*. Had he finished it, the work would have been a valuable document, for it dealt with an aspect of Chilean life different from those he had depicted previously.

To date, only three chapters of "Los trece meses del año" have been published: Chapter 1 and the "Plan de una novela" ("Plan for a Novel"), which were presented at the workshop at Concepción, were published posthumously in *Cultura*, Chapter 2 appeared in *Atenea* with the title "La poruña" ("The Large Spoon"), and Santiago's largest daily, *El Mercurio*, featured "Vianda de invierno" ("Winter Meal") on its front page on Sunday, February 23, 1964.[15]

In his last ten years Guzmán wrote popular columns in several different daily newspapers. From 1954 to 1956 his most famous *crónicas*, the "Estampas populares," appeared in *Las Noticias de*

---

read another paper, "El cuento y la novela chilenos en su expresión humana" (*Atenea*, 380–81 [1958], 371–74).

15. See *Cultura*, 96 (1964), 44–52, for the structural outline of the projected novel that was presented in the workshop, and pp. 53–57 of the same issue for Chapter 1 of the novel. For Chapter 2 see *Atenea*, 394 (1961), 138–51.

Última Hora. Between 1956 and 1958 Guzmán was hired by Domingo Melfi to write for *La Nación,* where during the last year he directed the Sunday literary supplement with the help of Ester Panay and his son Oscarín, who wrote articles. *La Segunda* ran Guzmán's articles from 1960 to 1962, and he concluded his journalism career at *Las Ultimas Noticias* (1963–64). He held these jobs in addition to his government position. During this same period Guzmán continued to travel extensively; after 1954 he went to Lima, La Paz, and Quito. He traveled throughout Chile as frequently as his health would permit, and he won several municipal prizes for his writings.[16] But finally his health failed to the point that during the 1960s he spent several weeks in the hospital each year and in 1963 he was virtually incommunicado throughout a long convalescence.

Guzmán left the hospital ruined physically, intellectually, and economically. He worked wherever he could, running errands, doing menial tasks. Irma Astorga, long-time friend of Nicomedes and winner of the 1971 Premio Municipal de Santiago for her novel *La compuerta mágica,* wrote that in April 1964 Guzmán was reduced to peddling men's ties.[17] At the same time he was also involved with writing or editorial obligations which included gathering stories for an anthology with a rapidly approaching deadline. But in spite of his fragmented labors, his income became so meager that he finally stooped to selling feminine apparel (apparently lingerie) in public office buildings, going from office to office in search of customers.[18]

Nicomedes Guzmán was finally defeated by alcohol. His drinking problem became so severe that he was sternly warned by a doctor that one more drink would kill him. This threat convinced him at last that he must abstain from liquor for his own life's sake. As soon as he stopped drinking he began to recover, but he had aged so severely that in a picture taken two weeks before he turned fifty he looks much older.[19]

16. Orlando Cabrera Leyva, "Nicomedes Guzmán: 'Se nace escribiendo porque sí . . .'" *Zig-Zag* (Santiago), April 10, 1964, pp. 14–15.

17. Irma Astorga, "Una dirección," *Las Noticias de Última Hora* (Santiago), August 9, 1964.

18. Interview with Hugo Goldsack and Irma Astorga (husband and wife), Santiago, August 5, 1971. Guzmán's wife, Ester, denies this, saying that she always made sure he had money.

19. *Cultura,* 96 (1964), 105; the picture also appeared in Oscar Vásquez Salazar, "¡Así era mi padre!" (*El Siglo,* June 26, 1966) and "Niñez y adolescencia de un gran novelista" (*El Siglo,* July 9, 1967).

The day of his fiftieth birthday, June 25, 1964, was celebrated with hope for a great new future. First, he went to the house of his second wife, Ester, for a celebration; then he visited with his family and parents at Lucía's, where there was a party. Guzmán's son Oscar explains the intimate details of his father's last day on earth:

> We had a dinner in his honor June 25. We were all pleased to be able to be with him at the table after his long illness. We didn't drink wine so as to not tempt him. Suddenly he felt ill and went home around ten P.M. The rest of us went out to have a drink at the bar "Mi compadre" which he always frequented. My brother Darío came there to inform us of his hemorrhage. My mother cried and applied coagulants. But it was useless. He handed me his watch, squeezed my hands, and later asked me to let him die. We had hopes of prolonging his life. We took him to the Infirmary No. 3. Then later we left. He died at four thirty-five in the morning of the twenty-sixth. They threw him in the morgue, naked, like a pariah.[20]

Apparently someone had opened some champagne in one of the homes and insisted that a little drink would not harm him; but the liquor was so poisonous to his body that it sent him into convulsions and he died within a few hours in the Quinta Normal Asistencia Pública.[21]

20. Ronnie Muñoz Martineaux wrote Oscar's story in a newspaper article (which I read without any indication of the source). Oscarín repeated these details of his father's death in an interview with me in Santiago, June 26, 1973, at which Muñoz was also present.

21. Interview with Enrique Lafourcade, Salt Lake City, Utah, January 4, 1970.

II

Nicomedes Guzmán and the
Proletarian Generation of 1938

4

Toward a Definition of the Generation of 1938

The Generation of 1938 was not fully recognized as a distinctive and forceful entity in Chilean literature until 1948, when Francisco Santana published his brief history of this group in *El cuento chileno*.[1] Nicomedes Guzmán had defined a smaller segment of the generation in 1941, when he published *Nuevos cuentistas chilenos*; yet it was not until the Primer Encuentro at Concepción in 1958 that an effort was made to identify all of the divisions.

Chile has provided a most fertile climate for the formation of literary groups. Because of the existence of several key generations, it has been common for Chilean critics to refer to every school, movement, or period as a generation.

Several philosophers have labored with the concept of dialectic generations, including José Ortega y Gasset and Julian Marías, but the first to establish a theory was the nineteenth-century German philosopher Wilhelm Dilthey. Yet, although it has been clearly defined, the term *generation* has been applied to all kinds of groups, very often with serious contradictions. Should one refer to the Movement of 1900 or the Generation of 1900? Or is the year for this group 1910, as some have insisted. Mario Espinosa refers to the Generations of 1900 and 1914, the latter being "Los Diez," which many feel is part of the Generation of 1900.[2] Fernando Alegría distinguishes "la Generación del Centenario (1910)," "the Tolstoy Colony, the group 'Los Diez,' and the so-called generación pictórica [impressionistic painters] de 1913."[3] Should Guzmán's group be called the Generation of 1938, 1940, or 1942? Small wonder the usefulness of the theory of generations is subject to question.

The Argentine scholar Aníbal Sánchez-Reulet suggested to me that the concept of generations originated not with Ortega y Gasset but in the early nineteenth-century radical "Joven" groups patterned after Mazzini's "Joven Italia" or "Joven Francia." Sánchez-Reulet

1. Cf. p. 29. Santana's essay was later reedited and amplified in book form: *La nueva generación de prosistas chilenos* (Santiago: Editorial Nascimento, 1949).

2. Mario Espinosa, "Una generación," *Atenea*, 380–81 (1958), 67.

3. Fernando Alegría, *Literatura chilena del siglo XX* (Santiago: Empresa Editora Zig-Zag, 1967), pp. 57, 177.

also gave Bilbao's "Sociedad de Igualdad" as an excellent example of a "Joven Chile" type of literary generation. This *joven* group of the 1840s has become the model for subsequent Chilean generations.

We will not attempt to pass critical judgment on the numerous so-called generations that influenced the Generation of 1938, but it will be valuable to list and discuss them briefly.

The Generation of 1842 was headed by José Victorino Lastarria, disciple of Andrés Bello. (Bello founded the University of Chile in 1842.) This movement began with the organization of the "Sociedad Literaria," also in 1842. The "Sociedad de Igualdad," founded in 1850 by Lastarria's confrère Francisco Bilboa, offered free education to the proletariat in politics, law, culture, and literature.

Though Guzmán personally did not recognize any literary generations between 1842 and 1900, he did praise in his talks and essays any writer of that period who promoted social values. He acclaimed Alberto Blest Gana as the "first great American novelist" and the father of all Chilean novelists because he introduced realism to Chile.[4] On the other extreme from Guzmán, Montes and Orlandi recognize a "Movement of 1842" in their *Historia y antología de la literatura chilena*, but in addition they insist that, beginning in 1837, new generations are formed every fifteen years in Chilean letters. Needless to say, their schematic outline produces some groups that were certainly not homogeneous generations: 1837, 1852, 1867, 1882, 1897, 1912, 1927, 1942, and 1957.[5]

The most widely accepted title for the socially oriented group of writers at the turn of the century is the Generation of 1900, though the dates of 1891, 1897, 1910, 1912, 1913, and 1914 have also been applied to this group. The Generation of 1900 embraced several of Guzmán's literary idols—Lillo, D'Halmar, Pezoa Véliz, and Pedro Antonio González. In stating his definition of the Generation of 1900, Guzmán lumps *naturalismo, criollismo,* and even *modernismo* erroneously together ("Miniatura," 23). Yet if these writers were

4. [Nicomedes Guzmán], "Miniatura histórico-informativa de las letras chilenas," in *Catálogo general de obras de autores nacionales* (Santiago: Editorial Cultura, 1946), pp. 15–30; cf. p. 22. This little catalogue was printed by the Editorial Cultura as an advertising promotion, and it includes Guzmán's brief fifteen-page history of Chilean literature as an added feature. Hereafter it will be cited in the text as "Miniatura."

5. Hugo Montes and Julio Orlandi, *Historia y antología de la literatura chilena* (Santiago: Editorial del Pacífico, 1965).

unified in any way, Guzmán clearly felt that it was in their spirit of disenchantment with the past and intense hope for social improvement in the future: "In synthesis, the Generation of 1900 represents a concern, an eagerness for great accomplishments, a nationalist passion at the service of literature." This attitude of Marxist hope as a key to future success can also be found in another group of turn-of-the-century writers: Jack London, Upton Sinclair, and others of the United States. Inspired, like several of the Chileans, by the works of Emile Zola, they created a new kind of novel and short story. With the advent of a new century, young radical writers in both nations were reaffirming socialism through new modes of expression, attempting to avoid the stereotyped efforts of the utopian socialists of the nineteenth century. They were greeting the turn of the century with great optimism for a revolutionary future.[6]

Although the social orientation of the Generation of 1900 was strong, Guzmán saw their focus on customs as a weakness; he insisted, however, that Lillo and D'Halmar were not to be considered among the "early Criollistas" (Miniatura," 23–24). This gives the reader a better idea of how Guzmán, an urban author, felt toward the criollista themes that his generation opposed. It also gives a better insight into the characterization of Pablo in *Los hombres obscuros* (cf. "Letter," Chapter 10, below).

The strongest and most important author of this epoch and the writer who inspired Guzmán the most is Baldomero Lillo, who, according to Fernando Alegría's research, was a socialist, in spite of critics' statements to the contrary.[7] Comments by Guzmán and Alegría leave no doubt as to the debt of the Generation of 1938 to the Generation of 1900.[8] They saw Lillo and the other writers of his time as the initiators of proletarian literature in Chile. The young writers of the Generation of 1938 looked to the fiction of the popular and successful Generation of 1900 for inspiration and guidance, hoping to find in it Socialist elements which they might imitate to continue a proletarian tradition in Chilean literature.

6. Walter B. Rideout, *The Radical Novel in the United States: 1900–1954. Some Interrelations of Literature and Society* (New York: Hill and Wang, 1966), p. 23.

7. Fernando Alegría, *Fronteras del realismo* (Santiago: Empresa Editora Zig-Zag, 1962), p. 22, and "Resolución de medio siglo," *Atenea*, 380–81 (1958), 143.

8. Alegría, "Resolución de medio siglo," p. 142.

Generational Criteria

Though the writers of the proletarian Generation of 1938 shared many interests, there were also many differences among them due to the various personalities involved. In order to interpret Guzmán and his group, it will be necessary to examine them in relationship to seven criteria that are generally considered to define a generation. Members of the Generation of 1938 were united by the following characteristics: (1) their birthdates were close together; (2) they had common backgrounds; (3) they were friends and associates; (4) they shared generational experiences; (5) they developed leadership; (6) they shared a generational language; and (7) they joined to suppress the previous generation. The following examples show in detail how the Generation of 1938 conforms to the seven criteria.

Birthdates.

Most of the writers associated with the Generation of 1938 were born between 1910 and 1920. None was born later, and only three or four were born earlier. These older writers had traveled or worked in their youth and had returned to school later in life. Thus, they were older when they made contact with the younger members of the generation in literary or cultural *tertulias*, or clubs. Also, the older writers' labor union experience guided the proletarian generation. Homero Bascuñán (born in the North in 1901) was working in a roof-tile factory in the Quinta Normal district when Guzmán included him in his anthology of the new generation (1941).[9] Gonzalo Drago (born in 1907) had been forced to travel extensively before he was able to establish himself in Rancagua where he became a member of Los Inútiles, contributing to the generation his famous novel, *Cobre*. The other older authors were close to Guzmán: Juan Negro (born 1906), Raúl Norero (born 1908), Nicasio Tangol (born 1906), and the physician Jorge Soto Moreno (born 1900). Guzmán aided Drago, Norero, and Tangol by publishing their works in the La Honda series.

Similar Experiences and Ideals.

Most of the writers were proletarian or were from the lower middle class and became identified with the proletarian cause. They

---

9. Homero is now the colorful journalist, folklorist, and bibliophile of the generation. He has published works under more than 250 pseudonyms.

attended public schools, and most of them lived at one time or another in Santiago. Actually, it would be logical to change the name of the generation to the Quinta Normalistas, for at one time or another most of the writers lived, worked, or studied, as did Nicomedes Guzmán, in the Quinta Normal district of Santiago. Once known as the Comuna Yungay, this large Lower West Side municipality is centered around a 330-acre park which includes two museums and other popular attractions. Home of several industries, Quinta Normal is a proletarian and lower-middle-class district. As the young generation formed in Quinta Normal, another group that merged with the youthful proletarians was the Oscar Castro group called Los Inútiles, which originated in the mining town of Rancagua and adopted as members Guzmán, Bascuñán, and others from the Santiago group. Out of the Instituto Pedagógico came another small group, headed by Juan Godoy and inspired by his Angurrientismo.

Personal Contact.

Extremely close associations were gained in groups like Los Inútiles or the Angurrientista movement. Since many of the writers had attended school together, they had also collaborated early in their careers on periodicals such as *El Peneca.* They later took over *Frente Popular, La Opinión,* and *La Hora* and made them organs of their generation.

The surviving members of the generation are still very close; they often collaborate on articles and are employed together on newspaper or government staffs. Most of them belong to the Sociedad de Escritores Chilenos (SECH), which offers the prestigious 50,000 *escudo* Nicomedes Guzmán Award each December 28 for the best novel entered in the new national contest. Several writers, along with their wives and widows of other writers, meet annually on November 1 in Rancagua, to commemorate Oscar Castro's birthday. And at any time it is possible to find three or four congregated in a newspaper office, at the SECH, or in a bar, exchanging memories and ideas.

Generational Experience.

The formation of the Popular Front, together with the victory of its candidate, Pedro Aguirre Cerda, was the main factor that molded these individuals into a homogeneous generation. The members' literary pursuits were encouraged through their participation in literary contests created by the Popular Front and in competition for national prizes offered from the first time in Chile by Aguirre Cerda and his successors.

Leadership.

The actual leadership of the Generation of '38 might be disputed; indeed, it is not necessary to cite only one leader in a group composed of over one hundred authors. The early and continuing leadership of the poets Braulio Arenas, Nicanor Parra, and Gonzalo Rojas is worthy of mention, as is the initial leadership in prose of the young "professor," Juan Godoy, who had over twenty Angurrientista disciples. Most critics, however, have consistently pointed out the leadership of Nicomedes Guzmán, not only as a successful author, but also as a promoter. It was his 1941 anthology that helped to define and identify the Generation of '38. His later labors as editor of several key works written by his colleagues established him as a definite leader. Because of his reputation and through his contacts, he helped lesser-known authors of his generation publish their works, and he encouraged the efforts of all his fellow writers. He also became a political and labor leader, working closely with Pablo Neruda and other distinguished Chilean figures.

During the last decade, Fernando Alegría has taken over much of the leadership and promotion of the generation. For many years Alegría was professor of Spanish American literature at the University of California, Berkeley, with a joint appointment at the University of Chile; more recently Alegría has taught at Stanford, and he was cultural attaché in the Allende government.

Generational Language.

The writers of the Generation of 1938 shared a recognizable vocabulary and neo-baroque style. The proletarian authors attempted to mix popular language with poetic style, including innovative images.[10] In addition, one of the common purposes of the members of the Generation of '38 was social reform.

Suppression, Negation, or Destruction of the Previous Generation.

This last element is the most disputed of the seven; many critics consider it unnecessary. The contradictory attitude of the younger generation toward the established writers, and especially toward the

10. One of the more complete works to deal with this aspect of the generation is by Luis Sánchez Latorre, *Los expedientes de Filebo* (Santiago: Empresa Editora Zig-Zag, 1965).

criollistas, is of major importance and will be carefully detailed throughout the rest of Part II.

Guzmán leaned toward previous generations to help define and outline actions for his own generation. Imitating Bilbao's Sociedad de Igualdad, Guzmán helped form his generation's Universidad Popular, where he taught "popular geography" and literature, Julio Moncada taught literature, and Hugo Goldsack taught economics. Taking a page out of history, their philosophy was that "la masa puede y tiene el derecho de ser culta."[11]

The critics' lack of agreement upon generational titles has led to some confusion. For example, Montes and Orlandi refer to Guzmán's group as the Generation of 1942. Another common title is the "generación del 40," a phrase first coined by Guzmán in *Nuevos cuentistas chilenos* (1941, p. 12). Ricardo A. Latcham, dean of Chilean critics, picked up the term and influenced many to think of the group as the Generation of 1940. Guzmán later dropped that tag in favor of the more popular Generation of 1938.

It would be helpful for critics to adhere more strictly to the generational criteria set forth in this chapter; otherwise, any writer born during the decade of 1910–20 could lay claim to being a member of the generation, which might thus wrongly be said to include as members Eduardo Frei and Salvador Allende, two Chilean presidents, since they were active authors and essayists in 1938.

A Beginning as Apprentice Poets

Chile produced very little literature of international importance until the advent of the "vanguard" or so-called Post Modernist period. Spain's great nineteenth-century critic Marcelino Menéndez y Pelayo called Chile "sólo un país de historiadores y juristas."[12] Between the years 1915 and 1930, however, the country produced an abundance of poetry that brought it stature as a newcomer among the foremost recognized Spanish American literary nations. In fact, Alan Price Jones of the *London Times* stated that in the field of belles-lettres Chile was "equalled only by Sweden."[13] Two Chilean poets, Gabriela Mistral and Pablo Neruda, won the Nobel Prize, and a third, Vicente Huidobro, was extremely influential in his

11. "Cultura chilena," *Voz de América*, 1 (May 1944), 2.
12. Cited by Mario Espinosa, "Una generación," p. 66.
13. Mario Espinosa, "Una generación," p. 66.

time. Nevertheless, this great movement of Chilean lyric poets was only a secondary influence on the Generation of 1938; the main influence, as has been outlined in this chapter, was the political and social orientation of the Generations of 1842 and 1900. Poetry was an indirect influence, however, for, as Fernando Alegría points out, the authors learned the value of the written word and how to overcome superficial localism; also, they realized that, in writing, the visual image was the major element, "victorious over pure conceptual knowledge."[14]

The stature gained by Chile's poets had made poetry extremely popular, and most of the authors of the new generation achieved publication first in the 1930s as poets. Although some never advanced beyond the stage of "teenage versifiers," they did write a considerable amount of verse and many of them published books of poetry.

The three great poets of this period, Mistral, Neruda, and Huidobro, did provide inspiration, though at times the new generation consciously rejected it. The young men thought their masters lacked certain fundamental values: "drama y condición humana auténticos, pasión verdadera del espíritu y profundidad consciente en el reconocimiento nuevo de nuestra tierra."[15]

A fourth poet who is cited regularly as a direct influence on the Generation of '38 is the leftist poet Pablo de Rokha. But he has failed to gain the international prestige held by the other three poets.

Gabriela Mistral, Chile's first Nobel Prize–winning poet (1945), published no verse between *Ternura* (1924) and *Tala* (1938). She was out of the country from 1932 to 1938, attached to Chilean consulates in Naples, Madrid, and Lisbon. She returned to Chile early in 1938, three or four months after Neruda's return, the same year that her book *Tala* was published and the same year that the Generation of 1938 finally began to take form. However, her influence was not as noticeable as that of Huidobro, who was directly influencing the new generation through his presence and his writing.

Volodia Teitelboim, a proletarian novelist of the generation who began as a poet, points out that Huidobro revealed to them "lo absolutamente moderno" when he returned from Paris in 1933. He held the majority of the young poets under his influence, teaching them

14. Alegría, "Resolución de medio siglo," pp. 142–43.
15. Miguel Serrano, *Ni por mar, ni por tierra . . . (Historia de una generación)* (Santiago: Editorial Nascimento, 1950), pp. 202–7.

to admire new European poets and to scoff at Darío, who had gone out of style. Teitelboim, who was a powerful Communist leader in the Chilean Senate during Allende's presidency, also states that neither Neruda nor Mistral was of significance to the generation during the early thirties.[16]

Huidobro continued to inspire these young poets, whom he attracted because he espoused a radical philosophy; however, his political sincerity was questionable and was later called into disrepute by his disciples when they became militant leftists.

Huidobro alienated himself from his followers one evening when he attempted to explain his theory of poetic creation (he had formulated in 1916 the concept of the international poetic movement of *creacionismo*). Huidobro insisted that poetic expression was often haphazard and arbitrary, not inspired and carefully polished; his disciples were amazed and confused. Then he ceremoniously brought out a shoe-box which contained folded pieces of paper, on each which was written a word: "aeronaut," "kiosk," "sorcery," "rubber," "monument," and so on. He explained that in recent years, in order to write, he had become accustomed to combining them by chance. A poem for him was a lottery, a game of dice played with infinity, a pure creation of one's spirit, a challenge to reason, a memory of worldly dreams that everyone else has forgotten, a magic act, the most pure totem, the great mystery, the unexplainable secret.

"That night doubt took form. So poetry is nothing more than play and chance. . . ."[17] Although the group lost faith in many things that night, they also awoke to a new light of rebellion and disbelief.

It was in this same ingenuous but revolutionary spirit that Volodia Teitelboim and Eduardo Anguita published in March 1935 the "rebellious and arbitrary" *Antología de poesía chilena nueva*. This anthology was the first publication to give a preview of the forthcoming generation's new works, although in many ways it was a literary farce. Teitelboim and Anguita represent the creacionista arm of the Generation of '38, the most faithful followers of Huidobro.[18]

Ultimately Huidobro lost nearly all his disciples, partly through

16. Volodia Teitelboim, "La generación del 38 en busca de la realidad chilena," *Atenea*, 380–81 (1958), 108–9.

17. Teitelboim, "La generación del 38," p. 110.

18. Alegría, *Literatura chilena del siglo XX*, p. 35

the deception that proved him not to be the great master they had hoped, and partly because his poetic and pseudo-socialist philosophies were not theoretically coherent. Huidobro played a revolutionary tune, but was hard to follow. He estranged himself even further from his disciples when they discovered that he felt himself to be an aristocrat and not truly a Marxist, while most of the young writers were sincere leftists and proletarians.

Pablo Neruda attracted the interest of several of the young writers, but allegiance to him was not as lasting as one would suppose in view of his influence upon world literatures. After several years of absence, Neruda returned to Chile from Spain on October 10, 1937. The Spanish Civil War had begun in 1936, and Neruda had witnessed its atrocities. When he returned to Chile, Neruda read his most recent poetical work, *España en el corazón*, in the Salón de Honor at the University of Chile. In photographs by Pedro Olmos and in Neruda's verses, which were to become part of his *Tercera Residencia*, the book showed the frustration of the defeat of the Spanish Popular Front government by Fascist forces. Of more direct impact on the young Chilean leftists than the political downfall of the Popular Front was the destruction of the youthful Spanish intellectuals by their own mother country. This became even more immediate to the liberal Chileans when the steamship *Winnipeg* harbored in Chilean ports laden with exiles of the Spanish Civil War. These war refugees strengthened Chile's Popular Front, however, for they were intellectual republicans who founded newspapers, publishing houses, and even universities during their "intellectual invasion" of Chile.[19] Embodied in the writings of Neruda and the presence of the exiles, the harsh political realities of the Spanish Civil War were instrumental in the conversion of many young Chileans to the Socialist, Communist, and Radical parties.

Luis Oyarzún explains how, during this time, he and several other "surrealist" poets of the "promoción *Mandrágora*" became disciples of Neruda. Moved and enthused by the new awareness of life he gave them, they learned, as did the other poets of the Quinta Normal, about Kafka, Malraux, and other writers; they took pleasure in learning about Stravinsky and the great contemporary composers; and they began to learn about theater when Margarita Xirgú brought her interpretations of Federico García Lorca to Chile in 1937. There

---

19. Enrique Lafourcade, *Antología del cuento chileno* (Barcelona: Ediciones Acervo, 1969), Vol. I, pp. 26–27.

was a great cultural awakening among the members of the new generation, and Neruda played a major role in bringing this about. Yet it was at this point that the apprentice poets felt they should find leadership among those of their own generation in order to avoid stereotyping themselves, or, as Luis Oyarzún puts it: "Corríamos el riesgo de cristalizarnos, de mirar el mundo desde el interior de un diamante."[20] According to Oyarzún the poetical segment of the group turned to two poets who still lead the Generation of '38— Nicanor Parra and Gonzalo Rojas. This group of writers who began as poets are best characterized by Fernando Alegría: "The young men who begin publishing around 1938 see in front of them a resplendent wall: that of Huidobro's creacionismo, and at the extreme opposite, the surrealistic tunnels which seem to lead to a revolutionary light."[21] While revolution was their ideal, surrealism was the major influence for the writers who published their works in the magazine Mandrágora, founded in 1937. When this review began a series of attacks on Neruda, the youthful poets had to choose sides, and most of them abandoned Neruda.

Neruda's poetic influence has never been renounced, however. He became the cornerstone and his disciples' verse became the foundation upon which the poetic novels of the generation were later built, for their poetical background is plainly evident in their fiction.

These influences on the young writers—their poet masters and the realists of 1900—were positive. The next chapter will examine the negative influences that acted on the generation when it attempted to establish a new type of prose in Chile.

20. Luis Oyarzún, "Crónica de una generación," Atenea, 380–81 (1958), 186–87.
21. Alegría, Literatura chilena del siglo XX, p. 35.

5

Toward a Rejection of Chilean Literary Tradition

The Generation of 1938 and the Critics

During the 1920s and 1930s, the critics in Chile generally lacked the aesthetic incentive or aptitude to keep pace with the movement of prominent poets. Many critics were autodidacts, and even though they read voraciously and wrote with great zeal, they failed to produce much more than impressionistic articles and reviews for newspapers and journals.[1]

According to Fernando Alegría—a Generation of 1938 novelist and one of the most prestigious new Chilean critics, who examines the criticism of this period with hindsight—the works of four reviewers were of value: "Alone" [Hernán Díaz Arrieta, b. 1891], Hernán del Solar (1901–73), Raúl Silva Castro (1903–70), and Ricardo A. Latcham (1903–64). Of these four, only Ricardo A. Latcham was instrumental in recognizing the new generation of writers.

Latcham had also been influential in guiding the *angurrientistas* and other young writers centered in the Instituto Pedagógico, where he taught. Though he was older, Latcham felt close to the generation since he was a leading figure in the Chilean Socialist Party; as the new generation took shape, Latcham did all he could to nurture its development, and his influence over Guzmán, both direct and indirect, is noteworthy. He published at least five articles on Guzmán, including reviews of his books; his review of *La sangre y la esperanza* was incorporated as a prologue into the later editions of the novel.

Since the Generation of 1938 felt that Chilean critics were generally superficial and missed the target, many of the young authors themselves began to review books. Ultimately—and more important —they delved into deeper research and published their own new critical essays. First a spirit of discontent, then a strong drive for national improvement motivated Guzmán and his colleagues.

1. Fernando Alegría, "Resolución de medio siglo," *Atenea*, 380–81 (1958), 141–48; see also Alegría, *Literatura chilena del siglo XX* (Santiago: Empresa Editora Zig-Zag, 1967), pp. 65, 129–46, 221.

In the prologue to his *Nuevos cuentistas chilenos* (p. 19), Guzmán attacks the essayists and critics as being slow to acknowledge the new generation; however, he praises the anarchist author and poet Manuel Rojas, who was the first to sow the seed of rebellion against the stereotyped ideas of the Chilean critics. An older and well-established poet and fiction writer, Rojas gained the respect of the generation with a biting essay, "Reflexiones sobre la literatura chilena," written previously but published early in 1938 in *De la poesía a la revolución*. It became an influential work for the new writers in denouncing the predominant literary tendency, criollismo:

> There are two types of critics: those that study books and those that study literature. We cannot complain that we lack the first (there is almost an overproduction), but we sigh for the second. Those critics of the first class are, in reality, writers' parasites. They live off of whatever the writers do. The others are the writer's companions; they march by his side, and occasionally they gain the lead.[2]

Rojas adds that he has not said this because of dislike for any Chilean critic. He feels that they have been overly kind to him; yet he feels that he must speak the truth.

Unanimously attracted to Rojas's radical thinking, the Generation of '38 soon began to confront the critics in open debate and to dispute among themselves—one of the few times that they ever disagreed. The resulting debate began when the established novelist Salvador Reyes ("Simbad") sharply attacked Miguel Serrano of the Generation of 1938 concerning an essay the latter had written.

Serrano had been disappointed in the results of a short story contest sponsored by the Santiago newspaper *El Mercurio*, so he responded with "Algo sobre el cuento en Chile," published in February 1938, in a Sunday supplement of *La Nación* (Santiago). In his weekly feature, "La huella de los días," in *Hoy*, March 3, 1938, "Simbad" said he had learned absolutely nothing from the *La Nación* essay: "Lo único que la crítica enseña en Chile es a darse cuenta de que la crítica no sirve para nada." While Reyes implied insultingly that the anonymous author seemed to know all about the short story without having written one himself, the irritated Serrano acknowledged in "Respondiendo a Simbad" (*Hoy*, May 12, 1938) that he was a short story writer, not a critic, and that he was the author of the unsigned newspaper article. He challenged *Hoy* to

2. Manuel Rojas, *De la poesía a la revolución* (Santiago: Ercilla, 1938), p. 122.

publish one of his own stories to show that he understood short story technique.

The editors acceded to his request and published as the feature "story of the week" Miguel Serrano's "La historia de Antonio," asking their "educated readers" to respond with opinions of the work.

Thirteen days later, May 25, 1938, two typical responses to Serrano's symbolic surrealist story were published in "Dos cartas: Una polémica acerca del cuento chileno." An editor's note explained the history of the debate to that point and stated that *Hoy* should never have asked for its readers' comments on the story. One of two representative letters they were publishing was by Emilio Walther (Serrano later suspected the name was a pseudonym for a critic); it was a scathing attack, suggesting that an insomniac should demand "Déme un cuento de Miguel Serrano" at the bookstore, instead of obtaining a sleeping pill at the pharmacy. The other letter was by Carlos Droguett, a fellow member of the Generation of '38. He agreed with Serrano that the short story did not currently exist in Chile, but he could not begin to admit that Serrano's story was good or that it could even qualify as a true short story. He claimed that it lacked a balance between interior narration (psychology, surrealism, existentialism) and the exterior world (realism and traditional narrative). Droguett was also impressed that Serrano was falling into the same error as the modernists in their escape to an ivory tower, or as the criollistas in extreme landscape descriptions; both were really "ignoring life."

The conclusion of Droguett's article is representative of the ideas of the proletarian faction of the Generation of 1938:

> I affirm and conclude. There are no short story writers in Chile, neither old nor young. The first are dead or are dying away, the latter have not been born yet, since they are still to be found in that great maternal womb of Vicente Huidobro.
>
> Well then, Miguel Serrano, one has to come down to earth a little, one has *to ascend* a little to the earth.
>
> Any other way is to live inside your own wardrobe [an ironic reference to Serrano's story of Antonio].[3]

In essence, Droguett, Serrano, and even Reyes were all obviously opposed to the previous Chilean critics, but their difficulty lay in

3. Carlos Droguett, "El cuento: cuentistas y cuenteros," *Hoy*, 340 (May 25, 1938), 59.

identifying the type of literature that represented the true short story.

In his prompt rebuttal, Serrano became aggressive and personal. He charged that Droguett, as a member of his own generation, should not have attacked him, especially since, he felt, Droguett had not understood his terminology.[4] Serrano was opposed to social literature, and he also criticized Russian literature, except for Dostoevsky. In repudiating Gorky and Lillo, as well as Manuel Rojas and Eduardo Barrios, Serrano illustrates how passionate and intensive the search had become in Chile for a "new literature."

Carrying Droguett's previous metaphor one step further, Serrano declared that if he himself were guilty of writing ivory tower, "white hand" literature, then Droguett and his misguided leftist colleagues were writing "literatura de manos negras," which was, in spite of their supposedly social intentions, socialistic only in a superficial sense. Serrano insisted that Droguett, in his "arte documento," was writing in the same vein as Franz Kafka. Ironically, this would seem to be a compliment, and even more ironical is the fact that in later years Serrano's writings were characterized as being very similar to Kafka's. And Poe, whom Serrano rejected as a writer in 1938 along with Chile's Latorre and D'Halmar, was a writer he acknowledged in 1950 as a precursor to his own surrealist tendencies.[5]

Carlos Droguett had the advantage of the last word in *Hoy*.[6] He was indubitably offended himself, and he reminded Serrano that if the argument had become personal and insulting, it was because Serrano had wanted to avoid abstraction and generalities by submitting himself as an example. Then Droguett proceeded to tear down Serrano's short story in terms of the same confusing four points Serrano had used in denying the existence of the short story in Chile: 1. "Nothing can be said about the short story in general." 2. "The short story is being born today in our America and especially in Chile." 3. "The short story constructed around exterior realities or impressionism in style is not a story." 4. "The authentic short story expresses a new and redeeming anxiety, a renovating, pro-

4. Miguel Serrano, "Literatura de manos negras (Un artículo más en la polémica suscitada alrededor del cuento chileno)," *Hoy*, 342 (June 9, 1938), 63–68.

5. Miguel Serrano, *Ni por mar, ni por tierra . . .* (*Historia de una generación*) (Santiago: Editorial Nascimento, 1950), p. 82.

6. Carlos Droguett, "Dúplica sobre el cuento en Chile (De Serrano a Serrano, pasando por Serrano)," *Hoy*, 344 (June 23, 1938), 66–69.

found, and authentically new reality; obscure feelings still about the new world." It is important to note that in negating Serrano's story, Droguett was ironically negating criollismo at the same time.

Droguett chided Serrano, stating that Serrano was feeling sad and dejected since his loss of face and so he had begun to write an essay. Droguett contended that if Serrano could write his short stories with the same enthusiasm he had shown in his essays, his stories would be outstanding.

The editors of *Hoy* did all they could during the polemic to belittle Serrano. Following Droguett's article they ran in the same issue "Sangre de cristiano" by Mariano Latorre, stating that they hoped to show that the short story did exist in Chile. They were also critical of the lack of conciseness on both sides, "since concision characterizes those writers who really have something to say." Serrano may have been sincere and even humble during the polemic, yet he sounded arrogant or juvenile at times and unable to diversify his arguments. Through his rhetorical ineptitude, for example, Serrano unwittingly placed Malraux on his side of the debate: "En la actualidad Malraux, para mí, es novelista, únicamente, y él lo sabe y lo acepta."[7]

Discouraged but not defeated, Serrano wanted the last word in the controversy, so he returned again to *La Nación*, where the debate had originated, and published an article appearing October 2, entitled, "A propósito del cuento en Chile y de las Antologías." It served a dual role, for Serrano also struck out against Raúl Silva Castro, one of the established Chilean critics, and his recent anthology *Los cuentistas chilenos: Antología general desde los orígenes hasta nuestros días* (Santiago: Empresa Editora Zig-Zag, 1938). Serrano reiterated his dissatisfaction with all previous Chilean short story writers, repeating essentially the same four points of his theory.

Apparently not satisfied with his *La Nación* article, Serrano retaliated against Silva Castro's anthology once more by publishing in November his own *Antología del verdadero cuento en Chile* (Santiago: Gutenberg, 1938). The title implies that prior to 1938 no true anthology of the short story had been published in Chile and no true short stories had been written.

In his preface to the anthology Serrano expressed a philosophy

7. Serrano, "Literatura de manos negras," p. 63.

that became a central doctrine for the whole generation. This does not imply that Serrano was the generation's philosopher, but rather that there existed a universal attitude of discontent among the writers that caused them to turn to socialist realism and to surrealism, which were both prevalent modes in 1938. However, Guzmán's socialist-realist movement soon triumphed and went on to dominate the generation's prose fiction.

The philosophy of Serrano's prologue appears to be moderate. The writer opposes capitalism, but he is a reactionary in stating that man is born into a hard life and must fight and work and that the radical writers "only aspire to a seat in the democratic parliaments." He also produces some interesting existentialist statements. Class is inferior to man: "El Hombre está por sobre las atrabiliarias y nominales ubicaciones de las clases: ES." The corollary, he declares, is that class theory is inferior to individualist theory. He mentions what his generation must do, and his philosophy is not too different from Guzmán's: "Tenemos el deber de vivir conforme a la verdad, de hacerla carne algún día. Por eso luchamos hoy contra la vida conformada en lo falso."

This generational philosophy of realism was paired with an intense spirit of nationalism. Serrano, the first to express these feelings, attacked the publishing houses Zig-Zag and Ercilla for not publishing works by Chilean authors. He opposed their spending Chilean money to publish foreign works. Guzmán continued this intense national fervor, similar to the spirit that carried Allende to victory. It showed in his editorial philosophy and in his business ideas. In charge of advertising promotions for Cultura from 1944 to 1946, he devised mottoes and slogans which he printed on promotional memo pads, calendars, and other mementos:

Es una gentileza de la Librería de la Editorial Cultura, el sello del auténtico libro chileno. (Compliments of the Cultura Press Bookstore, seal of authentic Chilean books.)

En la hora del libro chileno Editorial Cultura marca los segundos. (In the hour of Chilean books, Cultura Press counts off the seconds.)

Editorial Cultura: garantia de literatura nacional, selecta y chilenísima. (Cultura Press: a guarantee of national, select, and ultra-Chilean literature.)

El libro chileno de autor chileno es la más alta expresión del espíritu nacional. (Chilean books by Chilean authors are the highest expression of our national spirit.)

The essence of the argument proffered by these young writers was that a new national expression was trying to be born, attempting to take its first breath, but, as Serrano exclaims, it had no way to give vent to its birth cry: "Nuestra generación está desamparada, no tiene donde expresarse."

In the final pages of his essay Serrano attacks the previous generation, who, he felt, had tied up publishing facilities with useless landscape descriptions and *costumbrismo*: ". . . ¿Qué quiso, qué intentó, la generación anterior? Nunca he podido saberlo." Serrano insists that the older generation is trying to hold his own back by "opposing them decisively and sincerely, or with fondling, kindnesses, or fear."

Finally, he reiterates still again his argument that the short story does not exist and that his generation will accomplish the mission of the "*authentic vindication* and recovery [reivindicacion] of the short story." "The previous generation wrote poetry," Serrano concludes; "the new generation writes stories. Chile is a nation of short story writers." Though he sounds as if he is refuting his stand in the *Hoy* debates, Serrano's prophetic statement is correct, because the short story did become an important genre during the next thirty years in Chile, beginning with the Serrano and Guzmán anthologies. Because there were so many writers in his generation and Serrano knew so few of them personally, he wished his anthology could include blank pages so he could add talented writers. It is noteworthy that none of the authors Serrano selected appear later in Guzmán's collection.

Miguel Serrano followed popular sentiment in his anthology. Braulio Arenas already enjoyed great popularity, and one of the other writers included, Héctor Barreto (who had worked for *Hoy* and published a story in its pages),[8] had been assassinated in a street skirmish between fascists and socialists. This major clash, which led to the climactic and tragic confrontation called "La Matanza del Seguro Obrero," was a turning point in Chilean politics, contributing to the victory of the Popular Front and the formation of the Generation of 1938. Not only was this episode important to Nicomedes Guzmán, who interpreted it as an arousal to awareness of social problems,

8. Héctor Barreto, "El pasajero del sueño," *Hoy*, 279 (March 25, 1937),

bringing on a miniature renaissance,[9] but it has also been the subject of at least three novels by members of the Generation of '38: Carlos Droguett's *Sesenta muertos en la escalera* (Santiago: Editorial Nascimento, 1953), Fernando Alegría's *Mañana los guerreros* (Santiago: Empresa Editora Zig-Zag, 1964), and Guillermo Atías's *A la sombra de los días* (Santiago: Empresa Editora Zig-Zag, 1965).

Barreto became a symbol of the generation's ideals, and this first anthology of the generation's short stories was dedicated to his memory. Serrano also included a story by his main opponent in the debates, Carlos Droguett, feeling perhaps that his generous gesture would enable him to appear the victor.

When the Chilean critic "Alone" reviewed Serrano's anthology in *El Mercurio* (Santiago), he was of the unexpected opinion that the stories seemed to be the work of one person.[10] Indeed, the volume was markedly unified in style and technique, and it was this unity that pointed to the birth of a new generation. One by one, Serrano had attempted to destroy old and new literary idols, but in doing so he merely alienated himself temporarily from both the old and the new generations. While Serrano and his particular faction of the Generation of '38 do not represent the entire generation, his argument began a three-way division, causing the younger writers to focus their contrary thoughts. Serrano achieved at least three things. First, he alienated the new writers of his generation from the older writers (including the *marinistas* and the *criollistas*). Next, he made the public aware of a new literature; however, since the schism between political right and left increased as the new generation developed along with the victory of the Popular Front, a new reading public was created for leftist, not surrealist, literature. Third, Serrano alienated himself from socialist-minded authors such as Droguett, Guzmán, and others. These leftists carried the new revolutionary movement on into the forties, while Serrano ultimately took a conservative stand and spoke out against socialist literature.

Serrano's later history is rather interesting; he eventually assumed

76–78; reprinted in Miguel Serrano, ed., *Antología del verdadero cuento en Chile* (Santiago: Gutenberg, 1938).

9. Julio Mondaca, "Nicomedes Guzmán, un escritor en la línea de la sangre." *Vistazo* (Santiago), October 29, 1963.

10. Francisco Santana, *La nueva generación de prosistas chilenos* (Santiago: Editorial Nascimento, 1949), p. 12.

an aristocratic aloofness from the Generation of 1938. In 1950 he published *Ni por mar, ni por tierra* . . . , parenthetically subtitled *Historia de una generación*. This work presents a surrealistic, subjective interpretation of his generation, mentioning by name only a dozen of his colleagues, and never clarifying the mission of his generation. Serrano did not seem close to many writers, but by 1950 he lauded the generational experience as one of the most important factors in his life. It is paradoxical that Serrano should feel so socially attached to his generation, because in the polemic and in his later writings he attacks "social" writing but praises "generational" efforts, feeling that the individual and his generation have the same spirit: "Cuando uno muere, casi morimos todos" (p. 20). The book is intermingled with Serrano's new obsession with Chile and its people, the strong attractions of "the mystical emanations from his patria."[11] This change in Serrano from surrealism to a nationalistic pride is important, for one purpose of this study is to show that, beginning in the 1950s, Guzmán and the authors of his generation acquiesced to the critics' desire that Chile should be the theme of the literature produced. Serrano proved to be no exception.

Shortly after the Serrano polemic, several small splinter movements began voicing their philosophies in small reviews like *Mandrágora*. It was during this period that Nicomedes Guzmán also took the critics to task. He had been a disciple of angurrientismo, but his own proletarian movement was well under way when he compiled and published *Nuevos cuentistas chilenos* (1941), anthologizing twenty-five young colleagues. In his introductory essay on the nature of the short story, Guzmán openly contradicted Serrano's belief that the "cuento" had not existed previously in Chile. Guzmán summarized the history of the short story from 1900, the date that he felt realism and proletarian literature had begun with Lillo and other writers of his generation. Attempting to illustrate how a line of realism with socialist tendencies had continued from the time of the Generation of 1900 down to his own generation, Guzmán also hoped to demonstrate how similar these two generations were.

In this anthology, which brought a much needed unity to his

11. Thomas Edgar Lyon, Jr., "Juan Godoy in Chile's Generation of 1938: Theme and Style" (Ph.D. dissertation, University of California, Los Angeles, 1967), p. 62.

group, Guzmán laments the critics' lack of understanding of the new psychological types his companions had created:

> Por hoy, debemos conformarnos con una muy personal condición de nuestra literatura . . . que subsiste animada por la labor de algunos novelistas de proba sangre chilena. Mientras la seriedad y la adustez del ensayo han resultado siempre raquíticas en su fondo para soportar el brillante peso que representa este nuevo descubrimiento de Chile en el sentido humano y racial, nuestra novelística, en más de una oportunidad ha alumbrado en nuestro medio con rebencazos de luz nacionalmente viriles y significativos. (*Nuevos cuentistas chilenos*, 19)

While he feels that the critics and essayists had failed to comprehend the works and the characters created by his generation, Guzmán praises highly the novelists who have had to carry the load of literary criticism in Chile. Novelists like Manuel Rojas were his own colleagues' greatest inspiration in writing and criticism. More will be said about such novelistic influences and about Rojas in the following sections.

Guzmán's proletarian movement, much more than the poets or Serrano's group, represented the ideals and goals of the entire generation. Because of the optimism of the Popular Front, the socialist realism that Guzmán's group produced was wholeheartedly embraced by the Chilean reading public. Through Guzmán's leadership, his proletarian movement arose as the strongest force in the polemic.

Later, with the publication of the Honda series of novels, Guzmán hoped through his editorial efforts to immortalize his generation as the greatest prose innovators in the history of Chile. When La Honda failed, Guzmán's hopes were defeated. But the new generation was well established by then, and his own faction became its central force, the group that is most often thought of when the Generation of 1938 is mentioned.

The Influential Role of Hoy and Ercilla

After the five-year dictatorship of Carlos Ibáñez del Campo ended on July 28, 1931, Chile was able to print and import many foreign literary works that had been previously prohibited.[12] The youth

---

12. John Reese Stevenson, *The Chilean Popular Front* (Philadelphia: University of Pennsylvania Press, 1942), p. 49.

and the liberals now had ready access to the works of Dostoevsky, Gorky, Tolstoy, Gide, Sartre, Barbusse, Michael Gold, and Bret Harte. Several of the works that appeared in cheap paperback translations, such as the revolutionary writings of the American leftist Michael Gold, appealed solely to militant radicals, yet the scope of the new horizons of literature seemed endless. What was presented to the common people of Chile was a mixture of the popular and the erudite.

Many of the new radical and "proletarian" novels imported into Chile were extremely popular. The works of André Malraux, John Steinbeck, and others, including several Russian authors, were widely read.

In examining literary influences, it is often difficult to find out which works were read by which authors. This appears to be doubly difficult in leftist literature and especially when dealing with proletarian novels, since many of the oft-repeated literary and ideological concepts were transmitted orally in political groups, clubs, *tertulias*, or congresses of writers. Because of this oral transmission of ideas and because the guidelines for socialist realism are promulgated as dogma, Marxist works tend to resemble one another, even if there has been no direct influence of one work upon the other. Moreover, the problem is magnified because conservative critics seldom pay attention to radical literature or to the influences upon it.

For this reason, it is like discovering a gold mine to encounter in one of the Chilean journals of the 1930s, *Hoy*, a wealth of information on some of the socialist literature published in Chile and on the activities of the Popular Front. *Hoy* was sponsored by the publishing house Ercilla, which also published *Excelsior*, a bi-monthly literary magazine headed by Hernán del Solar. Several Marxist novels published in *Excelsior* were also bound and sold separately, such as *Tres camaradas* by Erich María Remarque, published in *Excelsior 7* (December 1937). Ercilla had as its literary advisor one of the leading Spanish American essayists and critics, Luis Alberto Sánchez.

Sánchez, a Peruvian Aprista, was in exile in Chile from 1934 to 1945 with several of his Peruvian colleagues. Although Apristas are considered by the Chileans to be a unique breed of leftists because, while avoiding communism, they interpret Marxism in their own manner, there is no doubt that the influence of Luis Alberto Sánchez on the Chilean Generation of 1938 is enormous. His work in writing, translating, adapting, and compiling is now seen as a remarkable, dynamic effort.[13] He rapidly translated recently published European works, such as *L'Espoir* by André Malraux, into Spanish, and as an editor of *Hoy*, Sánchez saw to it that current major novelists and short story writers were featured in the pages of the magazine. For example, in the "Cuento de la semana," a feature section in *Hoy*, there appeared weekly during the period from July 1936 to June 1938, stories by outstanding contemporaries from nearly every country in Europe as well as the United States, Chile, Peru, and India.[14] Although the slant of the magazine and its featured sections was predominantly to the left, not every author was a revolutionary.

Luis Alberto Sánchez also published several of his own works with Ercilla, and these, too, were of notable influence. Many were second editions of works that had appeared previously in Lima; his histories of literature and other history books went through numerous Ercilla printings. He even wrote philosophical works of a revolutionary nature, like his *Dialéctica y determinismo; la revolución y el individuo* (Santiago: Ercilla, 1938).

Another important aspect of Sánchez's influence is that in his well-known critical essays he has been most kind to Nicomedes Guzmán, Fernando Alegría, and their generational colleagues. It is mainly through his efforts, as well as the critical efforts of Latcham and Alegría, that the Generation of '38 has achieved considerable stature in Hispanic letters. Although most Chileans do not realize the influence Sánchez has had on them, like a kind and beneficent godfather behind the scenes, his contributions helped to nurture the young generation, opening to it a new panorama of ideas and concepts. Sánchez indirectly strengthened the socialist philosophies of the young revolutionaries and helped them to create literature that would be of a wider scope by introducing to them the best international works of the 1930s.

Hoy regularly reviewed authors such as Leon Trotsky and the young liberal Chileans of the Generation of 1938. Two of the Chilean works reviewed are Santiago del Campo's *California* and Fernando Alegría's historical essay, *Recabarren*.[15] In reviewing this

13. Eduardo Godoy Gallardo, "Diálogo con Enrique Lafourcade," *Mundo Nuevo*, 54 (December 1970), 67.

14. *Hoy*, 342 (June 9, 1938), 69, includes an index for the 100 issues beginning with number 242 and ending with 341.

15. "*California*, de Santiago del Campo," *Hoy*, 382 (March 16, 1939), 58; and "*Recabarren*, de Fernando Alegría," *Hoy*, 378 (February 16, 1939), 50.

last book, Luis Alberto Sánchez points out that Alegría writes with such a poetic style that his flowery prose contrasts strangely to Recabarren's violent life. This poetic neo-Baroque style which was so impressive to the reviewer is a trademark of the Generation of 1938.

Although Sánchez was trying to bring socialist culture to Chile through Ercilla, young authors like Serrano failed to see in his efforts anything but a "rapid, spectacular career based on a mishmash of titles . . . of Venezuelans, Peruvians, and tropical writers with or without fame." Ercilla's policy, he felt, was actually anti-Chilean; it was attempting "to impose a Spanish American criterion on Chile . . . when what it should do is draw together a criterion."[16] In other words, Serrano felt that Sánchez and his colleagues should print the works of young writers and thereby depict a new literature in the making. Obviously Serrano is partially correct, but Chile also needed to read foreign literature.

Despite the possible shortcomings of Ercilla's attempt to "Pan-Americanize" Chile, the company brought to Chile and the Generation of 1938 a great many influential books and did publish several Chilean works that directly influenced Nicomedes Guzmán: *Dos hombres y una mujer, memorias de un proletario* (1933), *Las barcarolas de Ulises* (1934), and *La estrella roja* (1936) by Jacobo Danke; *La viuda del conventillo* (1932) and *La mala estrella de Perucho González* (1935) by Alberto Romero; and *La fábrica* (1935) by Carlos Sepúlveda Leyton. Ercilla published Neruda's *España en el corazón*, which was important in the formation of the Generation of 1938; but what presumably disquieted the younger generation was that marinista or criollista works like Mariano Latorre's *On Panta* (1935) and *Hombres y Zorros* (1937) also bore the Ercilla imprint.

Among the foreign Marxist works that made an impression on Guzmán was the German proletarian novel, *Tengo hambre (Mich Hungert)* by Georg Fink, first published by Ercilla in 1933 and reprinted in 1938.[17] Fink's novel was extremely popular and was also translated into English, French, Russian, and Hebrew. Translations of other important proletarian novels introduced to Chile by Ercilla were *El chico Lonigan* by James T. Farrell, *Los perros de abajo* by Edward Dahlberg, and *Fiesta* and *Rahab* by Waldo Frank, most

16. Serrano, *Antología*, p. iii.
17. "*Tengo hambre*, de Georg Fink," *Hoy*, 330 (March 17, 1938), 62.

of which Guzmán read and had in his library. Ercilla published cultural works like Frank's *América Hispana* and *En la selva americana*, as well as novels by the American socialists Sinclair Lewis and Mark Twain. Some of the other authors the company published in translation were William Faulkner, Aldous Huxley, Somerset Maugham, Jean Cocteau, Alphonse Daudet, François Mauriac, André Maurois, and André Malraux.

The now-defunct weekly *Hoy* reflected some of the interesting events that occurred during 1938, a year of great social change in Chile. "Simbad" (Salvador Reyes) pointed out in his column the influence that the American movie *The Life of Emile Zola* had that year on the Chilean public.[18] He stated that since the showing of this motion picture in Santiago during the early part of 1938, the works of Zola had become scarce at the bookstores. In addition to the film, Henri Barbusse's biography of Zola was also published in Santiago in 1938.[19] This renewed interest in Zola's literature, his life, and his intervention in the Dreyfus case undoubtedly impressed the new generation with the importance of the ideological novel and an objective narrator. Once when Guzmán was asked his opinion of naturalism, he replied that it was a necessary evolutionary stage, as was criollismo.

Also included in the pages of *Hoy* were sections on national politics and major social issues, and occasionally the magazine was used by the new generation as a sounding board for socialist ideas. In its feature sections *Hoy* published information on the Popular Front, including its official platform, and propagandized strongly for its success.[20] *La Nación* and *La Hora* were the newspaper voices of the front, however.

An important article that caused all the younger Chileans to take note and re-evaluate Chile's stature in South America was an essay by the formerly radical American dramatist and poet Archibald MacLeish. MacLeish, an ex-Communist, had become a staunch supporter of Roosevelt (later he became Librarian of Congress and writer of the preamble to the United Nations' charter).[21] His article

18. Simbad [Salvador Reyes], "Zola," *Hoy*, 335 (April 21, 1938), 2.

19. Henri Barbusse, *Zola* (Santiago: Ediciones Ultra, 1938).

20. "El programa del Frente Popular," *Hoy*, 337 (May 5, 1938), 18–19; see also Johnatan [*sic*] Swift, "Lo que la derecha exigió en 1924 ¿Por qué no puede solicitarlo la izquierda en 1938?" *Hoy*, 337 (May 5, 1938), 19 ff.

21. See Daniel Aaron, *Writers on the Left* (New York: Avon Books, 1965), for MacLeish's evolution.

"South America, III: Chile" appeared first in the United States in *Fortune* and nearly simultaneously in *Hoy* when its author air-mailed one of the first copies to the editors.[22]

Still another Generation of 1938 theme was the *roto*. This Chilean term means "ragged" and refers to the traditional Chilean lower-class migrant to the capital who escapes the starvation of peasantry only to suffer the hardships of urban life. *Hoy* depicted the attitude of the new writers searching for a grass-roots hero in an article that tells of the new cult of the roto. "Simbad" (Salvador Reyes) reports in his feature column in *Hoy*, "La huella de los días," that on October 25, 1938, the younger generation gathered in the Yungay Plaza of Quinta Normal, Santiago, to pay homage to the roto. The Generation of '38 took this colorful Chilean type and converted him, for the first time, into a true proletarian, involving him in the revolution and showing him a "new road" leading to "*reivindicaciones proletarias*."[23]

As has been indicated, the magazine *Hoy* was the vehicle for the short-story polemic of 1938, it was constantly in the forefront during the elections, and it took an active part in the promulgation of the ideals of the young revolutionaries and the Popular Front. Although *Hoy* was not an organ of the Generation of 1938, it became a battle horn, sounding forth a first blare of combat—a call to colors for a generational clash to decide a new ruling literary force. Despite comments by Serrano to the contrary, the unspoken influence of this journal and Ercilla's publications on the formation of the Generation of 1938 was extremely important.

22. Archibald MacLeish, "South America, III: Chile," *Fortune*, 17 (May 1938), pp. 74–83, 148, 154–72; and "Chile," *Hoy*, 337 (May 5, 1938), 65–80.

23. Simbad [Salvador Reyes], "El Roto," *Hoy*, 375 (January 26, 1939), 2.

6

The Rise and Fall of the Generation of 1938

The world's critical economic and political situation prior to World War II strongly influenced Chile.[1] The world-wide depression and unemployment of the 1930s furnished verbal munitions to the revolutionaries who had been preparing seriously for class warfare. In Chile, the economic situation for the wage earner had improved very little, if any, from earlier years. During the late 1920s, foreign investors had begun to withdraw capital investments because of the unreliability of the government. Then, to make matters worse, Carlos Ibáñez had nearly bankrupted the nation financially during his dictatorship, which lasted until 1932. Ibáñez's successor, President Arturo Alessandri Palma (1932–38), was the middle-class leader who, during his first term as president (1920–24), had finally toppled the aristocratic oligarchy to establish a middle-class government for the first time in Chile. Alessandri improved the overall economic situation at the expense of the proletarian, whose fixed wages purchased less and less as the government-imposed inflation continued to raise the cost of living.

If the period of Alessandri's government from 1920 to 1924 is viewed as part of a dialectic process, it is seen as a first step in the evolution of a socialist state, the first time in the one-hundred-year history of Chile that the government was controlled by bourgeois interests. The second step began in 1931, when Ibáñez could not pay the army and public servants. There followed several months of chaos: army revolts, a navy mutiny, a series of juntas, and even the hundred-day Socialist Republic. At this time students, who were later the writers of 1938, played a major role, as they had a voice for the first time, and participated actively in the 1931 revolution. Through their action they gained respect and appreciation for revolutionary principles. When European Fascists like Hitler, Mussolini, and Franco began their power moves, the young authors were even more convinced of socialist principles, which were reaffirmed in the Chilean railroad workers' strike of February 1936, the first successful strike of a government union against the Alessandri

---

1. Ricardo A. Latcham, "New Currents in Chilean Fiction," *Américas*, 1 (October 1949), 39.

government. In retaliation, Alessandri banished the Socialist Party leader, Professor Ricardo A. Latcham, for his part in the strike. The evolution toward a working-class government had followed a dialectic-materialistic pattern up to 1938 when the masses elected a popular-class president, Aguirre Cerda; for some unexplained reason, it apparently ended there. Nevertheless, the Generation of 1938 expected the revolution to continue, and the writers optimistically reflected these hopes in their literature.

Latcham was not the only critic to encourage a socially based literature. In 1936, during the time Latcham was exiled, the Fourteenth International Congress of P.E.N. Clubs was held in Buenos Aires, and the Chilean delegation, headed by *Atenea* editor Domingo Melfi, promoted socialist ideals in literature. Melfi insisted emphatically on the social and revolutionary obligations of all authors. Paradoxically, however, he also stated that socialistic theses need not provide a constant theme nor should literature attempt to prove a thesis, "nor should it serve politics—rather it should show the blood, the marrow, the flesh of life."[2] On more than one occasion Nicomedes Guzmán cited Melfi's insistence that a writer must not escape into a world of purely aesthetic values. Melfi was one of the first to stress to the young writers of 1938 that literature should draw attention to injustices and class isolation.

The history of the proletarian novel in Chile differs slightly from its history in the United States. Major proletarian literature began to be published in the United States in 1930, but its career was only a short ten years and the output was superficial. For example, even though the true communist writers such as Michael Gold and Maxwell Bodenheim were hailed as revolutionary innovators, they were miserable stylists, and their experiments with the proletarian hero often produced awkward stereotypes. A second category of writers —the so-called fellow travelers—were much more successful in writing collective novels with casts of characters representing a cross section of American society. Established novelists like John Dos Passos and John Steinbeck fall into this category, but their works have not been considered to be true proletarian novels by such critics as Walter B. Rideout, who wrote the major classificatory work on the American leftist novel, *The Radical Novel in the United States: 1900–1954*. Because the overpowering economic problems

2. Domingo Melfi, *Estudios de literatura chilena* (Santiago: Editorial Nascimento, 1938), p. 209.

of the decade provided a Marxist inspiration, most U.S. proletarian novels were written during the 1930s, but the popularity of the genre ended abruptly with World War II. When Russia became an ally to capitalist powers, writers in the United States lost faith in the cause of communism.

Although in Chile the Generation of 1938 was the first proletarian literary school able to secure a foothold, the Chilean effort was more intense than the American, and undoubtedly more successful in the end, for in Chile a Marxist president was ultimately elected in 1970, owing in part to the propagandizing of Guzmán and his colleagues.

The main result of the delayed arrival of the proletarian movement in Chile was that, when it came, the Chilean effort was more concentrated. Young Chilean writers were motivated by the dogma of socialist realism that came out of the First Congress of Soviet Writers (1934), while the Americans were stifled by it and balked at such strict guidelines. There also seems to be a proportionate relationship between the fortune of the proletarian novel in a given country and the success of the Communist Party in the country. Manuel Pedro González cites the example of Mexico, "a country without proletarian writers of importance." Though Mexico has a colorful country life, folklore, and other customs that would adapt to a proletarian or a rural novel, its writers have not produced works of eminence like those published in sister republics. "Communism has not produced in Mexico a leader of the stature of those found in other countries like Brazil, Chile, and Cuba. Neither has the Communist party had the importance in Mexico that it has enjoyed in these three nations."[3]

In Chile, as soon as censorship was lifted, the young impressionable writers of 1938 began reading international works of proletarian literature, especially those written during the 1930s. They retained the more successful elements, and those who were inspired to write, such as Guzmán and Godoy, were able to create proletarian novels that were generally superior in style and content to the works produced in most other countries. In many countries Marxist literature has been poor in quality, and every group of proletarian authors has produced some poorly written propaganda novels, works of young writers inspired by the Marxist philosophy and a col-

3. Manuel Pedro González, *Trayectoria de la novela en México* (Mexico: Botas, 1951), pp. 402-3.

lective revolutionary spirit but lacking the ability of a talented artist.

The failure to produce a well-balanced, well-structured novel thus results from the desire of the novelist to subordinate the artistic interest of his novel to the propagandist purpose that his Marxist ideology imposes on him. Once the fighter comes forth in a man, the artist withdraws. This leads to the distinction drawn by Sartre between *engagé* and *enragé*. The more effective revolutionary has been the person who is actively *engaged*, like members of the Generation of 1938, not merely *enraged*, like some members of Chile's Generation of 1950.[4] In either case, however, when the artist withdraws in favor of the fighter, the product ceases to be literature. In such instances the communication channels between the author and the reader are weakened or severed since the narrator only expounds on social evils and is unable to convince his audience artistically. The arguments of certain enraged writers tend to be propaganda, not art; so such would-be artists become labor leaders in novelists' attire, not artists in the true sense of the word. Once art is suppressed to favor the propagandizing of a class war as it was in the thirties during the surge of extremist revolutionary writings, something vital is lost in literature.

Protest was not the main purpose of the works of the Generation of 1938, for style and art came first, especially in the novels of Guzmán and Godoy, the leaders. Guzmán mentioned often that it was his intention and that of his generation to produce art, not propaganda. Class revolution was an essential theme in the works of these young Chileans, but they were not controlled as strictly by the Communist Party as were writers in Mexico or Europe.[5] In Mexico a hard party regimentation forced leftist writers to conform to the discipline demanded by the labor leaders and the Communist International, but in Chile the Marxists were more fragmented, more independent, and were seemingly allowed more freedom by the party. Nevertheless, Chilean writers, including Guzmán, have been exploited by socialism over the years; several of Guzmán's friends have hinted at such exploitation.

The left in Latin America, as Jean Franco points out, also differed from the European left in that not all the leftist-inclined writers were

4. François Bondy, "The Engaged and the Enraged," trans. by Jean Steinberg, *Dissent*, 15 (1969), 49–58.
5. González, *La novela en México*, Chap. 21.

communists: "Even among writers who were not communists, the prevailing mood of economic depression encouraged a concentration on those sectors of society which seemed actually or potentially the most militant."[6]

In Chile, where several Marxist parties have existed and thrived, the Communist Party is the one that has become the most regimented, the most conservative; during the 1950s and 1960s it became progressively more demanding of its writers.

In the United States, when the Socialist Party nearly disintegrated at the end of World War I because of political persecution, the Communist Party attained predominance through the Great Schism. The history of the ideological novel corresponded loosely to the years of political domination by these parties. For example, the leftist novel of the first half of the twentieth century consisted of two waves: the socialist and the communist waves. The first period, 1900–1918, ended with the Great Schism, when the Socialist Party was dispersed by the reactionaries because of its anti-draft and anti-war sentiment. The second period encompassed the decade of the thirties; during the twenties there was little literary or political activity from the leftists, who were trying to regroup after the war. The twenties were dominated by Wobbly (International Workers of the World) and other anarchist writers, who carried on the Marxist literary tradition between the end of World War I and the Great Depression. The most important anarchist author in the United States and Spanish America was the cosmopolitan but mysterious B. Traven, whose identity was the subject of a multitude of legends. Traven appealed to English, Spanish, and German audiences, since his works were published in all three languages.[7]

Such political influences on the writers were major elements, for it was under the aegis of party ideology, especially through the John Reed clubs in the United States, that socialist realism was guided and developed during the late twenties and early thirties. In Chile, political ideology was also an important factor, but there were other traditions that exerted influence, both negative (such as criollismo) and positive (the poetry of Neruda and Huidobro or the realism of Lillo). Such traditional influences were as great or greater than the ideological ones imposed on the untrained novelists by Marx-

6. Jean Franco, *An Introduction to Spanish-American Literature* (Cambridge: Cambridge University Press, 1969), p. 231.

7. *Der Grosse Brockhaus* (Wiesbaden: F. A. Brockhaus, 1957), Vol. XI, p. 605.

ism, and it was, in part, because of them that Guzmán's generation produced art, not propaganda.

Having begun as poets, the writers of 1938 were torn between writing sociological novels and writing poetry. Since prose was the more effective means of communicating social evils, they hoped to synthesize poetry and prose in novel form. They found their main inspiration in two of the great Spanish American sociological novels of the twenties, *Don Segundo Sombra*, by Ricardo Güiraldes, and *La vorágine*, by José Eustasio Rivera. The reason given by the Generation of '38 for choosing these particular models for their own prose style is that Güiraldes and Rivera (and Miguel Angel Asturias) were also accomplished poets who wrote a "poetical prose" and whose works introduced a new sociological expression into Spanish American fiction.[8]

In addition to the poetic dominion of Neruda, Huidobro, and Mistral, and the great appeal of the highly stylized novels of Güiraldes and Rivera, the innovative works of Proust, Joyce, Dos Passos, Steinbeck, and Faulkner exerted stylistic influences. Non-Hispanic authors were generally read in Spanish translation, but they were nevertheless a "great discovery for the young generation." Though such writers influenced the generation in theme, point of view, and chapter structure, the proletarian revolutionaries—Fink, Gold, Dahlberg, Farrell, Malraux, and the Russians—held the greatest appeal for the generation because of their subject matter. They were the writers who had become most deeply involved with the problems of the thirties and were triumphantly prophesying class war.

While most Chilean prose of the twenties and early thirties (especially criollismo) was openly rejected by the Generation of '38, one Chilean author was a major model for Guzmán and others: Manuel Rojas, a novelist and accomplished poet. Rojas's influence was extensive, since it was he who first lashed out against the stagnant ideas of Chilean critics. Like Traven, whose books were in Guzmán's library, Rojas was an anarchist, reportedly a Wobbly, a member of the IWW, the most feared and the most militant of all the leftist groups.

Anarchism, which has been considered a variety of communism in Chile ("el comunismo anárquico"), was one of the most popular

8. Volodia Teitelboim, "La generación del 38 en busca de la realidad chilena," *Atenea*, 380–81 (1958), 115.

political movements of the 1920s. It attracted militant members from the proletarian and uneducated masses more easily than any other cause, and it was the ideology that offered a transition from the socialism of the days of Baldomero Lillo and the Generation of 1900 to the communism of the days of Guzmán and the Generation of 1938.

Manuel Rojas, together with José Santos González Vera and two others, founded the anarchist literary society Los Cansados de la Vida—un Club de Suicidas, whose first initiation included an escapade involving the severed arm of a cadaver.[9]

Guzmán admired both González Vera and Rojas. He used works of both authors as models for the point of view of *Los hombres obscuros* (see Chapter 10), and for the setting, a conventillo, as in González Vera's *Vidas mínimas* and Rojas's "El delincuente" (1929). The similarities between Pablo, the adolescent protagonist of Guzmán's *Los hombres obscuros*, and Eugenio, the narrator-protagonist of Rojas's *Lanchas en la bahía* (1932), are notable. Guzmán's plots and motifs, too, often resemble those of Rojas. Chapter 5 of *Los hombres obscuros* includes a scene where a drunk enters the conventillo, which is not very different from the situation in Rojas's story "El delincuente"; both stories begin in the present tense, and they share similar point of view. Rojas's protagonist accompanies the thief and the drunk to jail, a setting mirrored some twenty years later in Guzmán's "El pan bajo la bota."

Manuel Rojas was an eminent literary figure and a masterful novelist whose works represented a transition from socialism to communism, at least to Guzmán's thinking.

Except for Alegría and Guzmán, members of the Generation of 1938 have never publicly credited Manuel Rojas's influence. They have always preferred to acknowledge the poetical heritage of Neruda, for example; yet Rojas is also much admired in Chile as a poet.

Guzmán credits Rojas with his conversion to socialist realism, which for Guzmán means life artistically and faithfully portrayed:

> Manuel Rojas, nuestro gran novelista chileno, americano o, mejor, universal, ya me había dicho personalmente:
> No me explico cómo los jóvenes tienen el coraje de escribir tan largo.

9. Sergio Atria, "Los cansados de la vida," *Atenea*, 412 (1966), 205–12; also reprinted with other pertinent essays in José Santos González Vera, *Vidas Mínimas: Novelas*, 7th ed. (Santiago: Editorial Nascimento, 1970).

Su libro no es publicable, créamelo. Pero tiene una virtud: no es cursi. Y ya es bastante para usted. Trate de olvidar la lectura de novelas piratas. ¡Mire la vida!

Esto es: "¡Mire la vida!" ¡Y yo que creía ya estar cansado de mirar la vida! La verdad es que recién ahora estoy contemplando la vida. Y no la inmediata sino aquella otra vieja vida de mi infancia, la mía y la de aquellos heroicos seres que me rodearon. En ella están, por hoy, para mí los mejores potenciales de creación. ("Pequeñas notas auto-biográficas," 8)

Not only did Rojas show Guzmán the path of socialist realism, he was also one of the writers who taught him that artistry is accomplished only through hard work and discipline. Rojas, Melfi, and Danke also represented for Guzmán a true example of brotherhood. This leads to another theme of great importance to the present work. It was the principle of fraternal association exemplified in Rojas, Melfi—who published several of Guzmán's short stories—and Danke, Guzmán's inseparable comrade and compadre, that caused Guzmán to embrace many new friends as colleagues and comrades, publishing their works and organizing a fraternity within the Generation of 1938.

Divisions in the Generation of 1938

The seemingly unified Generation of 1938 actually consisted of several groups or cliques, which shifted somewhat as writers became discouraged with a given tendency or style and aligned themselves with different groups. Nine main divisions within the generation can be identified.

The above-mentioned *creacionismo* group, headed by Eduardo Anguita and Volodia Teitelboim, emulated Vicente Huidobro, but Nicanor Parra ironically refers to them as the "Grupo David."[10] The group identified itself early in the *Antología de la poesía chilena nueva* (1935).

Serrano's friends, described in Chapter 5, made up the surrealist group; but these writers were also committed to the revolution, since most of them had socialist tendencies. They appeared first in Serrano's *Antología del verdadero cuento en Chile.*[11]

The influential group known as Mandrágora (Mandrake) was

10. Nicanor Parra, "Poetas de la claridad," *Atenea*, 380–81 (1958), 46.
11. Cf. Miguel Serrano, *Ni por mar, ni por tierra . . . (Historia de una generación)* (Santiago: Editorial Nascimento, 1950), p. 113, n. 35.

named after the magazine it published from 1938 to 1943. The writers in this group combined creacionismo and surrealism. They claimed to have introduced surrealism into Chile, but it was already present in Neruda's poetry. Braulio Arenas, the founder, stated that their goal was to define more completely the human personality, including its thoughts, expression, love, and poetry. They tended toward escapist literature, but they also endeavored to instill protest in their lyrics; a revolutionary aspect is present in most of their writing.[12]

The obscure group Poetas de la Claridad, composed of many secondary poets, has only recently been identified by its leader, Nicanor Parra, now the most famous poet of his generation. He insists that it consisted of nonconformists: apathetic leftists, non-Catholics, non-surrealists, and poets who wrote too lucidly for the Mandrágora movement. García Lorca was their main guide and influence, and their work appeared in Tomás Lago's anthology, *Poetas de la claridad* (Santiago: Sociedad de Escritores de Chile, 1938).

A number of "fellow travelers"—middle-class writers—have been included in studies of the generation by Santana and Alegría. While their ideology is not Marxist, they write with a distinct revolutionary spirit. Included are María Luisa Bombal, who dealt the first death blow to criollismo with her novel *La última niebla* (1935), the humorist Enrique Araya, a latecomer to the generation, and Araya's colleagues Enrique Bunster, Juan Tejeda, and Carlos León, also late arrivals. Fernando Alegría also includes several essayists and other minor writers in his studies.[13]

The generation's experimental theater group was founded in 1938 by Pedro de la Barra at the Instituto Pedagógico of the University of Chile (TEUCH, Teatro Experimental de la Universidad de Chile). Later university experimental groups (ITUCH, Instituto del Teatro de la Universidad de Chile, and TEUC, Teatro Ensayo del la Universidad Católica) followed on its heels, but they created a middle-class theater.[14]

Commenting on the spirit of the new generation, Guzmán insisted that it included more than writers and dramatists: "Se fundó

---

12. Braulio Arenas, "La Mandrágora," *Atenea*, 380–81 (1958), 13.

13. Fernando Alegría, *Literatura chilena del siglo XX* (Santiago: Empresa Editora Zig-Zag, 1967), pp. 64–65, 121–39.

14. Hans Ehrman, "Theater in Chile: A Middle-Class Conundrum," *The Drama Review*, 14 (1970), 77–83.

desde el reducido plano de una orquesta afónica, el Teatro Experimental, hubo manifestaciones de arte múltiples, ballet, música, poesía. . . ."[15]

Among the large proletarian division were the Angurrientistas, headed by Juan Godoy.[16] This group attempted to write socially aware literature in a neo-Baroque style and to define the roto as a national archetype. Jules Romains's unanimism was the source of much inspiration for angurrientismo.

The Rancagua group of Los Inútiles, centered around Oscar Castro, was a small secret literary society patterned after Los Diez of the Generation of 1900. The group organ was the small review *Nada*; also the Rancagua editorial houses Talamí and Talcuni published the young writers' works.

Though Guzmán belonged to the Angurrientista and Inútiles groups, in 1941 he took the helm of leadership in his own "fraternity" with indisputable authority when he anthologized twenty-four colleagues in his *Nuevos cuentistas chilenos*. In the years following he gave these and other comrades opportunities for fame when he published their works in La Honda, Cultura, and other collections. Guzmán's efforts helped establish the image and ideals of the new generation in the minds of all Chileans.

The Demise of the Generation of 1938

In 1948, when Francisco Santana published his history of the Generation of 1938, he gave needed identity and publicity to the generation; but it was nearly too late. All of the major divisions had disintegrated, and only a few members remained active or popular: "It split into various factions and within fifteen years seemed to dissipate itself. . . . By the early 1950s the generation had spent itself."[17] Those whose popularity had survived the anti-Communist purge and the reactionary sentiment of the post–World War II years were forced to modify their writing, for their once-popular cries against nationwide injustices had lost mass appeal. There was a noticeable retrogression in the fiction of several Marx-

15. Julio Mondaca, "Nicomedes Guzmán, un escritor en la línea de la sangre," *Vistazo* (Santiago), October 29, 1963.

16. See Thomas Edgar Lyon, Jr., *Juan Godoy* (New York: Twayne Publishers, 1972), p. 42, for a list of the Angurrientistas which includes Nicomedes Guzmán.

17. Lyon, *Godoy*, pp. 36–45.

ists, and their modification of socialist realism—their concern with regional customs and types—became known as *neocriollismo*. The earlier enthusiasm was missing from their narrations, and they turned to the grass roots of Chilean culture, trying to discover its true essence and history in folklore or geography. Guzmán's *Autorretrato de Chile*, written by criollista and proletarian authors working together to define Chile, is a perfect example of this coalition with criollismo.

But criollismo was also losing ground. By 1950, the last two great criollista works, Eduardo Barrios's *Gran señor y rajadiablos* and Luis Durand's *Frontera*, had been published. In 1951, Manuel Rojas dealt the death blow to criollismo with his novel *Hijo de ladrón*. In 1950, moreover, a new literary generation was born. Most of the members of the Generation of 1950 (Donoso, Edwards, Giaconi, Heiremans, Lafourcade, Vergara, and others) were middle-class cosmopolitan writers who expressed themselves individualistically in existential and psychological novels. They attempted—with considerable success—to supersede both criollismo and socialist realism. Though some critics have declared that the Generation of '50 is only an invention of Enrique Lafourcade, it is obvious that generational similarities among the members do exist. Unlike the Generation of 1938, however, the Generation of 1950 is generally conservative.

In 1958, ten years after Santana's study of the Generation of 1938 was published in *El cuento chileno*, the University of Concepción held the Primer Encuentro de Escritores Chilenos in an attempt to regroup the generation, to inspire and laud it, and to define it as a generation. However, the papers that were presented gave a historical perspective on the generation, rather than depicting it as a current and progressive trend.[18] From 1950 on, socialist and criollista literature were rapidly replaced in popularity by the individualistic expression of writers like Eduardo Barrios in his psychological novel *Los hombres del hombre*, Manuel Rojas (*Hijo de ladrón*), and the Generation of 1950. From 1951 to 1956 the generation had some success with novels about the nitrate mines of the North (by Guzmán, Volodia Teitelboim, and Luis González Zenteno), and Guillermo Atías published the best novel about Santiago's middle class, *Tiempo banal*, but group efforts were suddenly turned

18. Gonzalo Rojas, "Segundo Encuentro de Escritores Chilenos," *Atenea*, 380–81 (1958), 209.

to individual success. Two of the more successful novelists after 1955 have been Carlos Droguett and Fernando Alegría, who had been out of Chile for several years.

Though no member of the Generation of '38 will admit that the revolution prophesied in 1938 failed to materialize, during the period from 1950 to 1970 the generation lost its impetus and its popularity to younger writers who hoped to vanquish the older generations. In 1973 Enrique Lafourcade of the Generation of 1950 published a novel *En el fondo*, making fun of certain professors and poets of the Generation of 1938 for withdrawing from the battlefield of ideological expression in 1970 just when they should have been taking action to establish Allende as president of Chile. Lafourcade was severe in his character delineation, depicting members of the generation as alcoholics, vagabonds, capitalists, homosexuals, and other decadent types. At any rate, the revolution in writing and thought stirred up by the Generation of '38 was dead.

7

Nicomedes Guzmán and Proletarian Literature

Leftist literature in the twentieth century has evolved rather slowly, in spite of the guidelines established by Marx and Engels. Before the Russian Revolution the boundaries of proletarian art were not as well defined as they were later during the dictatorship of Stalin. Even then, the standards and goals of socialist literature have been disputed continually as Marxism has grown and has been interpreted differently by political leaders and literary critics of different nations. Showing their idealist nature, many individual artists have also joined in the polemics, not wishing to violate Marxist principles, but unwilling to subordinate their art completely to the propagandist element that has been explicit up to now in all communist art.

On the one hand, Trotsky, Stalin, and Khruschev, the leaders and theorists, have added their interpretations (often dogmatic), assigned topics to leading Soviet writers, and purged artists who unfortunately failed to conform or who attempted to express their own ideas. Literary works were commissioned, for example, to be read at the dedications of dams or other public works; also, Stalin enjoyed being characterized as the protagonist of a historical novel where he might be compared to a czar, as, for example, in Alexis Tolstoy's *Peter I*.

On the other hand, many artists who have been attracted and freely inspired by socialist principles have written works of art as a result of their freedom (Steinbeck's *Grapes of Wrath* and the plays of Clifford Odets, for example), while many others have produced nothing more than propaganda. Some leftist extremists argue that all literature is propaganda, but Walter Rideout insists that "a novel is created by a far different process than is a strike bulletin."[1]

The forces that can influence a Marxist author's development can be categorized by order of Marxist significance into five basic classes. First in importance are the works of Marxist literature which, as

---

1. Walter B. Rideout, *The Radical Novel in the United States: 1900–1954. Some Interrelations of Literature and Society* (New York: Hill and Wang, 1966), p. 233.

"primitive masterpieces," have freely inspired writers like Guzmán because of their creativity and apparent revolutionary ideology; included would be the writings of Gorky, Fink, Frank, and Gold, and perhaps other more consciously artistic authors.

The international congresses, such as the First Union of Soviet Writers (1934) or the American Writers' Congress (1935),[2] actually stifled more writers in the United States and Russia than they inspired. Several writers in the United States were moved by the Marxist cause to write outstanding literature; yet revolutionary writers like James T. Farrell were the first to rebel at the American Writers' Congress, when dogmatic guidelines were established for Marxist literature. Nevertheless, we may consider the congresses a second source of influence, for they produced theories that established certain party guidelines for the evolution of socialist realism, like the influential statement of Andrey Alexandrovich Zhdanov, a puppet of Stalin, at the Russian Congress, or the most important document to reach Chile, Plejanov's *El arte y la vida social* (1936).[3]

The theorists, Marx, Engels, Lenin, and Trotsky, as well as others like Plejanov, or Stalin, through Zhdanov, are still a third influence in the establishing of acceptable boundaries for socialist literature. The *Communist Manifesto* is still the Bible of proletarian literature.

A fourth source of influence, reviews and journals are more spontaneous but less official interpreters of party doctrine; these periodicals have propagandized regularly and in many cases they have gathered together the nuclei of new generations. Such periodicals tend to convey the spirit (sometimes innovative and rebellious) of the generation. In the United States both *The Masses* and *The New Masses* were publications that resulted from the organization of communist groups like the John Reed clubs. These communist youth centers controlled the evolution of American socialist literature during the late 1920s and early 1930s, until they were disbanded at the time of the First Congress of American Writers in 1935. In Chile the major socialist publications were the *Frente*

2. Henry Hart, ed., *The American Writers' Congress* (New York: International Publishers, 1935) is the history of the event, but the unofficial happenings are summarized in Daniel Aaron, *Writers on the Left* (New York: Avon Books, 1965), Chap. 10.

3. Other major works were *El arte y la vida social* (1938) by Marx and Engels, and Stalin's *El marxismo y el problema nacional* (Moscow: Ediciones Lenguas Extranjeras, 1939).

Popular, begun in 1938, *Multitud*, published by the followers of Pablo de Rokha, and the *Aurora de Chile*, a non-communist review directed by Neruda. A later magazine that promoted proletarian culture was *La Voz de América*, first printed on May Day, 1944, with Latcham, Latorre, and Guzmán as three of its founders. In Russia, publications of the rebellious RAPP proletarian writers' union (1928–32) caused Stalin to form the Union of Writers in 1932 and to call the first congress in 1934 to establish party guidelines in literature.

Finally, many non-socialist writers, including "pre-October" and literary fellow-traveler Russians, have guided or inspired the evolution of proletarian literature. Occasionally Gorky is included here; other Russian writers in this category are Tolstoy and Dostoevsky. But Guzmán and his generation read and accepted many regional writers: Manuel Rojas in Chile, and some traditional (non-socialist) authors, among them Barrios, Azuela, Güiraldes, Rivera, and Faulkner. In fact, Guzmán ranked his preferences in this order. He was proud to refer to authors whom he knew were socialists; he did not seem to enjoy reading others, and he seldom referred to them.

Though not all of these levels of influence are necessarily discernible in Guzmán, most of them played a major role in his writings. The sources most easily recognized are those that influenced *La sangre y la esperanza*: Fink, Gold, Gorky. These writers, furthermore, influenced many other proletarian authors both in and out of Chile.

Modern socialist literature begins with the communist victory in Russia in 1917. In his book *Literature and Revolution*, Leon Trotsky explains the evolution of Soviet Socialist art from "pre-October" writers through futurism and formalism. Unfortunately, the magnificent literature Trotsky hoped his fellow Russians would create failed to materialize, as did his dream of a socialist utopia.

Trotsky attributes socialist realism to Osinsky; others claim Gorky originated it; but it was a form chosen by the establishment —Stalin:

At the First Congress of the Union of Soviet Writers in August 1934 socialist realism was much discussed. Bukarin's typically sophisticated address indicated a very permissive interpretation, one that would allow a wide range of creative freedom to the writer. But Stalin's mouthpiece, A. A. Zhdanov, couched his speech more in terms that suggested Stalin's idea of writers as "engineers of the human soul." In the wake of the congress many steps were taken "in the direction of suppressing all non-conformism and establishing totalitarian control over all manifestations of spiritual and cultural life."[4]

Two years eariler, in April 1932, the Union of Writers had been formed, with one of the statutes defining socialist realism as a literature "saturated with the heroic struggle of the world proletariat and with the grandeur of the victory of Socialism . . . reflecting the great wisdom and heroism of the Communist party. . . ."[5]

A more exact definition of socialist realism is given in a quotation by Abram Tertz in his book smuggled out of Russia, *On Socialist Realism*:

> Socialist realism is the basic method of Soviet literature and literary criticism. It demands of the artist the truthful, historically concrete representation of reality in its revolutionary development. Moreover, the truthfulness and historical concreteness of the artistic representation of reality must be linked with the task of ideological transformation and education of workers in the spirit of socialism.[6]

Though radical writers in the United States, Chile, Brazil, Cuba, Mexico, and other countries have attempted with varying success to employ forms and techniques of socialist realism, it is doubtful that socrealism (as it is called) can exist or survive anywhere except Russia.[7] And many critics question whether true socialist realism exists even in the USSR. Tertz's *On Socialist Realism* poses this problem and ultimately tumbles the sacred Soviet idol called socialist realism.

How valid is it, then, to speak of socialist realism? The answer undoubtedly lies in the fact that most terminology is useful mainly for classificatory or pedagogical purposes. For many people socrealism signifies the Marxist literature of the 1930s that depicts a class

4. Herbert J. Ellison, *History of Russia* (New York: Holt, Rinehart and Winston, 1964), p. 412. See also Edward J. Brown, *Russian Literature since the Revolution* (London: Collier-Macmillan, 1969), p. 213.

5. Gleb Struve, *Soviet Russian Literature 1917–1950* (Norman: University of Oklahoma Press, 1951), p. 239; see also p. 260.

6. Abram Tertz [Andrei Donatevich Siniavskii], *On Socialist Realism*, trans. by George Dennis (New York: Pantheon Books, 1960), p. 24. Tertz is quoting here from *The First All-Union Congress of Soviet Writers* (1934), p. 716.

7. Rideout, pp. 214–15.

struggle in process; thus socrealism is seen as the literary weapon of the revolutionary.

Socialist realism differs from nineteenth-century realism, which is also called "critical realism." Georg Lukacs and his disciples use this term because Balzac, Stendhal, Tolstoy, Gorky, and other nineteenth-century novelists used realism to criticize the bourgeois society of their day. Socialist realism is linked to critical realism, since the former is considered to be the final step in the evolution of literature, a product of the fusion of two Soviet creeds: "Belief in the mission of the Russian nation and belief in the mission of the (Russian) proletariat."[8]

The Russian Union of Writers prompted the First Congress of American Writers, held in New York on May 1, 1935. Socialist realism was not an issue at the congress, however, nor would it be debated in the United States until after World War II. The main issue at the congress became whether or not to support Russia and the Communist Party doctrine; delegates also made speeches on aesthetics and politics.

The development of the proletarian novel in the United States, which consisted of the adoption of elements of socialist realism by writers of the 1930s, is generally seen as a natural evolution. For example, most American proletarian novelists were not emulating Russian novelists so much as trying to supplement traditional realism—their predominant style—with their newly acquired Marxist philosophy: "The realism of the proletarian novelists cannot ultimately be equated with a mere straightforward photographing of surfaces; rather, their method approximates *independently* that 'socialist realism' which became the official technique in Soviet literature soon after April 23, 1932. . . . "[9] The similarity between the radical American writers of the thirties and the Chilean Generation of '38 is remarkable. In each group, the traditional realist literature of the country had maintained a position of importance. According to Guzmán and his generation, however, the Chileans had to look to an earlier generation—that of 1900—for their realist predecessors, although Rojas, Romero, Danke, González Vera, and Sepúlveda Leyton could also be considered realists.

Other factors—the distance of Chile from Russia, the difference

8. Czeslaw Milosz, Introduction to Tertz, *On Socialist Realism*, p. 17.
9. Rideout, p. 211; see also p. 208.

between Russian and Spanish (hence a longer period of time needed for translation), the censorship of the early thirties, and the need to wait for a political climate propitious for the Socialist victory of 1938—delayed the emergence of the proletarian novel in Chile from 1930 to 1938. This eight-year difference was advantageous artistically to the Chilean writers, for surrealist techniques affected the development of socrealism during the initial stages. Surrealist ideals were parallel in some ways to socialist realism, and surrealism reinforced in socrealism the value of shock. Both schools used sex, violence, and atheism. All these elements are present in the prose of Guzmán and Godoy—as are surrealist dreams.

The technical experiments of American and Chilean novelists are similar, as can be seen from a statement by the American critic, Granville Hicks:

> The realistic novels usually employ the traditional "biographical" or "dramatic" frameworks, or some combination of both; technical experimentation, as a rule, is connected with efforts to write the "group" or "complex" heroless novel.[10]

Hicks employs the term "dramatic" to describe a novel's framework in reference to Edwin Muir's *Structure of the Novel* (London: Hogarth Press, 1928). It is obvious that the majority of the novels produced by Guzmán's generation were spatial novels, with social types as characters, even though they attempt "dramatic" or "biographical" techniques. They are spatially structured, of course, because they are social and ideological in scope.

One of the generation's experiments, Fernando Alegría's *Recabarren*, was an experimental biography. Two of Guzmán's works imitated the innovations of Gold, Farrell, Dahlberg, and others in the first-person narrative. Several writers also experimented with the "complex heroless novel," as did Guzmán in *La luz viene del mar*.

Although the Generation of '38 experimented with literature, they did not reject the traditional Chilean modes of expression; rather they combined such elements with what they felt were the best characteristics of European and American proletarian literature. They also absorbed influences from the well-known regional novels that were popular during the 1920s, the sociological novels of Azuela, Güiraldes, Gallegos, and Rivera. This amalgamation of Chilean

---

10. Granville Hicks, quoted by Rideout, pp. 214 and 316, n.54.

elements with proletarian and traditional Latin American elements was characteristic of the Generation of 1938.

Chile's Pre-Proletarian Literature

Besides the several Latin American works which have been pointed out and the influence of the Chilean poets Neruda, Mistral, and Huidobro, several Chilean socialist novels influenced Guzmán and many of his contemporaries. In his various short histories of Chilean literature he referred repeatedly to certain key authors. His high opinion of Baldomero Lillo (whom he considered to be one of the most important of all Chilean fiction writers) and Carlos Pezoa Véliz was mentioned in Chapter 4.

In his comments Guzmán states that Augusto D'Halmar, a member of Lillo's generation, gave life to the novel with "the crude and moving realism" of *Juana Lucero*, "mensaje que fue como un grito desgarrador." He felt that D'Halmar's and Lillo's social awareness, the greatest of their generation, was lost after 1920. Guzmán emphasized that the prose fiction of his own generation was the first Chilean literature since Lillo's time to express such social awareness.

Between the two generations, however, a few authors did treat social themes, and Guzmán approved of their work to some extent. These writers were Luis Orrego Luco (author of *Casa Grande*), Eduardo Barrios (author of *Un perdido*), and Fernando Santiván, who was a socialist and a good friend of Guzmán's but whose fiction was too French and *costumbrista* for Guzmán's taste.

Guzmán insisted that intense social awareness did not begin to manifest itself in the novel again until the 1920s when Joaquín Edwards Bello published *El roto* and José Santos González Vera wrote the two stories, "El conventillo" and "Una mujer," which eventually became the two-part novel *Vidas mínimas*.

During the early 1930s three novelists came on the Chilean scene with proletarian or conventillo-inspired works. These books inspired Guzmán to write a greater conventillo novel, *La sangre y la esperanza*.

The first of these three writers was Alberto Romero, who published *La viuda del conventillo* in 1932 and *La mala estrella de Perucho González* in 1935. When Guzmán read Romero's works he found them inspirational: "Romero se adentra en los más transcendentales problemas del pueblo y expone su angustia con una sensibilidad que es la del propio hombre popular" ("Miniatura," 25).

Guzmán felt that Romero's *La viuda del conventillo* was of the stature of *El perdido*, his favorite novel by Barrios, and he considered it to be as important as Edwards Bello's *El roto*. He praised the three novels equally, for all three restored a social awareness to Chilean literature that had been absent during two decades of criollismo: "Aquí, sí, nuestra literatura hace sonar oro de buena ley entre sus manos. La realidad cruda y palpitante, como en los tiempos de *Juana Lucero* o de *Sub-Terra* se reincorpora a nuestra novela, con el rostro sañudo y fatal, moreno de chilenidad."[11]

The second inspiring writer was Guzmán's spiritual guide, Jacobo Danke, who published *Dos hombres y una mujer, memorias de un proletario* in 1933 and *La estrella roja* in 1936. Danke guided Guzmán's reading selections and gave his young protégé needed moral support in his projects of writing and publishing.

The third novelist—a kindred spirit of Guzmán's who initiated a movement Guzmán labeled "Reafirmación de nuestra novela social"—is Carlos Sepúlveda Leyton, obscure author of an autobiographical trilogy: *Hijuna* (Linares, Chile, 1934), *La fábrica* (Santiago: Editorial Ercilla, 1935), and *Camarada* (Santiago: Editorial Nascimento, 1938). *Hijuna* is very similar to *La sangre y la esperanza*, the story of a little boy in the conventillo. Guzmán was inspired by its realism: "Novela urbana, casi rural, alta y afortunada noticia de una infancia y de un pueblo. . . . Es todo la obra como un trozo de Chile."[12] *La fábrica* has a weak plot and is much less spontaneous. *Camarada* is the most proletarian of the three novels and, in Guzmán's opinion, was Sepúlveda's best book: "Más novela que sus libros anteriores, *Camarada* es una obra fuerte, viril, ancha."[13] Surprisingly, it is so similar in style and subject matter to Guzmán's works that it could have been written by him. Guzmán read and reread Sepúlveda's works and wrote an essay on him during the year he was involved in writing *La sangre y la esperanza* (1940–41).

Guzmán indicated that *Hijuna*, *La fábrica*, and *Camarada* complete a cycle; his vision of novels as part of a traditional cycle (a theme treated in several volumes) and as a circle (one or several

---

11. Nicomedes Guzmán, "Carlos Sepúlveda Leyton, novelista del pueblo," *Atenea*, 189 (March 1941), 355.

12. Guzmán, "Sepúlveda Leyton," pp. 355, 357.

13. Guzmán, "Sepúlveda Leyton," p. 360.

volumes completing a circle) was almost an obsession with him, but he died before he could complete the second volume in his long-dreamed-of cyclical trilogy.

Guzmán identified with Sepúlveda Leyton. Coincidently, both died at the age of fifty after publishing three novels. Sepúlveda, however, had a formal education as a school teacher. Guzmán erroneously considered him a fellow member of the Generation of '38:

> Lo grande de todos los compañeros escritores del 38, es su aporte general y particular a una definición de la nacionalidad . . . Hablemos, por ejemplo, de Juan Godoy . . . De Carlos Sepúlveda Leyton, hasta hoy tan maltratado por críticos políticamente ubicados en la Derecha chilena . . . [14]

Writing such as Sepúlveda's exemplified realism to Guzmán.

Realismo or Criollismo?

Although terminology in literature is essentially unimportant, it is a petty source of irritation to many people, and there is seldom perfect unanimity on the connotations of some terms. For example, the use of a word like *criollismo* is mainly a pedagogical device used to describe thematic concerns and to help classify or catalogue works in certain groupings so as to place and understand them better. Some terms have different connotations in different countries and to different critics. Too often arguments about the semantics and values of words render them useless because of their debatability.

Among the Chilean critics a wide schism in terminology has developed concerning the classification of the prose of the Generation of '38. Some feel that every narrative work written in Chile during the twentieth century should be regionalistic or criollista in scope; others, such as Guzmán and Alegría, see realism as a dominant tendency. Since many other terms have also been introduced, the controversies continue, and seldom have any of them been decided. The following pages will attempt to summarize the differences between *criollismo* and *realismo*.

Some of the critics have insisted that Guzmán's prose is merely naturalism, *à la* Zola; others have argued that the rebirth of sordid elements in some of the writings of the generation constitutes a

14. Guzmán, quoted by Julio Mondaca in "Nicomedes Guzmán, un escritor en la línea de la sangre," *Vistazo*, October 29, 1963.

movement of neonaturalism; but a surprising majority of critics have termed the writings of the Generation of '38 criollismo or at least have tried to relate them to the regionalistic Chilean tendency referred to by that name. However, it is essential to bear in mind that the Generation of '38 was attempting to negate criollista values and procedures through their revolutionary literature.

Another related term, *neocriollismo*, was coined by the Chilean critic "Alone" in his review of Guzmán's *Donde nace el alba*. At the same time, or almost immediately thereafter, Ricardo A. Latcham also adopted this term. However, neocriollismo is not accurate either, for in their first works the young writers were not attempting to renew criollismo, nor were they even related to it, except through their teachers, Latcham and Latorre. Hugo Montes and Julio Orlandi use *neocriollismo* and *criollismo popular* as synonyms, but it seems that the term "popular" referring to the masses distorts the meaning even further, as will be shown later in this section.

Guzmán conceived criollismo as a "necessary and essential step in the development of Chilean narrative":

> No se le puede desconocer puesto que la fuerza mental y humana que incorporó a nuestra literatura es el fundamento para las nuevas tendencias literarias; o sea, para lo que Alone ha llamado "neocriollismo" aunque no tenga mucha razón.[15]

Guzmán and Ferrero have disclaimed the term *neocriollismo* as the correct designation for the literature produced by their generation; therefore if the student and serious teacher are to have a valid term for classifying the early prose of the Generation of 1938, it is necessary to delve even deeper into the matter to come up with an appropriate label.

Many North American critics see "realism" as an empty bag into which all art and literature are too often cast. Perhaps because it is a term that is easily understood by the layman, it is employed frequently or even excessively.

Following the idea of Lukacs that realism has two connotations for the socialist writer and critic—critical or nineteenth-century realism and twentieth-century socrealism—Yerko Moretić argues that the short stories of the newest group of Chilean writers, the Genera-

15. Nicomedes Guzmán in an interview with Wilfredo Cassanova, graduate student at the University of Chile, 1958.

tion of 1960, are "realistic," like the fiction of their predecessors.[16] Alegría distinguishes twentieth-century realism from criollismo (regionalism) in *Las fronteras del realismo*, but the differences between critical realism, neorealism, and socialist realism are not well defined. His term *realismo social* for Lillo's writings is concrete, but *neorealismo* includes the works of Manuel Rojas, González Vera, Eugenio González, and Sepúlveda Leyton as well as the Generation of 1938. Enrique Anderson Imbert employs the term *neorealism* somewhat more broadly, as does Cedomil Goić (the Chileans Alegría and Goić spell it *neorrealismo*).

Guzmán and his colleagues considered realism a very important element in their writing. They saw realism as a method of objective observation and a way of showing the reader an honest, yet humble proletarian soul living in a "realistically re-created world." They were searching for the truth of Chilean life, hoping to discover it for themselves and their readers in realism. What bothered many of their critics and the reading public was that this realism revealed the low, the filthy, the repugnant side of Chilean life.

The arguments all seem to indicate that *realism* is, in fact, the most useful term. Many critics have wanted to expand the concept and have attempted to modify the word *realism* with an adjective to describe Chile's proletarian prose: *realismo popular, realismo populista, realismo sociológico, realismo proletario,* or *realismo materialista dialéctico.* For example, Mario Ferrero, the '38 critic who gives the best argument for naming this entire group of writers the "Generation of 1938" as opposed to Latcham's "Generation of 1940," also proposes convincingly that what Guzmán's generation produced was *realismo popular.*[17] As strong as his argument may be, the term could still be misleading, since *popular* can be defined as both "proletarian" and "in vogue."

Besides employing the term *neocriollismo,* Montes and Orlandi scatter *realismo populista* throughout their book as a synonym for it.[18] However, this term differs little from Ferrero's *realismo popular.*

16. Yerko Moretić "El realismo y el relato chileno," in Yerko Moretić and Carlos Orellana, ed., *El nuevo cuento realista chileno* (Santiago: Editorial Universitaria, 1962).

17. Mario Ferrero, "La prosa chilena del medio siglo," *Atenea*, 385 (1959), 97–124, and 386 (1959), 137–57. See p. 145.

18. Hugo Montes and Julio Orlandi, *Historia y antología de la literatura chilena,* 7th ed. (Santiago: Editorial del Pacífico, 1965), p. 167.

Fernando Alegría calls Guzmán's and Lillo's literature *realismo proletario*.[19] While this is a meaningful and useful classification, as is Mario Espinosa's *realismo sociológico*,[20] they are both subordinate to the official designation, *realismo socialista* (socialist realism or socrealism), which was adopted by the First All-Union Congress of Soviet Writers.

For the Marxist, "realism" is to literature what "materialism" is to philosophy. The Russians were left to decide on a proper modifying adjective. "It was discovered in 1932—no one knows by whom, but the inspiration was attributed to Stalin—that 'realism' might be qualified by the term 'socialist.' Socialist was the proper modifier because it had no negative connotation."[21] In Chile the term *socialist realism* would be applied mainly to the fiction that the Generation of 1938 wrote between 1938 (*Angurrientos*) and about 1950. Even after that date several socrealist works were published, like Guzmán's *El pan bajo la bota*, but generally socialist realism fell from popularity, as did some writers in the Generation of '38.

During their years of popularity, however, these writers indulged in stylistic experimentation, and Guzmán and Godoy developed the theme of the conventillo. Despite the term's popular connotation, socialist realism is not limited to theme; rather, "form and content are interdependent to insure the proper conveyance of the author's ideas."[22] In the United States, Russia, Chile, and other nations, authors like Michael Gold and Guzmán sought a revolutionary poetic style in an attempt to create a new and radically different literature. Their efforts involve experimentation with style, characterization (usually collective), and other techniques, and makes use of politics, philosophy (Marxism), humanism, and folklore. Socrealism attempts to depict the glories of the masses; ideally, it marvels at a nation living collectively. In a non-socialist country, such as Chile, it was employed to portray the harsh reality of social evils and a class war in the making; it aspired to motivate the working class toward vindication and revolution.

To show that both the objectives and the final result of the Gener-

---

19. Fernando Alegría, *Literatura chilena del siglo XX* (Santiago: Empresa Editora Zig-Zag, 1967), p. 64.

20. Mario Espinosa, "Una generación," *Atenea*, 380–81 (1958), 73.

21. Brown, p. 33.

22. Joseph T. Shipley, ed., *Dictionary of World Literature* (Totowa, N. J.: Littlefield, Adams and Co., 1964), p. 383.

ation of '38 were directed away from, rather than toward, criollismo, we may compare the philosophies and tendencies of the two movements. It is meaningful, but overly simplistic, to define criollismo as an observation of social-class conflicts during those years when Chile's economy was dependent on agriculture and to define socialist realism as an analysis of social struggles when Chile's economy became more dependent on industry.[23] The ideologies of the two movements must be examined.

The criollista school was formed by Mariano Latorre. It has often been stated that the criollista authors wrote in the spirit of Spain's realist author José María de Pereda. To support the premise that the criollista authors are similar to Pereda in their intent, one may argue that the terms *regionalism* (and sometimes *realism*), *criollismo*, and even *costumbrismo* are used synonymously when referring to a certain type of literature.

In general, this type of regional literature has been written out of a nationalistic or regionalistic desire to preserve an obviously fading reality (remember that Pereda was a reactionary who did not want his province changed):

> Es indudable que cuando los pueblos presienten que su realidad o contextura se va a modificar, y siempre que posean la fortaleza de espíritu suficiente, se apresuran de dejar estampada aquella realidad que será un antecedente, a fin de tener memoria de ella, y ejemplo, a fin de no perder de vista aquellos ideales o esas formas de vida que le fueron propios y formaron su carácter.
>
> El criollismo comenzó esta labor, sin duda, con el campo chileno. Cuando, dentro de cien años, las generaciones del porvenir lean las obras de D. Mariano Latorre, tendrán una imagen luminosa de lo que fue el agro chileno, en la misma medida en que ahora lo son de la Colonia las páginas del Padre Alonso de Ovalle o, del siglo pasado, la de Vicente Pérez Rosales y Alberto Blest Gana.[24]

In other words, criollismo may be defined as an attempt by a conservative element to record nostalgic realities in literature. The writers attempted to depict origins of regional customs, or they aspired to record with a sort of verbal photography certain essential customs and folklore that they feared would ultimately be lost.

Quite the opposite is the philosophy of the writer employing socialist realism. He is as nationalistic as his criollista teacher, but he

---

23. Mario Ferrero, "La prosa chilena del media siglo," *Atenea*, 386 (1959), 122.

24. Espinosa, "Una generación," pp. 72–73.

interprets national problems by means of "realism," not "regionalism":

> Una nueva corriente, igualmente nacionalista, hace la historia de ciertos problemas or realidades de Chile. Yo llamo a esta tendencia el "realismo sociológico" porque, teniendo, sin duda, caracteres de literatura realista, esta creación literaria se refiere principalmente a aspectos de nuestra vida que engloban a mucha gente, a compactos grupos humanos, con sus correspondientes problemas de índole socioeconómica.[25]

Even the term *neocriollismo*, then, is a contradiction when used to designate the proletarian novels of the Generation of '38 written between 1938 and 1960, for *criollismo* denotes conservatism and even a reactionary philosophy. Yet the majority of the writers in the Generation of '38 were revolutionaries or sympathized with the lower class and its Marxist ideology. Therefore, socialist realism is the most appropriate term to categorize those works which deal with problems of class revolution.

Future studies on Chilean prose would be wise to bear in mind that such an ideological schism exists between *criollismo* and socialist realism, and this antithesis should be shown when the two movements are interpreted.

Socialist Realism and Guzmán's Generation

Socialist realism was the force that motivated Guzmán to begin writing prose. Realism meant truth to him, and the only artful, truthful model was life; but life is so complex that it would be impossible to portray it with a single universal technique:

> Justamente la complejidad de la vida, materia prima de toda creación artística, impedirá siempre la rigidez de la técnica, a no ser que se desee falsearla, desposeerla de sus calores íntimos, arrebatarle su tembloroso gesto eternamente desgarbado y caprichoso.[26]

Guzmán's longest discussion of socialist realism, especially as a phenomenon that involved his generation, was the prologue to his *Nuevos cuentistas chilenos*. In this four-part essay, Guzmán at-

25. Espinosa, "Una generación," p. 73.
26. Nicomedes Guzmán, "Prólogo," *Nuevos cuentistas chilenos: Antología* (Santiago: Editorial Cultura, 1941), p. 7. Further references in this chapter to this anthology will be included in the body of the text.

tempts to demonstrate that his colleagues have written socrealism with all the varied literary aspects that it involves.

He first attempts to refute previous definitions of the short story based on the oft-repeated statements of Poe, Maupassant, and Bret Harte—they differ too greatly for all of them to be correct.[27] Then he argues that there are as many possible definitions of the short story as there are philosophies of life, but that the best narrative form is socialist realism: "Technique and method are often controlled by the author's feelings, his sense of well-being; sometimes a great work is created by the artistic instinct of the author; at other times, it is a product of his emotions." To support his theory, Guzmán cites Godoy's *Angurrientos* as an example. It is thought by all to be a novel, but Guzmán insists that it is a collection of short stories dictated by Godoy's life and his surroundings. Other authors experience the opposite when they feel that they are creating a short story but actually produce a novel (pp. 8–9).

Whereas Miguel Serrano had denied emphatically that a tradition of Chilean short stories ever existed, in the second section Guzmán praises the "cuento chileno," which he feels began with Lillo and the Generation of 1900. (He insists, too, that no literary generations took shape between 1900 and 1938, an opinion which is in agreement with the thesis proposed in Chapter 6 of the present work that Chilean literary generations are socially oriented and that they take form at times of fundamental social change.)

In the longest section of the prologue, Guzmán philosophizes subjectively on socialist realism and his generation, stating his belief that socialist realism began in 1900. He extolls the virtues of each of his colleagues, and he shows how they include in their stories each of the geographic regions of Chile.

Finally, Guzmán summarizes his colleagues' combination of socrealist and poetic elements. Then he states that he published this anthology of short stories to compete with the many collections of poetry that had previously been published by other factions of his generation.

27. Enrique Lafourcade carries on this theme in his *Antología del nuevo cuento chileno* (Santiago: Empresa Editora Zig-Zag, 1954); he asks for a definition of the short story from each of the authors in his collection of the Generation of 1950, and obviously each opinion differs. Lafourcade also acknowledges his debt to Guzmán in his bibliography.

Guzmán's second and third points are worthy of further discussion here, for he goes to great lengths to attempt to prove that socialist realism would ultimately bring about the extinction of *costumbrismo*.

In Chapter 4 we examined the basic influence of the Generation of 1900 on the Generation of 1938. Among the turn-of-the-century writers, in Guzmán's opinion, there was no one more masterful in his portrayal of Chilean life and in his characterization of the roto than Baldomero Lillo. Guzmán emphasizes the similarity of Lillo's generation to his own comrades—the prophets of the revolution "during Chile's literary meridian":

> Realmente no se había dado en Chile un caso de tan apretado y vital florecimiento literario hasta constatar la presencia colectiva de los valores novecentistas que hemos venido incorporando ligeramente a nuestras palabras. Su gesto tuvo la importancia de ser el primero que se adelantara para significar la existencia de una ancha y conjunta *realidad* en el proceso de nuestra novelística. (*Nuevos cuentistas chilenos*, 10; my italics)

Reality and *revolution* become synonymous for Guzmán, and he heralds them as the watchwords of the Generation of '38. Their origin, he finds, was conceived in Baldomero Lillo's concept of literature and in his portrayal of striking "cuadros mineros," which still speak prophetically for the revolution, even after forty years (p. 11).

Between Lillo's day and Guzmán's, however, the short story followed another course. It is this departure from the social scene that Guzmán is criticizing; he feels that the non-realist short story has failed to discover the "vital essence of Chile." Each previous tendency had focused on essential aspects of Chilean life, Guzmán continues, but it is not only the theme of psychological development (as in Eduardo Barrios) even when it is intermingled with love intrigue, nor is it regionalism or morbidity or any other combination of themes in themselves that makes for socialist realism; rather, it is the amalgamation of *all* these elements that portrays Chile in her greatest splendor as she searches for new solutions to her social problems:

> Es precisamente de todo este conjunto temático, y de tantas modalidades y condiciones nuestras que son, en suma, como la aorta de la crujiente realidad nacional . . . ; es del cúmulo caótico de sombras en que la raza está buscando sus nuevas rutas, en armonía con los elementos objetivos

reconocidos ya como patrimonios de nuestro mundo real; es de la
pasión y del apego a nuestra tradición heroica afluyendo al ceñudo y
bullente río de nuestra retorcida hora social, de donde emanará, lit-
erariamente, el verdadero informe de nuestro desgarbado y viril tranco
en la historia humana, y de las lámparas de nuestro destino. (*Nuevos
cuentistas chilenos*, 11–12)

Guzmán continuously interrelates the Generations of 1900 and 1938,
which he felt shared a spiritual affinity:

> Desde esta generación, que marcó un paso de curtida planta en nuestra
> cultura, no era posible hablar hasta ahora de una fusión de espíritus
> hermanados no precisamente por la edad, sino por el plano común de
> tiempo en que asoma su obra—, alzando una voz tan pareja, no obstante
> sus diferentes inflexiones, tendiente a continuar el intento de salvar
> los obstáculos para alcanzar la veta de la verdad nacional. (*Nuevos
> cuentistas chilenos*, 12)

After forty years' absence of socialist realism in Chile, a new
generation was being resurrected from the once-smoldering ashes
of social injustice; the new writers hoped to show with sincere reality
the "pure, suffering, and hopeful heart of Chile." The young authors
had different origins and backgrounds—a few were from the middle-
class. But their "reality"and their blood were not romantic or "es-
túpidamente azul" ("blue"—meaning "aristocratic" as well as
modernista). Rather it was "real and red":

> Roja en cuanto a pasión por la vida de su tierra y de sus hombres, y
> roja también en cuanto a sinceridad y a intención interpretativa. He
> aquí la similitud entre ambas generaciones: la 1900 y la actual, que
> podríamos llamar con propiedad, la de 1940. (*Nuevos cuentistas chile-
> nos*, 12)

"Red" has an additional connotation, for, besides being of lower-
or middle-class birth, most of the writers embraced communism,
associated with revolutionary blood red.

In the lengthy third part of his introduction, Guzmán enumerates
the virtues of each of the twenty-four writers he is anthologizing.
He mentions that Juan Godoy, who writes about the city, like Guzmán himself, is one of the more capable portrayers of the "heart of
the roto." Godoy aspired to characterize perfectly this archetypal
Chilean character. He argued that in order to discover the essence
of the nation and its destiny, one must study the collective archetypes
—the gaucho in Argentina, the *cholo* in Peru. Although he may
have failed to achieve his goal in many respects—according to Guz-

mán, at least—Godoy was still in accord with the goals of his generation. Guzmán was one of the few to have seen the essence of the Chilean people captured in Godoy's characters; several other critics only saw "tragic man in Godoy, caught between sex and alcohol."[28]

Another colleague, Abelardo Barahona, develops the roto from a psychological point of view, which is also an interpretation of the heart of Chile and of Latin America: "nuestra grandiosa América Latina, vientre potente y libre donde el porvenir está concibiendo tanta *realidad de luz y de esperanza*" (20, my italics). Guzmán felt that Barahona would ultimately discover the key to the roto's collective idiosyncrasies, to the "discovery of the Chilean race's spirit, of the national 'collective archetype' ":

> Potencialmente, el "roto" es el símbolo de la aventura, del esfuerzo, del impulso que no conoce retroceso, de la gracia, de la picardía, de la *fe* y de la *esperanza*. La *realidad* y el medio han condicionado su corazón dentro de un clima de fatalismo. Es ésta una característica psicológica que, por hoy, está presidiendo su gesto humano." (*Nuevos cuentistas chilenos*, 19)

Gonzalo Drago is pointed out by Guzmán as another member of his generation who artfully accomplished the mixing of essential universal and Chilean elements. He portrayed another Chilean type, the *arribista*, a unique social climber who could not wait for history to run its course so that the proletarian could take over as the ruling class. This "climber" is a link in the chain of dialectical materialism; he is a collective type who has been held down so long that misery makes him fight back tooth and nail. Ironically, the arribista is actually a rebel. Pushed against the wall, he has only one choice: revolution.

Guzmán praises individually the other twenty-one authors who write about the various geographical areas of Chile—the ocean, the small ports, the cities, the country, the mountains, the extreme South, and the North—and he goes to great lengths to interpret impressionistically the writings of each of the authors in his anthology who attempt to portray the social reality of those particular areas. Guzmán laments the fact that Baldomero Lillo did not complete his half-finished "La huelga," which would have been, according to Guzmán, the greatest novel about the North of Chile. Guz-

28. Thomas Edgar Lyon, Jr., *Juan Godoy* (New York: Twayne Publishers, 1972), pp. 132 and 155, n.

mán also regrets that none of his colleagues have written about the North; then he challenges them to produce a great novel about that desert region. His word seems to have been heeded, for many novels about the North appeared in later years, including Guzmán's *La luz viene del mar*.

Key words in Guzmán's descriptions of his colleagues' stories are *truthful, reality, rebel, realist, authentic, and truth*. Such "realistic" elements were essential for a true socrealist work. The opposite of socialist realism was criollismo, and Guzmán identifies Leoncio Guerrero as a convert to his generation from criollismo:

> Leoncio Guerrero, ingresado a nuestras letras en 1940 con *Pichamán*, colección de cuentos, maulino de la misma estirpe de Latorre, se nos descubre ahora con un claro horizonte marino, oloroso a peces, a verdad, a sangre. El cuentista de la pequeña aventura salpicada a ratos de crudeza—como se nos había demostrado en su primer libro—se torna ahora abiertamente familiar a un mundo real y humano. No ya la masturbación verbal ante la magnificencia de un paisaje. (*Nuevos cuentistas chilenos*, 15)

In these harsh words Guzmán characterizes the conversion of Guerrero from criollismo, where he had been a disciple of Latorre, to socialist realism, where such "verbal masturbation" does not occur. Even as early as 1941 the alienation between the criollistas and the Generation of '38 had become a major polemic; at least Guzmán appeared ready to attack criollismo without fear of the consequences.

In the summary of his introductory essay, Guzmán elaborates on the objectives of his generation. He emphasizes that his colleagues are prose writers, not poets, and that they will endow Chilean letters with a humanist voice and a socialist inclination:

> Con la generación de prosistas que recién surge a nuestro panorama literario, equilibrando las fuerzas y debilidades que la personifican, Chile en todo caso alza una estrella de rojos destellos frente al porvenir. (*Nuevos cuentistas chilenos*, 24)

The young anthologist continues in this prophetic voice, but then, for some unexplained reason, he states that these artists are not entirely proletarian. He also points out that his generation is not necessarily revolutionary, which seems paradoxical in the light of his previous arguments to the contrary. He emphasizes here that "according to Luis Alberto Sánchez the generation has a middle-class origin and a middle-class style." Perhaps Guzmán takes this stand so as not to build up any preconceived prejudices in his readers against the Generation of 1938.

Guzmán's final point is that his generation unites "heroic tradition" with social intent. In other words, traditional Chilean realism and elements of socialist realism are combined in their literature. This is a major premise of the present study, which proposes that such a blending is the key to the uniqueness of the works of Guzmán and his generation.

Although Guzmán was one of the first theorists of socialist realism in Chile, his rhetoric and impressionistic approach undercut much of his literary criticism; nevertheless his preface introducing his generational colleagues was important in demonstrating how his colleagues applied socialist realism to their literature and how they identified with it.

During the last half of the nineteenth century, according to Lukacs and his Marxist disciples, critical realism was the tool of bourgeois writers who were attempting to evaluate capitalist society. These "romantic realists" were attempting to show the relationship between the individual and his society with as much objectivity and verisimilitude as possible.

Nicomedes Guzmán points out in his essays that the nineteenth-century novelist Alberto Blest Gana has been designated as the father of Chilean realism and he identifies Augusto D'Halmar and Baldomero Lillo of the Generation of 1900 as more socially oriented realists.

In the 1930s realism took on a new meaning. Society was shown in a constant class struggle, for the lower classes were suffering from economic exploitation. A new force among the proletariat and the peasantry focused on changing the miserable conditions under which the masses lived and worked. This new type of realism was called socialist realism; yet it became a prevailing type of fiction during the thirties even among those Latin American writers who were not Communists. Many references have been made previously to the numerous "proletarian novels" written during this period in Europe and the United States, industrialized areas with large labor forces. "In Latin America, where the proletariat was almost non-existent [except for mineral-rich Chile], some writers found their Latin American equivalent in the small industrial enclaves such as oil and mine fields, amongst the dockers or the city *Lumpenproletariat*: more often, the writer found his material among the peasants and agricultural workers or the Indians."[29] In Chile, the Communist, Socialist, and Radical parties have originated in the mineral-rich regions of the North. There the homeless worker with no ties to the land or property has freely espoused Marxist ideologies, and as part of an isolated community miners have developed a closely knit social organization with a great deal of interaction between individuals. This is also true in the southern mining area of Concepción (Lota and Talcahuano) which has remained a liberal stronghold for decades. But in the other, predominantly agricultural provinces in southern Chile this liberal freedom has not existed, for the citizen has been too tied to his land, church, and tradition. This is perhaps why Guzmán and others felt that the proletarian novel in Chile must reflect the desert North and the social problems there. This, of course, is a paradox, since some of Lillo's best "proletarian" stories take place in the South; nevertheless many members of Guzmán's generation became obsessed with the idea of the perfect proletarian novel of the North. Santiago and the South have remained politically reactionary, and only ineffectual middle-class government and the movement of northern socialist mining families to the Central Valley has allowed Marxism to thrive in Chile and has created a large industrial and intellectual proletariat.

Other Latin American writers, such as Brazil's Jorge Amado, transformed the peasants into the proletariat; however, Marx and Trotsky always insisted that the peasant was bound by tradition to the earth and was not a true proletarian. Guzmán's close friend Jorge Icaza of Ecuador attempted to convert the Indians into proletarians in *Huasipungo*; but even though his novel is revolutionary, it is not successful in showing the Indians to be a true proletariat.

In Guzmán's generation each writer has searched for Chilean equivalents to the Marxist proletariat. Inspired by Jack London, the great American Marxist, Francisco Coloane portrays hostile men in the equally hostile regions and seas of Tierra del Fuego. Lomboy depicts unjust treatment of the *inquilino* or peasant in *Ranquil*. Oscar and Modesto Castro expose disgraceful exploitation of the miner in the Rancagua copper mines. But Guzmán and Godoy discover their working-class hero mingling with the urban *Lumpen-*

29. Jean Franco, *An Introduction to Spanish-American Literature* (Cambridge: Cambridge University Press, 1969), p. 231.

proletariat (Marx's fifth social class), struggling for existence, and longing for a revolution to free him. He is forced to exist in the conventillo with the outcasts of society—thieves and prostitutes, the unemployed and alcoholics—because social injustice has forced him down into the depths of an earthly hell.

Retaliating against social evils, Guzmán and his colleagues constituted a new generation of young writers raising a collective fist, hoping to become through their application of socialist realism the prophets of Chile's destiny.

III

Analysis of a New Proletarian Style:
Tradition Versus Innovation

8

Plot and Structure

Guzmán's works are characterized by many unusual techniques. Social and psychological conflict are predominant plot devices, even though most proletarian literature avoids psychological complications. Plot in Guzmán's novels evolves from the conventional chronological sequence of his first novel to the total destruction of the traditional idea of plot in *La luz viene del mar*.

The plot of Guzmán's first novel, *Los hombres obscuros* (1939),[1] concerns a few months in the life of Pablo, the protagonist and narrator. Except for a few flashbacks to events that happened a day or two previously, the structure of the novel suggests that of a documentary motion picture or television film, disclosing the details of the protagonist's daily life in a slum tenement in Santiago.

Pablo is an unskilled country boy, and the only work he can obtain in the city is shining shoes. He meets Inés, a working girl, and is physically attracted to her, but her father forbids them to see each other. Interspersed with the intense love intrigue are a party, an accident, and other episodes, including several dialogues about communism, strikes, and social injustice. Pablo's world of women's legs and neighbors making love is so sensual that he and Inés finally surrender to their emotions and agree to go to a cheap hotel together.

Throughout the story Inés suffers from a tubercular cough. Her health suddenly declines; when an anti-typhus brigade descends upon the conventillo, shaves off her hair, and takes her to a hospital which is too full to receive her, she quickly dies of exposure to the cold. Pablo is alone in a hostile world.

Up to this point the tempo of the plot is quite intense. It slows down in the last chapter, in which Pablo receives an irritating reconciliatory and admonitory letter from his father.

The last two pages of the novel show a complete conversion of

1. In Part III Guzmán's major novels will be identified in the text and notes by their key words only: *Hombres*, *Sangre*, and *Luz*. The editions used are the following: *Los hombres obscuros*, 6th ed. (Santiago: Empresa Editora Zig-Zag, 1964); *La sangre y la esperanza*, 5th ed. (Santiago: Editorial Nascimento, 1957); *La luz viene del mar*, 1st ed. (Santiago: Ediciones Aconcagua, 1951). The pagination of most of the Zig-Zag editions of *Hombres* is the same.

Pablo to proletarian ideals, and his concluding words are a shout of faith and hope that the working class shall ultimately triumph.

Though *La sangre y la esperanza* (1943) is structured in three parts—three periods of the narrator's life—the plot of Guzmán's "autobiographical" novel does not follow the traditional chronological sequence. Part II, "Las campanas y los pinos," takes place some four years earlier than Parts I and III. Outlined on a chart, the plot structure would appear as follows:

Sequence of Plot: I II III
Corresponding age of
Enrique: 8 4 9 or older

Part I of the novel, "El coro de los perros," begins with the unidentified protagonist, Enrique Quilodrán, recalling his years in the slums of Santiago. He vaguely identifies the period as the early 1920s, when he was eight. The first chapter of Part I moves with breathtaking speed through the appalling beheading of Enrique's playmate Zorobabel, the tragic death of Zorobabel's father, and finally the fatal rape of his eight-year-old sister, Angélica, by the alcoholic and mentally retarded lover of Zorobabel's unfaithful mother. These and many other episodes of promiscuity and violence are contrasted with a few pleasant scenes such as a proletarian payday with its carnival atmosphere and unexpected treats for the youngsters. Part I ends with the birth of Enrique's baby brother, which is contrasted with another childbirth, one that causes the death of a thirteen-year-old vagabond girl who sleeps among the neighborhood dogs with her grandfather, the memorable tramp Pan Candeal.

Because Part II shows the world of a four-year-old boy, it includes more episodes from the family's intimate life. These are the events that take place earliest in the novel's action.

One day a pious woman is found half-drowned in the sewage of the canal. It was rumored that she had once been a prostitute; she jumped into the canal because the parish priest did not love her. During the ensuing confusion when she is carried to the Quilodráns' room, someone steals their laundry basket, leaving them with only the clothes on their backs.

A lung congestion causes Enrique's father to be hospitalized. The labor union attempts to aid the distressed and starving family, but after a week or two the union treasurer runs off with the funds. Having no income, Enrique's mother has to take in washing, and as the situation becomes worse, she has to pawn her wedding ring to feed the family.

The family's stolen clothes eventually turn up in the room of an insane neighbor, but shortly after Enrique's father is released from the hospital, the infant sister dies. This is a purposely misleading event; the reader feels that this infant who dies in Part II is the same child born in Part I; such is not the case.

In the third part of the novel, "Suceden días rojos," Enrique is several months older than in Part I and several years older than in Part II. The family is living in a different neighborhood and the old grandmother has come to live with them, thus adding to their burdens.

As the plot moves rapidly through the summer setting with interspersed erotic episodes, Enrique tells of swimming in the nude, discovering a corpse, and slowly becoming aware that his older sister, Elena, has been having an affair with a married poet. This last situation is partly developed through letters that Enrique finds and reads.

The last two chapters embody the structural conflict that is the key and the title to the book—"Sangre" and "Esperanza." The chapter entitled "Sangre" describes a strike where demonstrators are killed and Enrique's father is hurt when the police attack. In a victory celebration that evening Elena's boyfriend, the poet Abel, is shot and killed while giving a speech. Men, women, and children are sent rolling and are fatally crushed by the charging mounted policemen. Enrique's father is struck on the back with a rifle butt and is hurt so seriously that he has to return to the hospital. Elena is pregnant with the poet's illegitimate child, so Enrique provides the only possible salvation for his family when he secretly quits school and goes to work in a foundry. His first wages provide the hope that his family can survive. This final note of Marxist "hope" in the closing chapter, "Esperanza," is bitingly ironic, completely abstract, and seemingly pessimistic.

The plot of La luz viene del mar (1951), Guzmán's last published novel, is much more complex, for the chapters concern episodes in the lives of a young girl named Virginia, her mother, and three or four older proletarian men. Some chapters (including several historical flashbacks) are devoted exclusively to labor union problems; some, in contrast, take place in a house of prostitution.

After an opening chapter of pure scenery (an *estampa*), the novel begins with a flashback to the birth of Virginia as seen through the eyes of Lorenzo Carmona, a link with the past, a witness of "time" in the novel who resembles a Fellini character. Virginia was born the night her father was shot and killed during a labor dispute. Her mother, Sofía, who arrived at the scene of the thwarted strike, collapsed from the shock of seeing her dead husband, and gave birth to Virginia on the street.

The plot then shifts to less remote time, a flashback to Sofía's life and the problems she encounters in a subsequent poor marriage which caused her alienation from Virginia's grandfather, a formidable man of Greek origin. The next part of the book centers in present time on this virile figure with a gold earring who, although he is in his sixties, is still the greatest lover in the city.

Most of the scenes deal with a thirty-six-hour period in Virginia's life. She is shown sunbathing, swimming in the nude (she had just seemed to discover her recently matured body in the mirror that morning), talking to Andrea, her closest friend, and strolling along the beach. Time is purposefully mixed in the narration. For example, Virginia met Eudocio on the beach in an early chapter; but during the main-plot time of the novel, when it seems that Virginia is still on the beach, Eudocio is actually working in the desert or is in the brothel. Such scenes are like fragmented cinematographic sequences interspersed with straightforward action narrative—or occasionally played in slow motion.

Focus is switched for shock effect to the hideous Cara de Pescado, an extremely ugly yet sensual man. He has a horrible face because he had cut out one of his eyes to please a girl who had only been joking with him. The plot next moves to another worker who had sacrificed part of his body because of a passion for a woman. When we first see Pedro Andrade he is holding his bloody arm in a bandage and relating his tragic life to Lorenzo Carmona. He had once seduced a young girl, Fresia, in Magallanes and planned to marry her, but she ran away just before the wedding with the first of Pedro's rivals, her cousin. Pedro followed her to Santiago, where he seduced Melania, whom he left when she became pregnant so that he could be with Fresia again. Distressed by Pedro's perfidy, Melania attempted suicide by hurling herself under the streetcar on which Pedro was driver-conductor; but instead of dying, she lost her unborn child and one of her legs. Recovered, she followed Pedro and Fresia to Iquique, where both women in this triangle finally became prostitutes. In spite of Fresia's aloofness, Pedro's desire to marry her was so great that to redeem her from the brothel he tried to obtain money from the mining company by self-mutilation. When he attempted to sever his finger in a machine, he became so nervous that his entire hand was amputated.

The second part of the book, "Las anclas de la noche," is central to the plot; it unites many of the major characters in a brothel orgy that ends in blood when Pedro's arm hemorrhages, leaving him dead in the arms of his naked Fresia.

Guzmán does not connect the episodes dealing with labor officials to any other portion of the novel until the morning after the orgy, when Cara de Pescado sees a man about to shoot into a group of labor leaders in an attempt to assassinate a visiting official, Ceferino López. Hoping to divert the shot, drunken Cara runs and staggers toward the assassin, but he can only throw himself in front of the bullet in a sacrificial attempt to save the heroic union leader.

When she discovers that her boyfriend has spent several nights in the brothel with an Oriental girl whom he had seduced away from her recently wed Chinese husband, Virginia suffers an emotional crisis. She attempts suicide in the ocean, but instead of drowning, she is pulled out of the water by an acquaintance who rapes her while she is still unconscious.

When several of the characters in the novel depart for the desert, a submissive and confused Virginia climbs the bell tower to see them depart and to orient herself once again by observing her cyclical world of sand and sea, parallel deserts. There is a possibility that she is again contemplating suicide as the novel closes. The narrator hints that the bell tower signified the same thing to Virginia as the sea, which had been the source of her first suicide attempt.

The plots of some of Guzmán's short stories are weak; there is no point summarizing them, since a few have been described elsewhere in this work and several are mentioned—together with excellent criticism—in an article by John P. Dyson.[2] There is little action and a minimum of motivation in the stories, and very often the

2. John P. Dyson, "Los cuentos de Nicomedes Guzmán," *Atenea*, 404 (1964), 228–49.

setting is static—a proletarian apartment, a shack—and character delineation is flat. "Extramuros" (1944), however, has one of Guzmán's finest plots as far as suspense is concerned. It is a story about four nameless vagabonds and a cat who have gathered one by one around the warm ashes and coals of a tarworks on a cold, drizzly night. One of the four is a boy, a "cabro," and it becomes more and more noticeable to his three unusual companions that something is bothering him. He is nervous, he cries, and finally, after the others try to discover and calm his unknown fear, he jumps up and confesses that he has just killed a man. He then runs away, leaving the money he had stolen. When the two older men scuffle for the abandoned money, the cat and the third man flee. After a short struggle the lame man stabs the old man and takes the loot.

In summary, it should be stated that Guzmán's plots are predominantly episodic. The autobiographical structure of the first two novels causes them to be extremely fragmentary. In *La luz viene del mar*, there is no clear climax, and continuity from one chapter to the next is weak. Guzmán was trying here to create a novel that would reflect the lives of several northerners and represent faithfully the enormous expanse of the arid North of Chile.

Structure

Various traditional structural elements are altered in Guzmán's novels. For the first time in Chilean literature, traditional forms are combined with socialist realism and baroque elaborations, such as contrast (*sangre* versus *esperanza*) and a first-person narrator of the type that has its root in the Spanish picaresque novel.

External Structure

A reworking of one-third of the original 300-page manuscript (possibly 600 pages at one time), *Los hombres obscuros* is divided into nineteen unequal chapters, the shortest of which is two pages (Chapter 6) and the longest and most intense of which is fifteen pages (Chapter 16). Though several reviewers mentioned the uneven structure,[3] only one major change was made after the work was

3. Guillermo Koenenkampf, "*Los hombres obscuros*, novel por Nicomedes Guzmán," *Atenea*, 170 (August 1939), 339; Milton Rossel, "*Hombres obscuros*, por Nicomedes Guzmán," *Atenea*, 180 (June 1940), 444; and Ricardo

published: the first four editions have eighteen chapters, but later Chapter 10 was divided into two chapters.

Guzmán used ordinal numbers as part of the chapter headings of his books, even up to the seldom used "capítulo trigésimoquinto" (thirty-fifth chapter; see the first edition of *Luz*). Chapters were also subdivided in *Los hombres obscuros* by inserting an additional space between paragraphs or "three garish little stars" in a triangle for the first edition, a symbol later dropped by Guzmán. Because the plot of *Los hombres obscuros* is structured entirely around time, these breaks signify only a passage of time: a shift in space is not possible in *Los hombres obscuros*, except in a chapter break, for the protagonist is narrating immediate present time only and can be in no more than one place at a time. Another use of such narrative breaks is to indicate the beginning or end of a poetic expression or description of the conventillo in the form of an *estampa*—a lyric stylization of the scenery—which will be studied later. These breaks also mark shifts from metaphorical description to Pablo's plain prose narrative. Thus, as we will see in later chapters, they are breaks in time or in poetic voice.

La sangre y la esperanza is divided into three nearly equal major divisions: Part I (eight chapters) has 129 pages, Part II (eight chapters) has 90, Part III (six chapters) has 88. The unusual element in this novel is the narrative progression. Narrative progression in the traditional Chilean novel, including the criollista works, is organized along a horizontal plane; *A* is followed by *B* and *C*, to the conclusion *D*, which is the last event in the temporal sequence of events. Beginning with Juan Godoy's angurrientismo the Generation of '38 attempted another technique, that of placing a character in the center of the narration, surrounded by his past, his present, his friends, his environment. According to Lyon, their goal "was a deeper penetration of man's psyche," and the several pages that Lyon devotes to concentric time in *Godoy* equally apply to Guzmán's *La sangre y la esperanza* and to *La luz viene del mar*.[4]

Although Guzmán was not as revolutionary in his prose style as Godoy, he attempted to change the static progression of Enrique

---

A. Latcham, "Dos novelas santiaguinas: *Los hombres obscuros*, por Nicomedes Guzmán y *Muerte en el valle*, por Bernardo Kordon," *La Nación*, Sunday [April or July] 25, 1943.

4. Thomas Edgar Lyon, Jr., *Juan Godoy* (New York: Twayne Publishers, 1972), p. 103.

Quilodrán's story by inverting Parts I and II, beginning the book, as it were, *in medias res*. The importance of this procedure has been overlooked by the critics. In Part I Enrique states that he is eight years old: "Mis ocho años se desencadenaban en gritos." Yet in Part II he has retrogressed from the third grade to preschool days with only a hint for reference, which is easily overlooked or misunderstood: "Yo, por entonces, no iba aún a la escuela. Y mi hermana no trabajaba todavía."

The relationship of Part III to the other parts is vague; the only reference point is the father's statement: "¡No hace tres años que me jodí, y ahora, de nuevo, la cama!" Because of the seasons of the year mentioned in the novel and because Enrique has completed at least three full years of school, we know that it is actually more than three years. The father was ill in Part II, so it would seem that the logical sequence is II, I, III; thus the chronological sequence of the novel is present-past-present. Since Parts I and II depict the late autumn and the winter and Part III the summer, it seems likely that Guzmán placed the third part six months or more after the first part, though otherwise he attempted to destroy evidence of historical time. Nonetheless, Guzmán's own biography is visible in spite of the intentional vagueness of the narrative.

In *La sangre y la esperanza* Guzmán defines his story by adding suggestive titles to the major divisions: "Primera Parte: El coro de los perros," "Segunda Parte: Las campanas y los pinos," and "Tercera Parte: Suceden días rojos." Also, the chapter titles throughout the novel recall the structure of Michael Gold's *Jews Without Money*. Most of the chapter headings in the first part refer to holidays or events ("El pago," "Primero de mayo"); in the middle of the novel they name characters ("Pan Candeal," "Leontina," "Elena"); but toward the end of the novel, abstract or symbolic headings ("Fantasmas," "La sangre," "La esperanza") hint at the evolution from concrete to abstract, away from names and toward the symbolic or thematic titles that most of his short stories and collections of stories will have after *La sangre y la esperanza*. To substantiate this statement, it might be mentioned that a short story published by Guzmán in *El Siglo*, January 26, 1941, bore the title "Mujeres." Later it was republished in *Una moneda al río* with the more abstract and symbolic title "Destello en la bruma."

In addition to the titled divisions and chapters, each chapter in *La sangre y la esperanza* is also divided temporally, thematically, or episodically into smaller sections identified by an arabic numeral, as in *Jews Without Money*. Juan Godoy subdivides chapters of *Angurrientos* with stars and occasional roman numerals, as does Francisco Coloane in *Cabo de Hornos*. But through Michael Gold's influence, it is Guzmán who has broken the usual Chilean tradition by employing arabic numerals in the subdivisions and utilizing ordinal numbers spelled out in Spanish—not Roman numerals—for chapter headings.

Guzmán's third novel, *La luz viene del mar*, comprises three extremely unequal divisions which the now-mature author prefers to call *climas* (though in his rough draft he designated them "Parte o clima primero," and so forth). The climas also have symbolic subtitles: Primer Clima, "Los mástiles del día" (24 chapters); Segundo Clima, "Las anclas de la noche" (4 chapters); and Tercer Clima, "El mar arrodillado" (7 chapters). The first clima (apart from the flashbacks) takes place for the most part during one afternoon; the second is an orgiastic night in the brothel; and the third clima is the morning after. There are thirty-five chapters in all, but the subdivisions of chapters are unnumbered once again as they were in the first novel, further demonstrating the structural influence that *Jews Without Money* had on *La sangre y la esperanza*. In *La luz viene del mar*, for the first time in Guzmán's novels, these breaks within chapters denote major shifts in space as well as time.

The element of space is also suggested by the use of the word *clima* (climate) instead of *parte*. The novelist intended *La luz viene del mar* as a dramatic or spatial revolutionary novel, while his first two novels were "biographical," with an emphasis on time.

Also unusual in *La luz viene del mar* and appearing for the first time in Guzmán's work are the repetitive thematic chapter headings. Since these headings continually reappear, they are not the traditional chapter headings like those in *La sangre y la esperanza*; rather they are signposts of the various thematic motifs. Each combination of chapters seems to have its own philosophy and to be centered on a particular character. In order of appearance the chapter headings are:

1. "En la brecha": the Marxist or strike viewpoint; appears six times including the opening *estampa*.
2. "Virginia y su mundo"; adolescent and erotic development; appears ten times.
3. "Medalla oriental": the problem of the Chinese in Iquique, exoticism, and social inequalities; appears three times.

4. "Un corazón soñador detenido en el tiempo": the development of Lorenzo Cardona, El Reliquia de la Huella; appears twice.

5. "Huracanes y estrellas": characterizes Sofía, Virginia's mother; appears three times.

6. "Los cinco jazmines del Huacho Fieroga": the characterization of an old ex-boxer now on the verge of insanity; appears three times.

7. "Canción de cuna": two distinct views of Basilio Cholakys; one is in juxtaposition with Virginia.

8. "La ternura terrible": the development of ugly one-eyed Cara de Pescado; appears four times.

9. "Coro de rameras": the brothel scenes, appears twice. The only chapter heading used only in Part II.

There are notable differences in orthography between the first and second editions. In the first Guzmán prefers to capitalize certain symbolic titles like "Brecha." Also he had the names of certain individuals like **Cara de Pescado** and **El Quemado** set in bold-face type. The editor of the second edition (perhaps Guzmán himself) preferred that everything follow more traditional patterns.

The evolution of Guzmán's indications of structure is simple but meaningful. He began with no chapter titles in his first novel; next he used simple titles; and finally he resorted to highly stylized symbolic headings, which he intended more to identify themes than to describe actions and events. In his short stories he preferred symbolic titles which indicated his message or statement. The titles of his nineteen short stories as they appeared in books exemplify this abstract approach: "Extramuros," "La ternura," "La angustia," "Destello en la bruma," "Donde nace el alba," "Sólo unas cuantas lágrimas," "Soledad," "Aún quedan madreselvas," "Rapsodia en luz mayor," "Una perra y algunos vagabundos," "Una moneda al río," "Leche de burra," "El pan bajo la bota," "La jauría," "Animita," "Perro ciego," "Pan de pascua," "La sagrada familia," and "La hora de la vida." Evident in Guzmán's titles is a penchant for contrast. The relationship of the title to the story, theme, or meaning is not always clear.

Internal Structure

Los hombres obscuros has a simple symmetrical structure: Pablo is a humble worker alone in the world; he meets Inés; their passion is intensified until the sensual climax of the novel when they finally give themselves to one another; Pablo loses Inés; once again he is a humble worker all alone. The symmetry is implicit in both the tone and the intensity of the novel. It can be best understood by comparing the plot to an arch or a triangle. Nevertheless, in spite of Pablo's loss of Inés and his ultimate sense of frustration, his character develops politically. He is converted to the proletarian cause, goes to work in a factory, and joins the Communists. The novel's symmetry also makes it appear to be cyclical like *La sangre y la esperanza*.[5] Pablo ends the novel where he began, having made a complete revolution on the wheel of dialectical materialism; he has "advanced" sociologically and ideologically.

In *La luz viene del mar* Guzmán adds to this cyclical structure a series of parallels. As we saw above, he builds a parallel development of themes, motifs, and characters. Guzmán's existential approach presents man alone, as in a tunnel, forced to scratch out his own existence and somehow progress. Yet if men's tunnels or paths cease to be parallel and somehow cross, the result is fighting and blood, because the man of the North is *ensimismado*: he has no concern for the existence of his fellow beings (*Luz*, 309).

The other structural parallel Guzmán experimented with in *La luz viene del mar* is characterization. Two of the men, Cara de Pescado and Pedro Andrade, are nearly carbon copies of each other. Both come from Magallanes in the southern tip of Chile. Both have been forsaken in the North, one working in the mines, the other in the sea. One sacrifices his eye for a girl; the other gives his hand. Both die tragically the same day.

A few moments before he dies, Cara de Pescado has a drink in the bar of El Quemado, inviting Quemado to have a few drinks with him. When Cara staggers away "as if walking on a cloud of anguish," Quemado thinks to himself: "Pobre Pescado—se dijo. Y se puso a secar unas copas. A fin de cuentas, El Cara de Pescado era un desecho humano igual que él. Y, pensando en esto, se dio a silbar" (*Luz*, 319). This example illustrates Guzmán's obvious intent to make several of his characters strikingly similar.

Finally there is the parallel of the ocean and the desert. Both are vast. Both are sand and salt (the desert salt is nitrate, the ocean salt sodium chloride). Guzmán states in countless metaphors and symbols—Virginia's bottles of sand and salt—that they are exactly the same. Both the pampas and the sea make man an island, never in

5. Though I also discovered it independently, the cyclical structure of *La sangre y la esperanza* was shown first by José Promis Ojeda, "El sentido de la existencia en *La sangre y la esperanza*, de Nicomedes Guzmán," *Anales de la Universidad de Chile*, 145 (1968), 65–68.

communication with others. Man is alienated both existentially and socially, for the North has been isolated for centuries; transportation by land or sea has always been difficult, undependable, and slow. In displaying the beautiful side of these two forces, Guzmán has used strange imagery and symbolism to evoke the action of light (sun and stars) on both the sea and the desert, and he makes the reflections from each stand out for the reader (*Luz*, 200, 310). In stylizing the North Guzmán creates a telluric protagonist that manipulates man's existence.

Structure by Contrast

Even before he wrote his novels Guzmán employed antithesis as a part of the structure in his book of poetry, *La ceniza y el sueño*. The same baroque contrast of past and future, of destruction and death versus faith and life, is intensified in *Los hombres obscuros*, where there are alternate elements of defeat and hope, with love or erotic episodes interspersed throughout the narration. Considering in addition the constant interplay of eroticism and Marxism, it is not surprising that when Pablo has a choice of reading Lawrence, Lillo, or Huxley, he chooses Huxley's *Point Counter Point*—also an obvious model for *La luz viene del mar*.

The critics immediately recognized that *Los hombres obscuros* ends on a note of hope,[6] as all good Marxist novels should, and one critic even pointed out the major structural element of contrast:

> Guzmán nos lleva a los rincones de un conventillo donde palpita *el dolor y la esperanza* de seres humildes a quienes la vida consume implacblemente.[7]

This antithesis is also the key to the structure of *La sangre y la esperanza*; in fact, all other elements of structure in the novel are subordinate to the contrast and counterbalance of suffering and faith, "actos que sublevan y desconciertan."[8]

An antithesis between blood and hope also exists in *La luz viene del mar*, but it has been elaborated and varied to such an extent that it is no longer basic in the work. There is no clear alternation be-

6. Lautaro Yankas, "Los libros: Dos libros chilenos," *Atenea*, 173 (November 1939), 247.
7. Rossel, "*Hombres obscuros*," p. 247.
8. Francisco Santana, "*La sangre y la esperanza*, por Nicomedes Guzmán," *Atenea*, 225 (March 1944), 283.

tween the two elements, nor does the novel end on an emphatic Marxist note of hope.

In spite of its seemingly transparent structure, *La sangre y la esperanza* is not a simple work. The combinations of contrasting elements are as numerous as the different shades of *sangre* (red) or *esperanza* (green), symbolic colors often employed on the covers of the novel. *Sangre* involves all of society's deterministic ills and all crimes and tragedies; *esperanza* includes all the Marxist elements of hope, even that of educating man. Both blood and hope as structural elements reflect (and are subordinate to) the great humanism and sensibility of Guzmán the novelist.

Autobiography

Both *Los hombres obscuros* and *La sangre y la esperanza* are structured as autobiographies or diaries.[9] This stance gives the novels verisimilitude, and it adds a personal tone of apparently objective testimony, which undoubtedly has more effect on the unsuspecting reader than the direct propaganda found in many less successful proletarian novels.

These structural elements and their complexity show that Guzmán was first and foremost an artist, and that he compromised nothing to achieve his goal of creating meaningful proletarian literature.

Interpolations

The interpolations in Guzmán's fiction offer keys to understanding some of the other structural elements, especially theme and tone. The most common interpolations are the quoted epigraph and the poetic song or verse; a minor item is artwork.

There is only one epigraph in *Los hombres obscuros*, although in the first two small editions there were originally two, the first of which was from Jacobo Danke's *La estrella roja*: "Yo digo a un arte con testículos." In all later editions Guzmán removed Danke's insinuation of *machismo*. The epigraph that has remained in all the editions is from *El escritor y el pueblo* by Ernesto Montenegro,

9. American bibliographers (in the Library of Congress, for example) have categorized a similar American novel that reached Chile, *Jews Without Money*, by the Communist leader Michael Gold, as history or autobiography and not a novel. It would be a grave error to consider *La sangre y la esperanza* or *Los hombres obscuros* to be true autobiographies.

an older established writer who had been an American newspaper-
man at one time:

> . . . si el escritor quiere que el pueblo le oiga y tome en cuenta sus
> palabras, *debe encarar su vida* y sus problemas con ojos implacables,
> con palabras firmes como el acero. Que las tiradas sentimentales y las
> frases de efecto queden para los oradores, o para los actores, para esos
> mercaderes que viven del trueque de fuegos de bengala por aplausos.

The italicized words in the epigraph also echo those of Manuel Rojas,
who reportedly told Guzmán to edit this same novel and "observe
life."

This quotation from Montenegro was not employed for the
traditional purpose of suggesting the theme; rather it was placed
at the beginning to help prepare the reader for the shock of the
bloody scenes to follow, and as a rationalization or support for the
novelist's philosophy of socialist realism.

The epigraph at the beginning of *La sangre y la esperanza* was
in the same tone, anticipating the socialist realism to follow:

> "Hablo de cosas que existen; Dios me libre
> de inventar cosas . . ."
> PABLO NERUDA
> "Estatuto del vino"

This epigraph, like Montenegro's, prepares the reader for an intimate
and truthful relation. In the manuscript of the novel Guzmán had
used the following quotation from Andrés Sabella's *Diálogos con
mi ternura*: "Unicamente digo que los héroes del pueblo representan
el arco de la eternidad, los más seguros colores del tiempo y el
espacio." Epigraphs are also included in the body of this novel to
introduce the theme: one motto by Charles Baudelaire heads Part II
and another by Lubicz Milosz is placed at the beginning of Part III.
An epigraph from Georg Fink and two from Lubicz Milosz are
arbitrarily placed at the head of one chapter in each of the three
parts. All of these quotations heighten the poetic symbolism of
the work.

About one-half of the short stories included epigraphs when they
were first published. When they were republished in *El pan bajo la
bota* (1960), Guzmán saw to it that each story was accompanied
by an epigraph. According to Dyson, "Guzmán's epigraphs generally
indicate the themes of the stories."[10] These epigraphs at first came

10. Dyson, "Los cuentos de Nicomedes Guzmán," p. 236.

from Marxist writers, but in Guzmán's later life they were scriptural quotations. Guzmán read the Bible regularly, and the scriptures were especially meaningful to him in his later years. Eleven of the nineteen short-story epigraphs are biblical, and those short stories written after he met Ester tend to have scriptural mottoes.

In *La luz viene del mar* the use of the epigraph has evolved to a regular and discernible pattern. Once again a quotation by Neruda was chosen to lead off the narration:

> Norte, llego por fin a tu bravío
> silencio mineral de ayer y de hoy,
> vengo a buscar tu luz y a conocer lo mío,
> y no te traigo un corazón vacío;
> te traigo todo lo que soy.

On the next page, the epigraph heading the Primer Clima, "Los mástiles del día," is of classical inspiration. Seemingly inspired by Danke's *Las barcarolas de Ulises*, Guzmán wrote " 'Titania' o la leyenda de Orfeo y Vilma" for *La ceniza y el sueño* and included a stanza as an epigraph in *La luz viene del mar*:

> Es aquí donde empieza la leyenda de Orfeo.
> Y es donde Ulises pulsa sus remos. Y el mar tañe
> su tambor de esmeraldas con los fémures rotos
> de los que en vida fueron audaces capitanes.

A poem by Lubicz Milosz is the epigraph to the Segundo Clima, "Las anclas de la noche," and the Tercer Clima, "El mar arrodillado," begins with two quotations, both statements and metaphors about the ocean by Jacobo Danke and Victoriano Vicario, two of the novelist's closest friends.

It is significant that poems by Neruda should appear only in those chapters on revolution and that epigraphs are used in no other chapters. Guzmán had just traveled to the North with Neruda when he began writing *La luz viene del mar*, and he became so influenced by the North and by Neruda's inspirational presence that he wanted to write a novel that would be a synthesis of the space, sea, brightness, poverty, labor conflicts, social problems, and total human alienation that the North typifies. He hoped to intersperse all this with poetry, songs, poetic imagery, and a multiple psychological portrayal of the proletarian inhabitants of the region.

The Chilean critic "Alone" sees Neruda's influence in more of *La luz viene del mar* than just the epigraph; in a review of the novel, he states that Guzmán is trying to become a poet in his prose, and that Neruda is the poet he is imitating.[11] "Alone" is wrong, however, for there is no imitation of Neruda in Guzmán's prose. Guzmán's language is very generational, extremely socialist-realist. Undoubtedly Neruda's greatest influence on the novel is simply his socialism.

One of Neruda's poems, which heads a subdivision in Chapter 24, shows how greatly Guzmán was inspired by the poet and by what he and Neruda had witnessed:

"Y me mostraron sus raciones, sus miserables
alimentos, su piso de tierra en las casas, *el sol*,
el polvo, las vinchucas, y *la soledad inmensa.*"
(*Luz*, 193; italics mine)

The novelist's choices of epigraphs can assist the investigator in two important ways. First, they can aid in locating sources and in determining the works and authors Guzmán was reading at a given period of time; and second, they can support the thesis proposed by this study that Guzmán's work is a synthesis of two strong influences, namely, the international Marxist writers of the thirties and the Chilean socialist writers, especially Neruda, Pablo de Rokha, Rojas, and the novelist's friends in the Generation of 1938. It would appear from the epigraphs that Guzmán received special inspiration from Pablo Neruda, Georg Fink, and Oscar Lubicz Milosz, the Lithuanian leftist poet whose works were translated into Spanish in Chile by Augusto D'Halmar.

In *La luz viene del mar* epigraphs mark narrative passages that are politically radical and describe labor meetings. Poetry or songs are also interspersed through these same Neruda-inspired paragraphs. As will be shown in the following pages, songs and verse usually indicate the most tranquil parts of Guzmán's prose—the scenes of hope—but occasionally they evoke sensuous sounds and parties.

Nearly a hundred poems, fragments of poems, or verses of songs are interspersed in Guzmán's prose fiction. Seventy-three appear in his first two novels, fifteen in his last one, and only eight poems in his nineteen short stories. The ninety-six interpolated stanzas consist mainly of popular verse, including Chilean *tonadas* and *cuecas*, old and new popular songs, "añejas canciones picarescas," children's

11. "Alone" [Hernán Díaz Arrieta], "Crónica literaria: *Los hombres ob-scuros*," *El Mercurio* (Santiago), August 27, 1939.

songs, nursery rhymes (a Chilean "Farmer in the Dell"), cradle songs, Catholic and Protestant hymns, labor union songs and anthems, and even a version of the Mexican song "Cielito Lindo" mentioning the Chilean president Arturo Alessandri Palma.

Poetry interrupts the narrative tempo and adds a dimension of space in the first-person novel to enable the narrator to comment on his parents, the children, the meetings, and the characters that sing the songs. The storyteller can then make reference to the surroundings in which the song is being sung. The songs also diversify the commentary and broaden it. Many of Guzmán's songs were familiar to the Chilean public, so the reader would become interested and nostalgic as he recognized them.

Popular poetry has played an important role in the writings of the Generation of 1938 and in leftist literature as a whole, for such popular expression has been referred to as the poetry of the masses. In recent Marxist literature, folk literature has often been a point of departure for a study of the origin and value of a culture. This is no less true in Guzmán's philosophy. He included songs for all purposes. At times it was for their folkloristic or evocative value:

> Desde lejos, se allegaba a los tímpanos una
> versaina graciosa, de entonación indígena:
>> Vamos a la plaza,
>> ¡ay, palomita!
>> que hay mucho que ver,
>> ¡ay, palomita!,
>> Un indio llorando,
>> ¡ay, palomita!,
>> y al amanecer,
>> ¡ay palomita!   (*Luz*, 128)

A still more earnest examination of popular poetry leads Guzmán to consider the song or cry of the street vendor as one of the most basic forms of popular verse, a form that contains the very germ of a powerful, popular poetry:

> Sería necesario dar forma íntegra al sentido social que guarda en sí el grito de los vendedores callejeros de Chile. . . . Como en toda manifestación de arte popular y primitivo, el pregón es una creación rotunda, una expresión categórica dentro de la simpleza, del espíritu colectivo en trance de realizaciones dotadas de espíritu. No se explica de otro modo la influencia profundamente vigorosa que tiene en las almas del suburbio.
> Y bien, aunque pareciera estar de más el delineamiento objetivo

de ciertos tipos populares y la referencia a asuntos también naturales al pueblo chileno, hay que reconocer cómo el estado espiritual de Chile es consecuencia de esos ciertos tipos y de esos asuntos. Exactamente por aparecer como comunes y vulgares, no se atiende a tales figuras y asuntos. *Mas, nada se conocerá de un pueblo sin ir a lo puramente popular, en su expresión más simple.*[12]

Guzmán was convinced that Chile's essence was hidden in the lives of these popular types and their street cries. And since they appeared common and vulgar, nobody before Guzmán bothered to heed their importance. He felt here that it was impossible to understand any people without searching for their "purely popular base," which he refers to as the "simplest expression": "Es menester mirar con mayor fervor a la vida del pueblo para deducir la verdad de Chile y las posibilidades que se asientan en el pasado de este pueblo."[13]

He goes on to state that even though these simple customs and gestures of the poor Chilean people are their least transcendent acts, it is impossible to understand a nation without examining its daily life patterns:

Hábitos y cosas dan pauta para serios estudios tendientes a lograr la interpretación de un pueblo. Lo humano desplazándose en los planos aparentemente más intrascendentes, resulta a veces lo más tracendente y significativo.[14]

Thus, when Guzmán interpolates the cry of a tinsmith or a vendor, he is attempting to include in his prose a "poetic expression" that he feels is essential. When he heard the cry of a street merchant, Guzmán would often write it down and use it in his books. On occasion he invited the man in and bought all of his wares in an attempt to try to find out more about him as a human being. Usually the vendor was skeptical of Guzmán's good intentions, for he did not realize that the writer was searching for further poetic and cultural elements in the peddler's life.

Some of the interpolated songs or verses evoke another aspect of the author's life. When his novels describe labor union meetings, Guzmán often includes several songs that were sung during these meetings. This is reminiscent of the musicality of the Wobblies, who were known for their songs and musical spirit; Joe Hill, the

---

12. Nicomedes Guzmán, "Encuentro emocional con Chile," *Atenea*, 380–81 (1958), 85. My italics.

13. Guzmán, "Encuentro emocional," p. 86.

14. Guzmán, "Encuentro emocional," p. 86.

"Wobblies' Troubadour," and other folk-composers gave the world songs like "Casey Jones" and others still available in the Wobbly *Little Red Songbook*.[15]

These anthems of the revolution, popular songs, and other poetic elements give a lofty and occasionally sensual spirit of hope to Guzmán's prose. In his works they appear mostly in scenes that suggest *esperanza*. Even thumbing through Guzmán's novels one can spot optimistic or pessimistic sections by the number of poems or songs included in that section, chapter, or story. Seldom do such interpolations appear in the bloody or tragic episodes except in ironic contrast, such as in the scene of *La luz viene de mar* where the dying Pedro Andrade bathes Fresia in his own blood from his arm stump. Then Pedro's other prostitute girl friend, Melania, comes out of her room singing a Protestant hymn about being washed in the blood of the Lord:

> Las venas puras de Emmanuel
> de *sangre* ofrecen un raudal
> y pierde, sumergido en él,
> sus culpas, todas el mortal.
>
> Hasta el ladrón placer sintió
> de salvación la fuente al ver,
> tan vil como él, canalla yo,
> mis manchas vi desparecer.   (*Luz*, 269)

In the rough draft the four verses of this hymn were placed all together (see pages 232–33 below for verses 3 and 4); then Guzmán drew arrows intercalating the verses at appropriate points in the narration.

Also interspersed in four of Guzmán's works are the sketches and drawings which are the result of an artist's interpretation of certain scenes: *Los hombres obscuros* uses art by Carlos Hermosilla Álvarez and Pedro Olmos in different editions; *La carne iluminada* contains artwork by the brothers Aníbal and Lautaro Alvial; *La luz viene del mar* includes the art of Osvaldo Loyola and Enrique Lihn (poet and Marxist leader in the Generation of 1950); and *Una moneda al río* also contains art by Osvaldo Loyola. It will be remembered that Guzmán had begun as an artist, sketching scenes for his own narrations. A similar type of interpolation is seen in the

---

15. Walter B. Rideout, *The Radical Novel in the United States: 1900–1954* (New York: Hill and Wang, 1966), p. 93.

strike poster and the newspaper print that Guzmán reproduced carefully and faithfully in the 1943 editions of *La sangre y la esperanza* to add a realistic effect. Later editions used standard type.

Often Russian Communist works, like Gorky's *Mother*, include pictures, as do many books of fiction that are directed to the young or to a popular audience. Guzmán wanted his work to appeal to the masses and to be read by all. He felt that the interpolation of art work would help make his books more popular without lessening their artistic and aesthetic value.

Structure and plot in Guzmán's works are innovative and original. Guzmán and his generational colleagues broke away from traditional forms of Chilean prose by employing lyric interpolations of various kinds and by experimenting with radical innovations in plot and narrative structure.

Throughout Guzmán's prose fiction an additional element reappears continually, interrupting the plot structure. In his novels and most of his stories, the traditional flow of narrative is broken at the beginnings and ends of chapters and other structural divisions by the lyric *estampa*, a contemplative poetic description of the background scenery of the story. This element, to be studied further in Chapter 10, together with the episodic nature of Guzmán's novels, creates a loose plot framework. Recall in addition the break in narrative progression mentioned earlier (II, I, III in *La sangre y la esperanza*, for example) the concentric progression of *La luz viene del mar*. Generally, it might be stated, the cohensiveness of Guzmán's plots are subordinate to unity of theme.

Since the central figures in his novels are everyday proletarian individuals, not strong heroic characters, plot is not a dominant feature in their delineation. More important for Guzmán are social awareness and individual psychological conflict. Parallel or counterpoised themes become predominant structural tools. While structure is Guzmán's forte in *La sangre y la esperanza*, and it is well balanced in *Los hombres obscuros*, it becomes purposely complicated and cyclical in *La luz viene del mar*.

The interpolated verses and songs add rhythm and rhyme, folk motifs, and vernacular tone to Guzmán's fiction. They break the normal rhythm of his prose structure to help create a sort of poetic surge. The narrator is also able to recall to the reader previous actions through a song inserted into the narration, or he can place a present action in ironic counterpoint by juxtaposing song and narration.

Guzmán also uses communist songs to great advantage, for as a poet he is able to propagandize indirectly by incorporating protest songs in their proper narrative setting. He is able to express his own philosophy through appealing characters, leaving the unsuspecting reader unaware of this maneuver.

9

Theme and Motif: Unity and Familiarity

Theme is the most important element in Guzmán's fiction. The term *theme* and the related term *motif* have different meanings for different critics. For some, theme is structural unity; for others, it is thought, concept, or purpose; and for still others, semantics becomes an issue. I shall deal with Guzmán's themes and motifs as one would approach their counterparts in music, but without ignoring the other definitions.

Theme

In Guzmán's works two basic types of themes appear: Marxist themes and the author's personal themes. The latter reflect Guzmán's own individual sensibility; the Marxist themes, typical of those in most proletarian literature, include class struggle, work as salvation, proletarian integrity, socialist ideals, and revolution. In using these collective themes, Guzmán attempts to be a spokesman for his society. As Northrop Frye says in discussing thematic literature, "The poet may devote himself to being a spokesman of his society, which means . . . that a poetic knowledge and expressive power which is latent or needed in his society comes to articulation in him. . . . In poetry which is educational in this sense, the social function of the poet figures prominently as a theme."[1]

Because Guzmán's novelistic structure is centered on a thematic axis, we must ask whether the critical approach to his works should be primarily thematic. Such an approach carries the risk of showing the work to be allegory or, worse still, of oversimplifying it—lessening its value. When a reader dissects a novel only to discover an overly facile thematic structure—*sangre* versus *esperanza*, *civilización* versus *barbarie* (*Doña Bárbara*), *menosprecio de cortes, alabanza de aldea* (*Doña Perfecta*)—the value of the novel depreciates in his mind. Such has been the case with two of the most widely read works by students of Hispanic literature, *Doña Perfecta* and *Doña Bárbara*, both of which have been considered thematic or

1. Northrop Frye, *Anatomy of Criticism* (New York: Atheneum Publishers, 1965), p. 54.

thesis novels. In spite of their greatness and popularity, their reputations have been hurt by critics who have emphasized the shallow thematic-structural antithesis of good versus evil.

The reader should be careful not to categorize *La sangre y la esperanza* as tendentious. While the desire of most proletarian novelists has been to show the establishment as evil and the masses as virtuous, Guzmán is not so inclined. For example, in *Los hombres obscuros* he depicts a kind and humble policeman whose wife suffers humiliation at the hands of the typhus corps. Guzmán's proletarian is anything but perfect or idealistic; only the Marxist ideology is perfect. Even Marxism and labor unions do not perfect men automatically; a union secretary absconds with the union's funds in *La sangre y la esperanza*. From a Marxist point of view this is a highly unorthodox situation for Guzmán to depict in a proletarian novel (*Sangre*, 202). Elena, the father, the mother, all have their faults, as does the "hero," Enrique. In fact, the family as an entity is probably the predominant theme. On the other hand, Guzmán is not a Manichaean who sees all the characters except the narrator as bad; rather, he finds poles of good and evil in each human soul.

Although the novel may group opposing elements beneath the banners of *sangre* and *esperanza*, this structural device of contrasting themes in no way lessens the importance of *La sangre y la esperanza*. The structure of the work opposes the values of one way of life (those of the prostitutes, for example) to those of a noble proletarian life (the humble goodness of the Quilodrán family), which inspires Enrique, the son.

Two of Guzmán's themes, *sangre* and *esperanza*, which were examined as structural elements in Chapter 8, are Marxist themes; their intertwining, however, constitutes a theme in itself, as it would in a musical composition.

To satisfy the student who feels that theme is "idea," the central theme of *La sangre y la esperanza* could probably be stated as follows: "A young boy, faced with crime and oppression on all sides (*sangre*), ultimately achieves salvation when he chooses to reject the destructive influences of his environment and to follow the good example of his father and the other influential laborers in his neighborhood by going to work in a foundry so that his family can survive on his income."[2] The theme of the novel is much more complex than

2. José Promis Ojeda, "El sentido de la existencia en *La sangre y la*

this, however. The Marxist concept of antagonistic social forces, depicted by the author as *sangre*, includes the elements of class struggle, frustrated strikes, and acts that violate human dignity. In the end all of these minor subthemes will terminate in revolution. Indeed, everything else is subordinate to revolution, and an extreme Marxist interpretation of Guzmán's theme in *La sangre y la esperanza* might be stated in these words: "Proletarian existence is impossible in the light of the horrendous atrocities of upper-class domination (*sangre*) unless all workers of the world unite in revolution."

The theme of *Los hombres obscuros* could be summarized in the same words. In this case, however, a more meaningful statement would be that "a young man, having been exploited in the country during his youth by his father's bourgeois class and having discovered that the poor have little right to their own dignity because of social injustice, chooses, after a short and tragic love affair, to become a worker and join a labor union in order to be able to promote the inevitable revolution."

A statement of the theme of *La luz viene del mar* is much more difficult if, in fact, a single theme exists: "The once great North, with its vast ocean and arid desert, is a deterministic element on the minds and bodies of the men and women who are forced to live and work there, for it alienates men from one another and from the rest of the social world. The nearly impossible life, due to the heat and living conditions, produces a sterile, hostile world without women. Work and life in the North will continue to devastate and alienate men unless a revolution improves social and economic conditions, and raises wages to make them equitable to the demands made on the laborer."

One of the author's more important Marxist themes is that of "proletarian integrity." Marxist theory dictates that the basic qualities of human goodness and integrity pertain to the proletarian class. Guzmán, who claimed to be more humanist than militant, took no such unilateral point of view, but he did frequently employ the concept of proletarian integrity—if not as a theme, often as an important element of characterization. In his short story, "La hora de la vida," it is the main structural theme.

Guzmán stated in his autobiography that the characterization of

esperanza de Nicomedes Guzmán," *Anales de la Universidad de Chile*, 145 (March 1968), 58–68.

Enrique's parents in *La sangre y la esperanza* was a reflection of the integrity of his own good mother and father. José Promis Ojeda ascribes Enrique's character development to his ability to make the proper moral choice at the end of the work. He is able to struggle and win because he chooses to accept the good example of his family. Guiding parental inspiration is the best possible route to salvation. Enrique chooses the upward path rather than falling victim to the temptations and negative attractions produced by the destructive environment that almost overwhelms him in the conventillo. In Chapter 1 of the novel a malicious youngster hands Enrique a knife during a fight, but Enrique cannot bring himself to stab his opponent. This is one of his first personal conflicts. Enrique could have become a criminal because of the influence of his school companions, but had he done so, he would have destroyed the author's Marxist purpose. Enrique is the opposite of Studs, James T. Farrell's protagonist in *Studs Lonigan*.

In Guzmán's attempt at a sequel to *La sangre y la esperanza*, the first chapter—though incomplete at the time of his death—shows the father, who has just recovered from his illness of "luengos meses," in a Christ-like image, shining the shoes of his son who stands before him, crying. Enrique's habitual crying is probably more symbolic than real, for he breaks into tears at the slightest provocation or even in the mere anticipation of problems. This weeping comes near to irritating the reader, but it confirms the emphasis that Guzmán places on Enrique as an innocent child. In *La luz viene del mar*, several of the adults weep, often to intensify irony, but usually to symbolize proletarian integrity.

The novelist had the ironic intention of ultimately destroying the godlike image of the father-hero at a later point in his unfinished novel. This handsome but humble, poor but prim proletarian would tarnish his reputation by having a love affair with Graciela Tagle, a wealthy woman who lives in one of the elegant residences on his trolley route. She is beautiful and would attract any normal man; he is bewildered, perhaps blinded, and caught in an ever-tightening net that will allow the novelist to introduce a new theme, a social phenomenon latent in Chilean social life: "el acercamiento o la nivelación de las clases sociales, si no en el orden económico, en el afectivo o pasional."[3] It appears that Guzmán is intent on negating

3. Nicomedes Guzmán, "Plan de una novela: 'Los trece meses del año,'" *Cultura*, 96 (1964), 46–47.

two of his most important themes: proletarian integrity and class struggle.

A basic element in the proletarian novels of the 1930s is the theme of hope, an element similar to Christian faith. The worker who embraces proletarian hope will not lose sight of his ultimate goal and will finally be able to redeem himself through revolution.

> The marrow of Guzmán's thought, that which distinguishes him from all his literary predecessors, is his philosophy of hope. . . . Guzmán is convinced that the Chilean city masses can triumph over their misery; that there are spirit, free agency, and possibilities for regeneration from within; but not with the precarious help of politicians or journalists. It is precisely that which gives Guzmán's novels their beauty.[4]

Hope takes many forms in Guzmán's works. It appears as a motif in every novel and several short stories, especially at the conclusion of the story; however, it is often disguised so that it is not always discernible in the traditional definition of the term.

André Malraux, the noted French leftist, used the word *hope* as a title of his novel *L'espoir*, a story about the Spanish Civil War, but Guzmán structured his novel around *esperanza* as only one part of the antithesis between hope and defeat. In the end, hope wins out and becomes a metaphor for victory:

> Y, en el aire, parece que existieran campanas, claras *campanas de esperanza* que repiten nuestras voces:
> —¡El triunfo! . . . ¡El triunfo! . . . (*Hombres*, 209; my italics)

Hope, then, is a unifying element that permeates Guzmán's novels. It could soon tire the credulity of the reader, but it appears in constant interplay or contrast with violence and sex. This antithesis between blood and hope, a sort of dialectic struggle, makes each match and rematch of *sangre* against *esperanza* in the book bring the poor proletarian one step lower toward animalism, thus one step nearer unavoidable revolt and class war. The contrast is thus a new look at the thesis-antithesis of dialectic materialism. The ultimate decision of characters like Pablo to overcome forcefully those deterministic and depressing forces is a fitting Marxist victory with which to end the novel.

The element of blood, which is contrasted so often to hope in the

---

4. Arnold Chapman, "Perspectiva de la novela de la ciudad en Chile," Arturo Torres-Ríoseco, ed., *La novela iberoamericana* (Albuquerque: University of New Mexico Press, 1952), p. 203.

book, produces several problems of ethics in literature. Does Guzmán use the shock element of his bloody scenes as a way to popularity? Or is gore a vehicle for expressing true-to-life tragedy which will ultimately lead the proletarian to revolution?

As to the first question, the important thing to remember is that Guzmán is writing socialist realism. The entire first chapter of *La sangre y la esperanza* is intended to shock the reader into following the narration in order to discover what other atrocities could possibly happen in the neighborhood of Enrique Quilodrán.

As to the second question, it appears that if hope is Guzmán's thesis, blood is its antithesis; it is the only means of eventually arriving at the thesis of hope, or revolution. The masses will react only when they have no other recourse. Thus when blood is cause, hope is effect, for bloody acts by the government can cause a revolutionary response from the proletarians. Hope is an abstract spiritual element that the proletarian must retain in order to survive and defeat the attacks of tyranny.

Other answers become evident after a further examination of theme. Since this problem is important in interpreting Guzmán's novels, it may be apropos to compare the hypothesis advanced in the previous paragraph to Northrop Frye's distinction between the thematic and the fictional.[5] In this light, one element, hope, is *thematic* (abstract, propagandist); here Guzmán, the poet of social compromise, the prophet of the revolution, adjusts his narrative materials to the propaganda of his Marxist ideology. The other element, blood, is fictional (involving plot and action); here Guzmán the storyteller records the many atrocities leading toward class war. Somewhere in the middle is Guzmán the poet, who narrates the estampas, transposing his slums or the northern desert to a poetic image through the use of metaphors and flowery prose.

Though it is obvious that the element of blood becomes a motivational tool, an attention getter, "hope" also offers motivation to the characters and to the reader. The bloody episodes hold the attention of the reader who virtually wades through a swamp of blood to receive a celestial shower of Marxist hope at the conclusion of the novel.

The thought that Guzmán might have prostituted his art for popularity is untenable. He was, however, attempting to reach as

5. Frye, *Anatomy of Criticism*, pp. 52–53.

many readers as possible by writing of subjects with which they could identify. He was not always successful in this goal, however, for the inclusion of pessimistic elements often brought down the wrath of the reactionary public and the critics. Had Chile been more inclined to accept surrealism (which used similar shock elements), the works of Guzmán and his generation might have been rejected because of the propaganda implicit in them. However, the time was ripe for socrealism, and a sizable number of Chileans embraced it as an art form for nearly a decade.

Guzmán's only goal was the creation of socialist art. He hoped to help create a new proletarian culture in Chile. He might easily have exploited the element of gore more than he did, but his works would then have appealed to the reader only through sensationalism, and this was never the case. Guzmán's use of violence was limited by his great sensitivity. In *La luz viene del mar* Guzmán causes the reader to anticipate the horrible slaughter of a mother and toddler by their beloved yet insane father-in-law and grandfather, Huacho Fieroga. However, Guzmán wisely saves them from an inopportune death; in a moment of love and tenderness, the old man's reason returns. A lesser artist might have erred by allowing the tragedy to occur.

As Guzmán matured, his fiction contained fewer shocking elements. His later short stories are still classifiable as socialist realism, yet they contain fewer jolting passages than the novels. About half of Guzmán's short stories might be considered bloody; the most violent are "Extramuros," "Perro ciego," "La jauría," and "Animita." Many others have no violence, including "La hora de la vida," "Una moneda al río," "Sólo unas cuántas lágrimas," "Dónde nace el alba," and "La ternura."

Barrow and Olstad list four principal groups of themes in Spanish literature: "universales, nacionales, epocales y particulares."[6] Guzmán's themes of love, hope, and the family are universal themes, like those found in the Bible. The predominant national theme in Chile is criollismo, and Guzmán goes often to that well for some water of inspiration; but more commonly he gathers ideas from novels like the naturalist-inspired *El roto*, by Edwards Bello, as well as from several other Chilean works that deal only coincidently with criollista ideas and situations.

While many Chilean critics have considered Guzmán's first works

6. Leo Barrow and Charles Olstad, *Aspectos de la literatura española* (Lexington, Mass.: Xerox Corp., 1972), p. 11.

to be criollista because they depict the conventillo of Santiago, it is not until *La luz viene del mar* that Guzmán actually relies on criollismo as a theme. The northern region of Chile with its symbolic overtones unifies the whole work.

The Marxist themes examined in this chapter belong in Barrow and Olstad's "epoch" or "period" group. Similar themes were common to all the proletarian writers of the 1930s, the decade of class struggle. The principal theme of Juan Godoy foreshadows the central concept of Guzmán and the entire Generation of 1938: "Man is a struggling, agonized being, striving to raise himself from misery to decency and nobility."[7]

Besides these generational and social-realist themes, Guzmán developed his own personal statement of the human condition. One of his favorite themes, repeated and abstracted until it became a symbol, is *ternura*, an innate loftiness discovered in old people, children, animals, pregnancy, love, and kind acts. Such "tenderness" is, perhaps, an extension of proletarian integrity, but Guzmán's approach to *ternura* is uniquely his own and exhibits his artistic sensitivity:

> Creo que la literatura tiene una responsabilidad vital: crear el clima propicio a la paz, al mejor entendimiento entre los hombres, esto a trueque de describir sus luchas, decir sus verdades, *incidiendo, incluso en lo que hay en los seres de corrosivo, enfrentando los aspectos de negación humana, con las virtudes, particularmente la ternura* que, a mi entender, es el don más varonil del hombre, el basamento de todos los actos de la existencia. (*Una moneda al río*, 9–10; my italics)

In other words, literature should be humanistic and realistic; it should describe man's conflicts and portray even the evil and negative side of his personality in contrast to his virtues, the greatest of which is *ternura*:

> La ternura es el origen de los mejores méritos humanos. El trabajo mismo, sin ternura que derive hacia la pasión, no tendría razón de ser, como el amor, como el ansia de superación. (*Una moneda al río*, 10)

John P. Dyson points out that *ternura* can be found in all of Guzmán's stories:

> Aunque hay gran variedad de temas y maneras de abordarlos, todos los cuentos se caracterizan por la ternura y el contacto humano. En

---

7. Thomas Edgar Lyon, Jr., *Juan Godoy* (New York: Twayne Publishers, 1972), p. 121.

algunos casos estas cualidades se hacen presentes por medio de algún sacrificio de parte de un individuo. A menudo hay un beneficio común, no por medio de un sacrificio particular, sino sencillamente, por el contacto entre dos seres solitarios.[8]

Dyson also elaborates upon several themes similar to *ternura*: human contact, kindness, and the kind almost human animal. Other major Guzmán themes are the prostitute and the conventillo.

Two of the stories from *Donde nace el alba* (1944) are excellent examples of the theme of tenderness; each story develops the feeling in a different way, yet both portray it as emanating from children. In the first story, "La ternura," disillusion because of adultery is destroying a home; then a child appears on the scene and reunites the couple. The solution of the story is similar to that of *La sangre y la esperanza*, for in both a child brings about a sort of temporal salvation. In the second story, "La angustia," the unfortunate death of a child brings the hero to the sudden realization that his own intended suicide will not be the answer to his marital and economic problems. Children in these stories represent the element of tenderness that is missing in many adult relationships. When children are involved in Guzmán's plots, they become the true proletarian essence of life. Existence is meaningless without them, for man has no future without children.

Ternura is often stylized verbally into a symbol, and the author also employs it metaphorically to represent the life principle in the following example of an abandoned pregnant dog:

> Pero, sin embargo, se presentía una especie de espesa y destellosa luz en su vientre inflado, una especie de *luz de ternura ampulosa* que abarcara su cuerpo desde la última de sus costillas . . . .
> . . . Era así, flaca, redonda de vientre y llena aquí, en éste, como de una espesa y tremolante *luz de ternura*, la misma luz que se advertía en sus ojos verdosos. . . .
> . . . La bestialidad y lo absolutamente humano se identifican las más de las ocasiones, cuando *la ternura* rompe ciertas barreras de la vida.[9]

Folklore and folk motifs also become themes in Guzmán's works. A hopelessly poor proletarian man in "Una moneda al río" feels

---

8. John P. Dyson, "Los cuentos de Nicomedes Guzmán," *Atenea*, 404 (1964), 229.

9. Nicomedes Guzmán, "Una perra y algunos vagabundos." Cited version is from *El pan bajo la bota* (Santiago: Empresa Editora Zig-Zag, 1960), pp. 137–38, my italics; also in *La carne iluminada* (Santiago: Ediciones Amura, 1945), pp. 66–67.

there is little purpose in life until he meets an equally indigent woman who has recently lost her husband. Their attitudes and fortunes seem to change, as does the tone of the story, when the protagonist follows an old folk custom and throws a coin in the Mapocho River as he crosses the Pío Nono Bridge.

Though folklore and songs are more often motifs than themes, one of Guzmán's stories, "Animita," from *Pan bajo la bota* (1960), involves a folk theme. In this story, an old bootblack, Pantaleón Quintanilla, is hit by a train one foggy night as he returns home drunk. The accident severs his legs, and witnesses, assuming that he is dead, take him to a morgue. But he miraculously survives because his wife has prayed intensely for several days at "his" *animita* (a rustic shrine placed where a violent death has occurred).[10] For the old man, the *animita* symbolizes a true miracle.

In summary, most of Guzmán's themes serve a structural rather than a moral purpose. In a few of Guzmán's stories, such as "Animita," the title serves as a brief summary or abstract of the theme. Also it should be remembered that the epigraphs in Guzmán's short stories often introduce the theme, and that in certain chapter groups of *La luz viene del mar* the themes are specified in chapter headings.

Motif

A smaller structural element in Guzmán's works is motif, a device that expands the narrative by using a situation or incident familiar to the reader either because he has seen it earlier in the work or because it plays on his emotions more generally, as sex does. *Motifs* are to Guzmán's structure what *types* are to characterization. The interpolated songs examined in the previous chapter are motifs; they allow the narrator to expand his story, both through his commentary and the familiarity that the song provides. In music and art, the term *motif* has other meanings, which are adaptable to literature: a repeated melodic phrase, a prevailing idea or design, or a subject for a detailed sculpture.[11]

One of the first motifs that Guzmán employs is the classic image of the moth and its shadow as it flies around a candle:

10. Guzmán devotes a whole page to the folklore element of the *animita* in his article "Encuentro emocional con Chile," *Atenea*, 380–81 (1958), 86.

11. William Flint Thrall and Addison Hibbard, *A Handbook to Literature* (New York: Odyssey Press, 1960), p. 294.

Me entretengo en observar los giros y revoluciones de la polilla y su sombra. De pronto se quema las alas y cae aleteando en la palmatoria chorreada de esperma. Este percance ocurrido a la polilla me sugiere pensamientos que merodean alrededor del hombre, la vida y la muerte. (*Hombres*, 16)

The author clarifies the symbolic implications that this image has for his protagonist: life contrasted to death; a lofty flight thwarted by a fall. But it has other implications as well; the moth's free flight is the ideal, while the burning destruction and fall is the opposite, the real. This antithesis of ideal and real is similar to the contrast found in *La ceniza y el sueño*, the author's youthful book of poetry. The candle also reflects the indigence of the conventillo; Guzmán uses candles and images seen by candlelight to recall to the reader the poverty of the Chilean proletariat and the dark and destitute nights of the slums.

Guzmán uses the candle-moth image more than once in this same novel (he also includes it at least twice in his short stories) converting it into a highly stylized and individualized motif:

Me recuesto. Una mariposa revolotea alrededor de la vela. De repente, cae aleteando. En la palmatoria se empeña, desesperada e inútilmente, por emprender de nuevo el vuelo. Luego, deja de aletear: ha muerto. ¡Inés no está bien! Hay mariposas que no se queman nunca las alas. Sí, claro. Me sorprendo diciendo:
—Sí, sí, sí . . . —en voz alta.[12]

Although Guzmán has changed *polilla* (moth) to the generic *mariposa* (butterfly or moth), the image remains the same, except that the narrator has added an explicit moral, which in the earlier version had only been suggested. The classical image of Psyche is also implicit in these images, for Pablo is tormented by sensual love, which leads him and Inés into a moral and psychological conflict.

Some motifs are employed mainly to show social injustice or to introduce odd proletarian characters. One such motif is the stealing of clothes from other poor souls, an element that Guzmán could have acquired from González Vera. In *Vidas mínimas* González Vera introduces one of the worst conventillo types: Adolfo, who steals the miserable rags of the poor and also cats—to eat them. The first such thief in Guzmán's fiction is La Gringa Pobre, an alcoholic tramp, who steals clothes to sell them (*Hombres*, 179–84). The robbery

---

12. *Hombres*, p. 130. Cf. Carlos Sepúlveda Leyton, *Hijuna. Novela* (Santiago: Austral, 1962), p. 140.

she commits costs the newly widowed Yolanda her only income, since she makes money by washing clothes, and it causes her to take her own life and the lives of her children.

In *La sangre y la esperanza* the clothing thief is Doña Eufemia, who suffers a sterile marriage like that of García Lorca's Yerma. The insane Eufemia steals the Quilodráns' clothing, not to sell it, but to revere it, because the Quilodráns have many children while she has none (*Sangre*, 165–68, 205–10). Another motif used by both Lorca and Guzmán (suggesting Lorca's influence on the Chilean) is the *lagarto*—the folkloric lizard superstition—which has a sexual connotation. When Andrea in *La luz viene del mar* sees the lizard, she is fearful for her virginity.

Guzmán's works often include such socrealist (the generally accepted adjective) motifs as strike scenes and the prophecies of the revolution. Such recurring elements become structural motifs. Moreover, several violent motifs are used purely for their shock value. In the preface to his first anthology, for example, the young Guzmán exclaims that in Tierra del Fuego the men castrate sheep using their teeth: "—¡Es una tierra tremenda! . . . ¡Allí vi yo castrar los corderos con los dientes! . . ." (17). Compare this to the metaphorical analogy that Pedro Andrade makes concerning his aching mutilated arm: ". . . Me duele, ¡cómo decirte! . . . , ¡cómo les dolerán a los corderos las verijas cuando los capan con los dientes! . . ." (*Luz*, 209).

Another shock motif is human mutilation. "Animita," "Extramuros," "Donde nace el alba," "La hora de la vida," *Los hombres obscuros*, and *La luz viene del mar* depict characters who lose or have lost one or both legs, often through a train or streetcar accident. Self-mutilation appears as well. In *La luz viene del mar* Cara de Pescado cuts out his eye for a girl (132); Pedro Andrade cuts off his hand to get money to marry Fresia and later bleeds to death, bringing about the climax of the novel (215, 256–60). Another shock element with social intent is the poor washerwoman who deforms her hand through constant scrubbing. Mutilation is usually the low point of the proletarian's development in Guzmán's stories. In another novel a *lavandera* is forced to wash fine monogrammed linen by candlelight; unfortunately, she also has to clean up the gruesome and soiled wastes of humanity:

> Una de las mujeres suspira, alisándose los pelos flojos. Coge un "paño higiénico" de un montón que tiene al borde de la artesa, y se pone a desangrarlo. (*Hombres*, 120)

The washerwoman motif, which originated with Zola's *L'Assommoir*, is a popular one in the proletarian novels of the thirties. The mothers in Gold's and Fink's novels have to turn to washing clothes to support their families, as do several women in Guzmán's narrations. Guzmán's mother did not take in washing in real life (she took care of vacant bourgeois houses) but in the novel, Enrique's mother has no other recourse than to wash clothes for an income. In *El roto* by Joaquín Edwards Bello, Esmeralda's mother must wash brothel bed linen by day and play the piano by night. Paula in *Vidas mínimas* by González Vera is also forced to become a *lavandera*, and, in general, the clothes-scrubbing scenes in the conventillo novels of Chile are plentiful. Many scenes like the above example appear in Guzmán's novels, described in the most frank language, for the writer shies away from nothing. Many themes and motifs —such as toilet scenes—avoided by other authors came into the open with Guzmán and socialist realism.

One motif employed twice for shock value and humor—since it is both comical and distressing when it happens in actual life—is the image of a dog urinating on a person:

> Los perros olisqueaban, orinándose en todas partes.
> —¡Guarde, señora, que la mea el perro!
> —¡Ja, ja, ja!
> Los chiquillos burlaban de una anciana a cuyos tobillos se apegaba, con la pata parada, un perrillo de pelaje comido por la tiña.
> —¡Ja, ja, ja!
> —¡Chiquillos condenados! ¡Zafe, perro, ah, ah! (*Sangre*, 31)

This dialogue dramatizes the vicious nature of the children present in the scene where Zorobabel is hurled against the buzz saw. It also is a light humorous contrast to the excessively bloody scene that follows. More important, however, is the implication that dogs and humans live at the same social level in the conventillo. "Pero tanta o más miseria que gente. Y perros también que olían todas las piernas y que paraban la pata donde mejor les placía" (*Sangre*, 196). The motif comes from a folk saying—"meado de perro"—a forecast of bad luck. In the first case, it foreshadows Zorobabel's death; in the second, it emphasizes the bad luck of the poor people in the neighborhood of pawnshops. A third use of this motif also draws on its implication of future misfortunes for the downtrodden: After one of the women in the conventillo loses a child, the neighborwomen say "—¡Está meada de perro! . . ." (*Hombres*, 176).

These examples will give the reader an idea of the extremely harsh socrealist motifs that pervade Guzmán's works. Motifs of adultery and insanity, illness and starvation oppose comforting family situations, joy, work, love, and folk elements. Humane acts are contrasted to inhuman deeds as exemplified in a scene from "El pan bajo la bota." In kindness Enrique hands his father a sandwich through the jail bars; the jailer knocks it to the floor and stomps on it. This scene can be compared to Edwards Bello's *El roto*. In both, boys see their fathers in prison, but for different reasons. In both works bread is thrown on the floor, but with different symbolism.

John Dyson examines motifs at some lentgh in his article on Guzmán's short stories. In every case, those that he mentions are also important in the novels. "Otoño," "Guzmán's favorite season of the year, is a prevailing motif in *Donde nace el alba* as well as in the novels *Los hombres obscuros* and *La sangre y la esperanza*. Guzmán especially singles out the characteristics of a rainy, foggy autumn day in his metaphorical estampas.

Sounds and odors are other motifs that Dyson studies. Sounds are interwoven with another motif—music—and music harmonizes with light in several of Guzmán's stories, for example, "Rapsodia en luz mayor." In *La luz viene del mar* light is the main motif; it is reflected, poeticized, and revered in the pages of the novel, and it is blended synesthetically with sound. Sounds and odors both take on social significance at times, as, for instance, when urine splatters like a tambourine, leaving a fetid smell. The sound of a tambourine (*pandereta*) is a poetic motif in almost all Guzmán's works. Most commonly, urine falling into a basin, toilet, or bucket, or even onto a wooden floor is compared in similes to the sound of tambourines.

One motif that appears in *Los hombres obscuros* and *La luz viene del mar* has romantic overtones of coincidence. Guzmán may personally have observed such an incident, but it resembles something Alberto Romero included less dramatically in *La viuda del conventillo*. In the first of the above novels, Pablo is made aware of a murder in his neighborhood. When the victim's elderly mother arrives at the scene of the crime, she suffers a heart attack (*Hombres*, 52–59). In the second, Virginia's father is killed by a nightwatchman when a group of workers attempt to begin a wildcat strike. When Virginia's mother, who is pregnant, discovers her husband's tragic death, she goes immediately into labor from the shock (*Luz*, 25–26). In both scenes, one tragic situation leads to another in a chain reaction. The author is able to vary this motif with a note of Marxist hope in "La jauría." The women of the neighborhood join the offended wife in beating and kicking the mistress of her husband. They stop short of killing her on discovering that she is going into labor as she lies on the ground. Suddenly demonstrating tenderness, the women come to their senses and help her.

The final motif to be examined here is sex. Sex is a mainstay of most contemporary literature, but socialist realism included many explicit love-making scenes of a kind that had only been implied in earlier literature. As a result, the public often considered socrealist works pornographic, and Guzmán especially suffered in Chile because of such attitudes.

The limitations of space allow only the main erotic motifs to be examined here. In *Los hombres obscuros* Pablo is continuously tormented by sensuous thoughts. He must look up at women's bare legs all day long as he shines their shoes. He even grazes their skin slightly as he works, and he examines women's legs as he seeks customers who need their shoes shined or repaired. At night he can hear sensual parties in the conventillo and listen to the sounds of his landlords making love. Freely associated sexual images flash through his mind. At such moments, tormented by his forced abstinence from kissing or even seeing Inés, he burns with a sensuous anguish that can only be soothed by visiting a prostitute. Perhaps even then he is not calmed but is actually further frustrated.

Pablo's blood often symbolizes his sexuality, but it is not always directly connected with sensuality:

> La sangre me corre a torrentes por las arterias. . . . Pienso que, en realidad, debería ingresar a alguna institución política obrera. Sobre todo ahora que la sangre me corre a torrentes por las arterias y los pulmones se me ensanchan. Pero no me decido: el recuerdo de Inés me llena la cabeza. (*Hombres*, 66)

Compare this psychological or physiological phenomenon in Pablo to Guzmán's image in his estampa of the slums: "Por las arterias del suburbio, la sangre corre a torrentes, depurando el ambiente" (64).

Blood is also an erotic symbol-motif. When Pablo and Inés meet they are mutually attracted by a psychological and physiological intensity that ultimately leads them to bed: Pablo's blood boils, it howls ("aúlla," p. 69). Pablo's world becomes so sensuous that he has not even the inner peace to be able to read. The ultimate intensity is evoked in a metaphor: "En mis venas, la vida pulsa sus más jocundas guitarras" (77). Later a more generic metaphor appears because of his jealousy: "Me siento un hombre diminuto. Pero al mismo tiempo, me sé una inmensa bestia movida por los resortes del instinto. El hombre de las cavernas me tranquea por la sangre" (102). This primitive desire for sexual gratification overcomes both Pablo and Inés, but when they go to a cheap hotel to make love, they are temporarily stopped by a surge of morality. Eventually, however, they give in to their desire, unable to resist the suggestions of the erotic pictures on the wall and the sound of another couple making love elsewhere in the hotel.

Enrique's development in *La sangre y la esperanza* is depicted largely through a series of sexual awakenings. Sex is meaningless to him at first; later he understands but cannot act. His anxieties lead to such complications as the dream in the chapter entitled "Fantasmas." These frames of the novel are intensely erotic, and they are especially intriguing to the young adolescent, who might be led to read the book because of the erotic passages and thus be swayed toward the author's socialist and humanistic ideals.

Enrique's sexual awareness is typical of that of slum children as depicted in proletarian novels. In *Mich Hungert*, for example, Teddy recalls sneaking into a dark room where his father is making love to a prostitute. The boy begins to cry as he visualizes his dishonored mother, and he is literally kicked out of the room by the couple. The narrator remarks: "We children of the proletariat are healthy-minded. Nothing we experience makes us physically sick. We grow up hardened. We laugh about things as being funny which children of the upper classes mull over tragically. . . ." Guzmán selected this passage from Georg Fink as an epigraph to head the chapter of *La sangre y la esperanza* that contains Turnio's murder-suicide and the implicit seduction of Elena.[13] In Chapter 1, when Enrique kisses Angélica, who is crying because of her father's death, the neighbors and the two mothers who come upon the scene interpret the situation erroneously. Enrique's mother suspiciously lifts Angélica's dress, a situation which causes Enrique to recall a time when he was with another little girl, Leontina, who had learned the value of sex

13. Georg Fink, *Thirty-One Families Under Heaven*, trans. of *Mich Hungert* by Lillie C. Hummel (New York: Liveright Publishing Corp., 1931), pp. 52–53, 62.

almost as an infant. In exchange for the bread he gave her, she had let Enrique feel her nakedness under her dress; she was too poor to have any underclothing.

Enrique witnesses and conveys to the narration many things that the narrator, as a child, would not normally have understood at such a young age. The reader may still not understand these elements completely, even after a second reading, for Enrique is an objective first-person narrator who comments much less on the situations than did the first-person narrators of Fink and Gold. The description of Elena's loss of virginity is a good example of innocent objective narrative. Enrique recalls the scene in a dialogue, and the reader must be alert to realize what the conversation implies:

> Tocaba todo su cuerpo por sobre las ropas, con pasión, casi desperado.
> —¡Elenita!
> —¡No, no, no me toques ahí, me duele todavía! (*Sangre*, 137)

Elena is hinting indirectly that she has lost her virtue to Abel. This could have happened previously—the night she was late coming home from work and her father accused her of "estar pololeando" (dating):

> Mi madre ya estaba sirviendo la comida cuando regresó Elena. No sé qué tenía de extraño mi hermana. Estaba como transfigurada. Sus grandes, exóticos y dulces ojos café, que en la noche parecían negros, dispensaban un trémulo resplandor de ternura. (*Sangre*, 100)

Enrique's intuition finds in a now-mature Elena the tenderness which, as has been shown, became a theme and a symbol of love, pregnancy, and children's personalities in later stories.

It is apropos to compare the similarities and differences between Guzmán's scenes of early sexual awareness and those in two socrealist works that influenced him. In *Jews Without Money* the first-person narrator, Mikey (Michael Gold), is initiated to a world of sex at the age of five by looking through a keyhole at a man with a prostitute:

> Nigger and I followed them. It was on the ground floor of my tenement. Stealthy as detectives, we stared through the keyhole. What I saw made my heart beat, my face redden with shock.
> Nigger snickered. He saw I was hurt and it amused him. The couple rose. We sneaked through the hall back to sunlight.
> "You got scared," said Nigger.
> "No," I said.

"Hell," said Nigger, "everyone does it. That's the way babies are made."

"No," I said with unaccountable bitterness. "That's not the way!"

"Yes," said Nigger, "what do you want to bet?"

"But that's like saying my mother is like that! You're a liar, Nigger."[14]

This quarrel develops into a fight. When Mickey returns home, he cannot bear to look at his mother, partly because of his fresh black eye, but also because he feels that she has betrayed him—she is like the prostitute, because she is a woman.

Although Enrique, in *La sangre y la esperanza*, does not become fully aware of sexual intercourse until he is eight, it should be remembered that at an earlier age he had experienced intimacies with Leontina, described in the inverted second part of the novel. Nevertheless, Enrique is still a very naïve eight-year-old when he first becomes fully aware of the sex act. It is on an occasion when Antonieta bribes him to play hooky with her. After they have gone to her boyfriend's house, Enrique innocently walks into the house from the patio, where he was told to play, while Antonieta and the boy are having intercourse. Though he surprises them in the act, he is still unaware of what has been going on, and they send him outside again. Though he feels something is wrong, he does not realize the more violent implications of sex until a few moments later when the boyfriend's drunken father comes home, curses everyone, and rapes Antonieta.

As they return home from this frightening experience, Antonieta has to do some fast talking and bribing to keep Enrique from informing on her:

> —Mira, Enriquito, lo que hacíamos—seguía explicando ella—no era nada malo. No era nada malo. ¡Lo hacen todas las mujeres con los hombres!
> Qué me importaba a mí aquello. Lo cierto era que había faltado a la escuela y el miedo me devoraba las vísceras. Tenía ganas de orinar.
> —¡Suéltame! —¡grité a la chiquilla—¡Suéltame!
> Cuando me sentí libre de su mano, me allegué a una tapia derruida. Humearon contra los adobes los orines calientes.
> —¡Eso no es nada de raro, mira Enriquito! Tú también lo harás cuando seas grande! . . . (*Sangre*, 58)

14. Michael Gold, *Jews Without Money* (New York: Avon Books, 1968), p. 14.

When Enrique returns home he is fearful of his mother, as Mikey was in Gold's novel, and, like his model, Enrique cannot look his mother in the face. Aware that he has missed classes, she beats him with a belt. The next day he has a fight, as did Mikey, but not because of sex; he is harassed by his classmates because he has played hooky. To divert his friends' hostilities he picks on Turnio Llanos, whose mother runs a brothel. Like Fink, both Gold and Guzmán emphasize the awakening of their child protagonists at a tender age through an awareness of sex and violence. Implicit in both stories is the shattering of the child's pure-mother image, the harsh realization that his mother belongs to the opposite sex. Gold, however, like Fink implies that, since the proletarian learns early about sex, he becomes cold to it. Guzmán, as a Latin American, reflects another attitude: sex is always exciting, enticing. As Godoy theorized in angurrientismo, the Chilean hungers endlessly for sex.

The proletarian novelists of the thirties sought other sexual motifs of socrealist value. James T. Farrell includes a masturbating scene in *Young Lonigan* of the *Studs Lonigan* trilogy. He never mentions the word *masturbate*, because the dialogue presents the situation indirectly:

> "Well, Hennessey was under the Fifty-eighth Street elevated station. . . . lookin' up through the cracks to see if he could get an eyeful when the women walked up and down the stairs . . ."
> "Yeh, and we know what he was doing. That's nothing new," said Johnny.
> "He once had a race with Paulie, and they both claimed the other had fouled," said Studs, and they laughed.
> "But this time it's funny . . . You see, a dick caught him and shagged him down the alley. Three-Star got away because nobody could catch him anyway, but the guys told me it was funny, him legging it, with his stockings hanging . . . and he didn't even have time to button up," said Danny.[15]

Guzmán's narration, much more direct, is one of the most shocking for its time in Latin American literature. It appears in the third part of *La sangre y la esperanza*. During the summer in Santiago, while Enrique's gang is swimming in the nude in the Mapocho River, one

---

15. James T. Farrell, *Studs Lonigan* (New York: Signet Books, 1965), p. 76. The Chilean edition that Guzmán read is *El Chico Lonigan: Una niñez en las calles de Chicago*, trans by Inés Cane Fontecilla (Santiago: Editorial Ercilla, 1940), p. 140.

of the boys spots two girls above them on the bridge, who are enjoying the nudity. The daring boy invites the girls to come down:

> —¡Bajen, no más! ¡Hay donde escoger! ¡Aquí tienen!
> Carcajeaba el chiquillo, agarrándose y batiendo el pequeño miembro.
> Ellas reían. Risas frescas. Anchas. Campesinas. La baranda del puente
> era rala de tabla. Y desde abajo podía apreciarse la potencia de los
> apretados muslos jóvenes y tostados.
> —¡Aquí también hay! —gritó una, tapándose la boca fresca para
> acallar las carcajadas—. ¡Aquí también, y bueno! . . .
> Y se golpeaba las nalgas duras.
> Sus pasos fugitivos sonaron en el entablado del puente con ecos de
> pandereta. . . . (*Sangre*, 240)

As in *Studs Lonigan*, looking up at the girls' legs through the boards excites the young boys, who keep yelling at them until they are in the far distance. Then Enrique's friends begin to tell or invent their own stories of conquest and seduction:

> La fiebre de las sabrosas historias no tardó en sazonar sus frutos:
> los mayores de los muchachos convinieron en realizar una competencia
> y ante la expectación de los más pequeños, dieron suelta a la mastur-
> bación, haciendo apuestas inverosímiles. Rolando venció, rechinando
> los dientes. Apenas pudo ponerse los harapos. Yo lo veía tambalear.
> —¡Puchas —reía—, me siento jodido! . . .
> Se sentó en una piedra y se agarró la cabeza a dos manos.
> —¡Puchas, pa qué lo haría! —se dolió, pelando los dientes, riendo
> nerviosamente—. ¡Me da vueltas la cabeza!
> Estaba muy pálido. El otro experimentaba lo mismo. Pero se aguan-
> taba. Se animó a decir, sin embargo:
> —¡Chitas, que jode esto! ¡Es rico, pero lo emborracha a uno! . . .
> (*Sangre*, 240–41)

Although the two stories are dissimilar—undoubtedly because of situations the authors had witnessed or envisioned—each writer expressed himself as fully as the publisher and the printing industry would allow. Today neither story would be considered shockingly audacious. Both authors, however, for purposes of socialist realism, were using a sexual motif that had rarely been employed before in legitimate literature. Socrealist authors had various reasons for using the motif of sex in their literature: it is shocking; it has some prurient appeal to readers, especially to juveniles; and it can convey to the reader an idea of the bad environment which social evils produce. In summary, it is part of the attempt of the socrealist author to portray life faithfully, no matter how shocking the situation may be. Enrique's objective attitude is also important. He passively observes both evil and good situations; his objectivity causes him to delay his choice between good and evil until the end of the novel.

To show Guzmán's evolution as a writer, we may examine his use of a linguistic motif, the repeated word or phrase. For example, Don Juan's "¿Tan largo me lo fiais?" is a motto-motif in the *Burlador de Sevilla*. In Guzmán's first two novels, epithets are seldom used, because the narrators are objective. His short stories and *La luz viene del mar* use omniscient third-person narrators, and both narrators and motifs help define certain characters. The narrator repeats "el buen viejo" five or six times at the beginning of "La ternura" in anticipation of the sacrifice that the old man makes for his crippled grandson.[16] In *La luz viene del mar* the narrator refers repeatedly to Lorenzo Carmona as "La Reliquia de la Huella," and the two brief chapters that tell his story both carry the title-motif "Un corazón soñador detenido en el tiempo."

The evolution of Guzmán's use of motifs demonstrates that he has somewhat more freedom structurally in his later works where the omniscient narrator appears. He can elaborate and expand the narrative, and he is not limited in either time or space.

Generally Guzmán's motif is a phrase or concept, a circumstance or situation, rather than an image in the poetic sense. It can be the repetition of a ballad line, a leitmotif, or psychological or vocal repetition of an idea ("Acaso ella amara a Eudocio"). On the other hand, it can be a structural item, a sort of minor theme, an element the poet chooses to elaborate, strengthen, color, or contrast to the main theme. This does not mean that it cannot be an image (like Guzmán's moth and candle); however, many structural motifs, like "boy meets girl"—or love—are abstract or situational until their repetition breeds familiarity.

By combining all the motifs, Guzmán has been able to weave the total story. The motifs are not extraneous material; rather they are a basic part of the structure and as such can help the reader understand both the characters and the author.

It is essential to reiterate that Guzmán's motifs are drawn from Marxist literature, including both Chilean socialist literature and international proletarian literature. It would be naïve to say that

16. Dyson, "Los cuentos de Nicomedes Guzmán," p. 236.

Guzmán plagiarized from Gold or any other writer. He narrated situations from his own life, and he was inspired by themes, motifs, structure, characters, and countless other elements from works by Carlos Sepúlveda Leyton, Alberto Romero, and González Vera, as well as by other Chileans and the various foreign Marxist writers who have been mentioned. He combines national themes with Marxist themes and the period themes of his generation, which were very much in vogue. These predominant themes show the unique proletarian-Chilean synthesis that makes Guzmán an important figure who should be studied through new approaches. He did not emerge spontaneously from the Santiago slums, as most Chileans have been led to think. He consciously and artistically employed universal themes and created his own unique theme of *ternura*.

We can conclude that in Guzmán's literary production, theme and motif serve principally to increase the "illusion of reality," which Guzmán felt was the aesthetic function of a work of fiction. They unify his composition and make it appear realistically motivated. Sex especially adds needed motivation to his pages and allows him to work with innovative psychological and social situations. Unlike the average propagandist, Guzmán has been able to weave together his minor elements into a unified, tight structure. A few of his short stories may be episodic and weak, and occasionally some of his themes and motifs seem unconvincing and banal, but generally he is successful because he puts the artist ahead of the propagandist: "In art, seeming is even more important than being."[17]

17. René Wellek and Austin Warren, *Theory of Literature* (New York: Harcourt, Brace and World, 1956), p. 218.

10

Narrative Evolution in Nicomedes Guzmán
A Change in Point of View

The evolution of Nicomedes Guzmán as a writer is most notice-able in his selection of narrators. He begins with a very complicated first-person, present-tense narrator; then for diversification he chooses a different kind of first-person narrator, a child; he then uses a third-person omniscient narrator. This evolution parallels that of several modern authors.

First-Person Narrative

The characterization of Guzmán's two first-person narrator-pro-tagonists will be discussed in Chapter 12. Here we will examine only aspects of narrative point of view: the presentation of the story or myth, the sketching of the milieu, and the narrator's delineation of the other characters.

A first-person narrator always participates or has participated in the action. Although first-person narration is extremely variable, the narrator-protagonist always imposes his subjective view of the world upon the reader.

This technique is especially apparent in *Los hombres obscuros*, where the protagonist, Pablo, shares the spotlight with the environ-ment and its collectively characterized inhabitants, the proletarians or *hombres obscuros*. If Pablo did not stand out so forcefully as the main character, it would be possible to say that he is in competition with milieu and collectivity as the central focus of the novel. Espe-cially is the collective protagonist a strong feature of the novel in light of the unanimist trend of the work. Guzmán and all the an-gurrientista group were inspired by Jules Romains's philosophy of united group effort in his novel *La Vie Unanime* (1908) which gave unanimism its name. Collective and telluric protagonists were also created in the Spanish American regionalistic novels of the 1920s which inspired Guzmán and his colleagues.[1] In the outlines of his

1. Paul J. Carter, *Waldo Frank* (New York: Twayne Publishers, 1967), p. 180, n.16.

novels as he began writing, Guzmán would list as protagonists "the conventillo" or "the North."

Guzmán's choice of a first-person, present-tense narration for *Los hombres obscuros* is the most objective method of presentation he could possibly make. He chooses Pablo, an adolescent, as the limited narrator of the novel,[2] and restricts him even further in his narrative ability by having him describe almost all the action in the present tense, to convey immediacy. The use of the present tense places the reader close to the action; also, the combination of present tense and first person obliterates entirely the temporal and physical distance between Pablo, the participant, and Guzmán, the story-teller. There is an indefinable, infinitesimal distance and time between Pablo as a lens and Guzmán as film, a separation in space and time between Pablo as a notebook and Guzmán the editor—except that an editor *never* appears in the narration. Nor is it accurate to say that *Los hombres obscuros* is not fiction because it lacks such a time lapse and narrative distance, often assumed necessary for a traditional first-person point of view.[3] Guzmán was innovative and capable in handling this unusual viewpoint, but he was following a tradition, one found only in Chile's conventillo fiction. No critic, to my knowledge, has ever realized that González Vera's *Vidas mínimas*, Manuel Rojas's "El delincuente," Sepúlveda Leyton's *Hijuna*, and Nicomedes Guzmán's *Los hombres obscuros* all record a substantial portion of a first-person narrator's voice in the present tense (Sepúlveda Leyton's *Camarada* is written in the present tense but from a third-person point of view). Moreover, three of these novels open with similar statements: "I live in the conventillo." Past-tense narration often gives a definite impression of present action; furthermore, few hints even appear in most stories to make the reader aware of the grammatical tense of the narrative. Thus the majority of readers and critics fail to notice that *Los hombres obscuros* is entirely in the present tense while *La sangre y la esperanza* is in the past, except for dialogues and the estampas, which are in the present.

2. "Limited" is used here in every sense. The narrator is restricted in his power of comprehension—he has neither omniscience nor foresight. He is limited in both time and space, and in his intellectual equipment as a narrator.

3. Bertil Romberg, *Studies in the Narrative Technique of the First-Person Novel* (Stockholm: Almqvist and Wiksell, 1962), p. 100.

Guzmán also places additional limitations on his narrator. Pablo is to be politically unbiased at the beginning of the novel. Guzmán's insistence on Pablo's objectivity is most obvious in his deletion (after the fourth edition) of the closing paragraph of Chapter 2 of *Los hombres obscuros*:

> ¡Oh, arrabal, pueblo mío, de tu entraña sórdida, del fondo gris de tu aparente impasibilidad, yo sé que un mundo de luz viene naciendo!

This exclamation was not in keeping with Pablo's observant and stoic character in the beginning of the novel, so it was removed (perhaps at the suggestion of Latcham, who noted similar passages in his review of the third edition in 1943). Guzmán's attempt at objectivity has been successful, because Pablo usually seems apathetic. Toward the end of the novel, however, Pablo is allowed to remark:

> ¡Inés no se libró!
> ¡Canallas!
> Me muerdo y lloro hacia dentro un feroz llanto de impotencia.
> (*Hombres*, 191)

Though this is partly a candid dialogue of the narrator with himself, it is one of the few times that Pablo is allowed to make personal comments concerning social injustice. Also when he talks about strikes, Pablo becomes more emotional; at least a change is noticeable in the narrative.[4] Pablo does not become a laborer until the end of the novel, so he is not a participant in the strikes. However, the few pages that depict strikes and social scenes include less dialogue than the other narrative sections. As the narrative shifts (perhaps unconsciously) to propaganda, the narrator tells instead of showing, and the narrative tempo is increased (see *Hombres* 140–44).

Aside from the series of conventillo novels in the first-person present, few Chilean novels have ever been written in the first-person present. As to world literature, the only novel Romberg mentions in his study of the first-person novel is Schnitzler's *Leutnant*

---

4. This point, which I noted independently while preparing this study, is substantiated by the Chilean critic "Alone" [Hernán Díaz Arrieta] in one of the first reviews of *Los hombres obscuros* (*El Mercurio*, August 27, 1939): "La claridad de la prosa se mantiene. No así la sencillez: cuando llega el momento de discutir ideas sociales, el estilo se infla y toma las entonaciones declamatorias, adopta el énfasis pedantesco, ingenuamente confuso, propio de los discursos en las asambleas demagógicas."

Gustl (1900).[5] However, one Chilean novel should be pointed out because of its lyric quality and because of the importance of its author, who was a close friend of Guzmán's. The work is *El habitante y su esperanza* (Santiago: Editorial Nascimento, 1926) by Pablo Neruda. Not only is *esperanza* in the title of Guzmán's second novel, but Neruda's surrealistic novella features a poetic first-person narrator using the present tense; it also includes letters. The similarity ends there, for Neruda's work is a poem in prose, with no firm plot and no social intent. However, only Neruda and Guzmán are consistent in maintaining the present tense. Rojas's short story "El delincuente" establishes through the preterit what Wayne C. Booth calls "narrative distance" and what Bertil Romberg refers to as "epic distance": the distance between the roles of the first-person narrator as narrator and as character.[6] Traditionally this is a present to preterit distance, established at the moment the narrator leaves off his introduction to assume his historical role in the action. González Vera and Sepúlveda Leyton twist and invert this epic distance in *Vidas mínimas* and *Hijuna*, but readers have failed to catch an error that has become a tradition in the novel of the conventillo. Following these models, *Los hombres obscuros* consists of a sequence of events as if from a diary, all on one narrative level, but without actual diary references, such as dates or entries. As there is never mention of an author behind the narrator, Pablo stands alone, even more obscure to the reader than the title of the novel suggests. While first-person narratives traditionally begin with some sort of introduction (even if it is purposefully vague, as in *Lazarillo de Tormes*), most of Pablo's personal history comes out only at the very end of the novel, in the exchange of letters with his father. His presentation of himself is brief. In fact, Pablo introduces himself almost entirely through others, and he even allows himself to be a product of the environment, which he stylizes as if he were a being spontaneously produced by the slums (which he is not):

> Ciertamente que hay seres insignificantes que tienden a elevarse. El conventillo extático en su actitud de viejo en cuclillas y de cara acongojada, en la imposibilidad de elevarse, se entretiene. . . . (*Hombres*, 18)

5. Arthur Schnitzler, *Leutnant Gustl: Novelle* (Berlin: S. Fischer, 1926). Trans. as *None But The Brave* by Richard L. Simon in Arthur Schnitzler, *Viennese Novelettes* (New York: Simon and Schuster, 1931), pp. 393–433.

6. Romberg, *Studies*, p. 33; Wayne C. Booth, *The Rhetoric of Fiction* (Chicago: University of Chicago Press, 1961), p. 156.

The conventillo is a collective entity comprising all of its inhabitants, who are trying to rise from a position of "nonexistence." Pablo is merely an individual arbitrarily selected to represent the slums and narrate the situations and events that he observes there.

Rotating points of view, like those in Juan Rulfo's "El hombre" and Gabriel García Márquez's *La hojarasca* have appeared, but as far as I have been able to ascertain, no work with as complex a first-person point of view as *Los hombres obscuros* emerged in Spanish American fiction until Carlos Fuentes published *La muerte de Artemio Cruz* in 1962. In both novels the protagonist is fragmented into multiple voices. In *Los hombres obscuros* Guzmán creates a complex of four narrators present in the personage of Pablo. The four sections that follow will examine these points of view: the poet-narrator of the estampas; the "I-protagonist," who functions here as a camera; Pablo's ego; and Pablo's conscience, or the narrator's superego.

The Narrator of the Estampa

No Chilean critic has yet dealt seriously with the estampa, which is a short poetic-metaphoric description of the conventillo in a present-tense lyric voice. In an interview (Viña del Mar, July 21, 1971), Claudio Solar theorized that the estampa originated with Maupassant, who was read widely by the Generation of '38; however, such a genre does not seem to be present in Maupassant's fiction. Even Guzmán and Godoy failed to indicate origins in their praise of the form, and Guzmán only wrote about the estampa once, in his "Plan de una novela" for his "Trece meses del año." There are indications that the estampa is typical of proletarian literature and that it was completely developed for the first time in the proletarian novels of the *conventillo santiaguino*.

Michael Gold attempts to fix the image of his New York slum tenement through metaphors in the opening pages of *Jews Without Money*:

> . . . A tenement canyon hung with fire-escapes, bed-clothing, and faces. . . . It roared like a sea. It exploded like fireworks. . . . Earth's trees, grass, flowers could not grow on my street; but the rose of syphilis bloomed by night and by day.[7]

7. Michael Gold, *Jews Without Money* (New York: Avon Books, 1968), pp. 5, 7.

Waldo Frank opens and closes many passages of *Holiday* with lyric descriptions: "The waters of the bay go red to the blue gulf where swims the bloody sun . . . sunset on Nazareth."[8] By 1941, Waldo Frank was the most translated living North American writer in Latin America,[9] but the Generation of 1938 never acknowledged a debt to him.

Carlos Sepúlveda Leyton appears to be the first writer to have developed the estampa, which takes form for the first time in his novels nearly halfway through *Hijuna*:

> Al lado de mi casa, de cuadra a cuadra, se estira un conventillo como un reptil escamado de piedras, sucio y frío.
>
> * * *
>
> El viento guapea ronco y desafía al viento. . . .

This metaphoric comparison of the conventillo to an animal seems to create beauty in spite of filth, an elaboration which Guzmán will continue. Its title, meaning *stamp*, *print*, *or engraving*, seems to come from a paragraph appearing at the end of a chapter which later inspired Guzmán to use the estampa to open and close chapters:

> Una mujer se aparta de la carretela y atraviesa hacia el conventillo, hecha una flor en su percal: la calle y la niebla y la cordillera *sinfonizan en gris* y la mujer, afirmando un repollo en la cadera redonda, y llevando una mano en alto, y en la mano una media luna de zapallo barnizado en ocre, hace estallar la *tarjeta postal* de una *oleografía barata*.[10]

The synesthesia of the sound and color of the Andes, the plastic beauty of the slum and its surroundings, and the final statement comparing the entire scene a picture postcard all foreshadow Guzmán's interpretation of the conventillo through the estampa.

Among the different voices of the narrator of *Los hombres obscuros* there is, first of all, that of the stylist or poetic narrator. This impressionistic metaphorist of the slums appears to originate from somewhere between the narrator and the fictional author. Although Guzmán intends these metaphors and poetic images to be part of Pablo's observation of the slums, the tone changes ever so slightly,

8. Waldo Frank, *Holiday* (New York: Boni and Liveright, 1923), p. 9.

9. Carter, *Waldo Frank*, p. 178, n.1.

10. Carlos Sepúlveda Leyton, *Hijuna: Novela* (Santiago: Austral, 1962), pp. 72, 79, 123. My italics. See also the first paragraphs of Chapters 4, 6, and 13 of Alberto Romero's *La vinda del conventillo*.

and the flowery style of the poetic passages resulting from Pablo's ecstatic contemplation actually exaggerates the difference between the poetic interpreter of the conventillo and the uneducated, youthful bootblack narrator of the rest of the action. These estampas are occasionally set apart from the action by a space or three stars. The most notable distinction between the two narrators of Los hombres obscuros is made when the author sets the scene as in a drama, preparing the reader rhetorically for this change:

> Los cerrojos de la noche están echados. El arrabal y su chato caserío se amodorran bajo la mano tibia de las estrellas.
> Digo:
> Cosas hay poco menos que veladas para los hombres. . . . (Hombres, 75)

The insertion of the obtrusive "Digo" does more than just change the tone and prepare the reader for the dialogue that follows; it alerts the reader to a change of narrators—the poet leaving off and the prose narrator beginning.

The estampa effectively begins with Guzmán, Godoy, and the Generation of 1938. The prose style that Nicomedes Guzmán assimilated was first evolved by Juan Godoy, who modified the techniques of the criollista school led by Mariano Latorre, Godoy's professor at the Instituto Pedagógico.[11] Godoy and Guzmán rebelled against the criollista movement, yet they sought a means to describe Chile poetically. Godoy and Guzmán wanted to begin and end their narration within a frame, which they gave the name estampa. Their fiction is structured around an oscillation between action and contemplation, which ultimately evolved in Guzmán's works to a predictable pattern, the estampa appearing in the first and last of the chapters or subchapters with the plot action in between:

> La tarde se inflaba, enlazando entre sus brazos poderosos gruesos cadejos de sol. Esplendía todavía la luz, madura, bella, jugosa y espesa.
> * * *
> La ciudad, se hallaba llena de rumores, palpitante de ímpetus sonorosos. Parecía deternerse en ella el tiempo y se alumbraba de esa luz espesa que asiste a los ánimos en las grandes batallas.[12]

11. For the closest approximation of a criollista estampa see Chapter 4 of Mariano Latorre, Ully (Santiago: Editorial Nascimento, 1954).
12. The first paragraph cited is a fragment of the estampa that opens Chapter 24 of Luz; the second closes the same chapter.

The difference between Guzmán's estampas and the verbal contemplation of nature used by Mariano Latorre and the criollistas is enormous. Guzmán's poetic statement is always brief, usually a short paragraph (though longer estampas may begin a novel or head a major section), and it is detached stylistically from the body of the fiction. The criollistas interweave description and action with no definite pattern.

Guzmán's estampa often personifies time, nature, or the *arrabal* as an animal or a human "La campana de la parroquia cercana denuda sobre la brisa su claro sexo de sonidos, despertando los deseos en el corazón de los creyentes" (*Hombres*, 19). Through the use of metaphor, he hopes to fix the slums and their intense misery in concrete terms in the mind of the reader. Otherwise, the landscape would be nothing more than pure description and it would be entirely abstract for the reader.

The narrator of the estampa represents the author's ability to see beauty in everything. Though others only saw an immense sea of ugliness in the slums, Guzmán was able to transcend the temporal misery of the conventillo and catch the beauty of its collective spirit. The author's own personal interpretation of the estampas would seem to uphold this theory; note also that he sees the estampa as the key to showing life as it really is through socialist realism: "La fijación de la estampa en la novela pudiera ser la clave para destacar en forma más profunda la vida. La obligación más servera de la novela es reproducir la vida."[13] In this, the only statement he ever made on his own personal use of the estampa, Guzmán connects the poetry of the "frame"—his unique expression of Chile—with an attempt to reproduce life faithfully. The estampa amplifies the image of Chilean life and the Chilean soul; it depicts the degrading milieu in elegant poetic terms, contrasting the conventillo setting with socrealist action.

Guzmán hoped to portray in his prose the dual nature of the conventillo. It is a brutal deterministic environment that damns its inhabitants, a magnet that attracts both the poor and the lawless. But at the same time it is the cradle of Santiago's folk songs, folklore, popular lyrics, poetry, and people; it gives expression to the humble and obscure proletarian soul.

13. Nicomedes Guzmán, "Plan de una novela," *Cultura*, 96 (1964), 45.

To summarize, the technique of the estampa belongs entirely to the Generation of 1938, thanks to the innovations of Guzmán and Godoy. In the hands of the criollistas the elements of the estampa had never been refined. The influence of Frank, Gold, and Sepúlveda Leyton led the generation of socrealist authors to synthesize their images and metaphors into a most unusual narrative technique to open and close their action episodes.

The "I"-Pablo

Except for the camera-like use of the present tense, the second narrative level in *Los hombres obscuros* is that of a traditional narrator, the "I-narrator," a participant in the action with the role of protagonist, whose name is Pablo. Through the device of the first-person narrator, Guzmán has been extremely successful in concealing his own presence in the novel and thus creating an impression of reality. Moreover, the dominance of the protagonist's point of view allows Guzmán to experiment with the narrator's reflection upon and analysis of his own psyche.

It has been mentioned that an unusual feature of *Los hombres obscuros* is its failure to establish what Romberg calls "epic situation."[14] Pablo's role is innovative because of the absence of "epic situation." Because Pablo is narrating in the present tense and has such a close perspective on the action—in addition to being a participant in the action—there is no room for the author in the fiction. The use of this short or non-existent narrative distance approximates a genre in which the epic situation runs side by side with the action, such as the rapid narrative of a sports commentary; there is no room for editorializing. The reader of *Los hombres obscuros* has immediate action thrust upon him and is never entirely sure of its origin. The novel is similar to a diary; as the action develops moment by moment, it allows no glances into the future and little time for retrospection. Yet Pablo's story is not a diary. It is never presented as a summary of the day's events; rather it is a moment-by-moment, blow-by-blow account of the action. There is some editing, but it is not obvious; Pablo sometimes lets two or three days pass, allowing flashbacks to fill in for missed action. In *Hijuna*, by contrast, excessive time passes—as much as two years during a short sentence—making the point of view untenable. Guzmán's fictive technique is similar to that of a tape recording or a documentary on radio or

14. Romberg, *Studies*, p. 33.

television. Nevertheless, it is more complicated than just a commentary, for it comprises different narrative levels.

The novel progresses chronologically. To avoid the possible monotony of a continuous narration, Guzmán includes amorous episodes and shockingly bloody scenes that do not ordinarily occur in the bourgeois sections of the city; it is more credible to the middle-class reader that such happenings might occur in an "exotic" environment such as the slums. The estampas, too, tend to make the narration less commonplace.

Psychological reflections are common in the work. But only a minor portion of the narrative is traditional interior monologue, even though the entire novel could theoretically be considered interior monologue. The narrative of this second-level narrator is like a reproduction of Pablo's thoughts, so the novel reads almost as if Pablo were thinking aloud.

Narrative distance makes itself felt in the letters near the end of the novel, but the author-editor has completely camouflaged himself behind the narrator, so that the reader accepts Pablo as the bona fide weaver of the tale.

Pablo, then, is entirely objective, as if he were a camera lens. However, he does allow the reader to participate in what is going on inside his psyche, to examine the various levels of his ego and to see how exterior situations (especially sex, jealousy, and social conflicts) affect these additional dimensions of his character.

Ego–Pablo

In this light then, *Los hombres obscuros* is essentially a psychological novel. In addition to glimpses into the intimate recesses of the protagonist's mind, the author shows Pablo debating with an interior psychological narrator hidden within his own mind. At times, several paragraphs flow with a stream-of-consciousness technique, as Pablo's inner narrator from the hidden depths of his subconscious seems to take over the narration in the form of additional interior monologue. Guzmán employs quotation marks to indicate the presence of an internal narrator, while the exterior or dramatic dialogues which Pablo quotes as coming from himself and other characters in the novel are designated in the traditional Hispanic manner with a dash:

—¡Pablo!
—¡Inés!

This subordinate narrator, whose expressions are presented within
quotation marks, appears in the emotional passage when Pablo is
waiting for Inés to go to the hotel with him:

> "¡Carajo!"
> En uno de mis bolsillos, suenan algunas monedas. En el recuerdo,
> se me caen difusas imágenes de otro tiempo.
> Allá en el fondo mío, la niñez corretea a la caza de lagartijas. Una
> fragancia espesa de peumos en brote llena el ámbito de mi corazón.
> Olor a vida pura, sin complicaciones. . . . Bella vida, que es como una
> sortija que luciera el recuerdo.
> "¡Ah pequeño Pablo de entonces!, ¿en dónde te cobijas?"
> Los minutos tranquean con una calma desesperante. Hundido en una
> sensación de aletargamiento, me afirmo contra un poste. Miro un
> montón de piedras, sin verlo. Un desfile de imágenes hace en mi cabeza
> un rumorío de torrente distante.
> "¡Ah, sí, claro, los torrentes son bulliciosis y bravos! Una vez un
> hombre se cayó a un torrente. Yo lo vi. ¡Bah, pero no, no era un hombre:
> era un tronco de árbol! Ja, ja, ja. . . ." (*Hombres*, 157–58)

Pablo allows this interior narrator to lead him (and the reader)
on a stream-of-consciousness journey. He is awakened or made
aware of reality by Inés whispering his name in his ear. This
awareness of external reality is similar to Pablo's awakening on
another occasion from a subconscious trance to find his ego speaking
out loud, "Sí, sí, sí," when a moth burns its wings.

The Narrator's Superego

The fourth narrator, Pablo's conscience, speaks in parentheses.
Occasionally this internal voice is allowed to become rhetorical,
using expressions like "(. . . Ah, ¡carajo!)":

> Y yo, simple y pobre hombre, como si aullase a mi propio tormento o
> a mi propio fantasma, heme aquí a la borda de mi *conciencia*, vacilando
> bajo los fustazos de la pesadumbre.
> (¿No comprendías que era necesario reprimirte? ¡Aún te queda mucho
> que aprender, pobre niño! Ja, ja. ¡Cualquiera diría que la vida no te ha
> enseñado su silabario! ¡*Mira, Pablo, camarada*, acuérdate de que la vida
> no volverá a enseñarte su silabario!) (*Hombres*, 127; my italics)

On another occasion, this superego level even takes part in a three-
way debate with the Pablo-narrator and the psyche or ego-narrator:

> De pie en una de las esquinas, una prostituta mira con ojos supli-
> cantes a los transeúntes. . . . Mi imaginación pone a Inés junto a la

ramera. . . . Trato de desviar los pensamientos que me asaltan en tumulto de insectos exaltados.

"¡Ah Inés, tardas demasiado!"

Pienso que ella no vendrá. Se me allegan al ánimo unas ansias terribles de destruir. ¡Ella ya no viene; se arrepintió!

"¿Para qué aceptaste venir, entonces, Inés?"

* * *

¡Inés ya no viene; es demasiado tarde!

Sin embargo, espero. Acaso haya tenido que trabajar sobretiempo.

(¡Eh, hombre, vete, Inés ya no viene!) (*Hombres*, 156–57)

This kind of imaginative creativity had been lacking in Chilean prose before the advent of the Generation of '38, and it was not developed completely in Guzmán's primitive manuscript, "Un hombre, unos ojos negros y una perra lanuda." The generational experience allowed Guzmán to diversify an otherwise traditional point of view.

On another occasion Guzmán demonstrates his humor as well as his emphasis on the immediate present stance of his narrator:

Nos despedimos. La obscuridad vela los cuerpos que largan hacia adentro. Ya estoy en mi cuarto. Un olor a subterráneo me hurguetea las narices. Me pongo a reírle a la obscuridad. Sin duda si algún niño me sorprendiera riendo así, se asustaría. Me acuesto y me digo:

—¡Buenas noches, Pablo! . . .

Pero no alcanzo a contestarme, porque ya me he dormido. (*Hombres*, 90)

Here the narrative borders on the dream, another level of the subconscious; yet it also exaggerates and draws attention to the fact that the narration constantly remains in the actual present. Only on a few occasions does the narrator remove himself from the present to summarize an event that happened in past time (pp. 95, 107–12, 174). These brief flashbacks add variety to the narrative; and such a story within a story slightly expands the horizon of the prose, yet it keeps it inside the boundaries established by the author. However, these flashbacks do not supply narrative distance, nor do they completely violate the author's established pattern as happens in González Vera's *Vidas mínimas* and Sepúlveda Leyton's *Hijuna*.

Many more comments could be made on *Los hombres obscuros*, but some of the evolution of Guzmán's point of view is more discernible in *La sangre y la esperanza* and can be shown in a comparative examination.

In his second novel Guzmán attempted still another innovation. He had been successful with Pablo, the youthful narrator; next he turned to a completely impartial child narrator, Enrique Quilodrán, who has been a highly successful protagonist since the reader can easily identify with him.

Once again the use of the first-person narrator allows the socrealist author to maintain a "strictly objective" stance by "concealing himself behind the subjective presentation given by the narrator."[15] In *La sangre y la esperanza* Guzmán carries this technique one step further in that the narrator adds very few personal comments.

The forcefulness of both Pablo and Enrique as narrators has been recognized by Arnold Chapman, who feels Guzmán communicates his compassion through an intimate "I" chosen with a sure instinct, never embellishing reality. "His Whitmanesque embrace encompasses even the dogs."[16]

While Guzmán had ventured to experiment with obvious psychological levels in Pablo, creating conscience, subconscious, and unconscious levels, he became more subtle and indirect in Enrique's narration. Psychological elements are present, but they are often discernible to the reader only through Freudian associations and dreams. Therefore, Enrique makes an important contribution to his self-characterization when he recounts his dreams and his thoughts at particular moments. Since there is no interior monologue in this second novel, Enrique must state his feelings through direct narration or insinuation:

> Sufría. Temía. Estaba lleno de fantasmas. El dolor de Elena me aullaba en el pecho y el miedo parecía mutilar los brazos de mi espíritu como a aquel mismo mutilado del crimen [the dismembered body of a murder victim shown in the daily newspaper]. Y allí, encima de todo, estaban las velas de las ánimas, alentando demonios en mi mundo, animando bestias dentro de mi pecho, creando imágenes con tripas al aire en mi cerebro. Mordíame. Y sentía que el tiempo era un potro infernal pateando todos mis segundos. (*Sangre*, 283)

At this moment of internal turmoil, Antonieta tries to seduce Enrique, thus adding to the confusion of his mental state. Later that night he has a surrealistic dream, but he is comforted when his

15. Romberg, *Studies*, pp. 130–31.

16. [George] Arnold Chapman, "Perspectiva de la novela de la ciudad en Chile," in Arturo Torres-Ríoseco, ed., *La novela iberoamericana* (Albuquerque: University of New Mexico Press, 1952), p. 202.

sister Elena lies down with him to calm him. He then recalls an earlier occasion when Elena had calmed him (returning to a Freudian association of Elena with his mother):

> Elena tenía una maravillosa condición de madre. Mi instinto de hijo advertíamelo. Muchas veces me gocé, adurmiéndome en su falda y apegando mi rostro goloso de tiernos calores a su pecho, en el que una nueva vida comenzaba ya a definirse en dos brotes duros y promisores. (*Sangre,* 184)

Compare this erotic, future-mother motif with a petting scene between Pablo and Inés in *Los hombres obscuros:*

> La noche nos encuentra en una esquina cualquiera. Mis manos emprenden la aventura de coger sus pechos por encima de las ropas. Pechos de suave dureza, en los que la vida corre presurosa, como al encuentro de un proletario del futuro. (*Hombres,* 115)

Enrique's mother-image of Elena is reinforced in the last part of *La sangre y la esperanza*, where Elena is pregnant and thus on the threshold of motherhood, which also entails Marxist "hope." She is an attractive female, and Enrique's curiosity is continually centered on her sexual development; in fact, Guzmán purposely makes narrative cross references through Enrique to times when Elena was first maturing and to her later mature role. Finally, she is proletarian, and as a woman-child in Guzmán's fiction, she is the image of all motherhood, maternity in embryo. This last interpretation is supported by Guzmán's comments in *Los hombres obscuros* (34): "Y a lo lejos, como un pañuelo musical batido en lontananza, el coro de las futuras madres proletarias":

> Yo no quiero verde, porque es muy triste
> yo lo quiero calado para que pinte.

Such a search for a girl-mother image was strongest in *Hijuna*, where the orphan Juan de Dios seeks such a symbol in his ideal, the proletarian princess Lucía. Guzmán used Juan de Dios as a model for both Pablo and Enrique.

Enrique is a more controlled narrator than was Pablo; he is a child, so his point of view must remain limited. However, Guzmán is not able to hide entirely behind Enrique as he did behind Pablo, and thus he appears to be telling a true story:

> En lo que toca al cuadro, tenemos la obligación de recordar que, cuando se publicó nuestra novela *La sangre y la esperanza*, recibimos una nota

llena de reproches, con extraña firma, es decir casi anónima, donde se decía que tal libro no era una novela. Quizá hubiera razón en ello.[17]

The author is accused of passing off autobiography as fiction. Yet Enrique is the only storyteller present in the narration, and Guzmán attempts to make his own voice so vague as to be obviously fictional:

> Era el tiempo, el recio tiempo del despertar de nuestros padres, del despertar de nuestros hermanos. Rodaban en ensordecedor bullicio los vigorosos días del año veinte. O del veintiuno. O del veintidós. (*Sangre*, 16).

This paragraph on the second page of the novel establishes Romberg's "epic situation," the distance from the fictional author to the first-person protagonist. Behind the child narrator there is a mature Enrique who remains unknown and does not speak again except for two or three brief statements (pp. 148–49, 171). The narrative distance is not clear, but there are probably about twenty years—roughly 1920 to 1940—between Enrique as an innocent child and Enrique the mature poet-narrator of the estampas.

Because he is a child, Enrique is a more naïve witness than was Pablo. Enrique is too young to comment on social wrongs; he merely presents such situations, though he and Pablo both make limited comments on the action and summarize remarks made by others in dialogues. As a rule, however, neither one makes character judgments. Pablo dislikes Inés's father right from the start, but his passion for Inés prejudices him in this regard. Even in Chapter 10, when Maestro Mercedes dies, he fails to add flowery adjectives. Missing is the quick summary of a character or a situation in a few opinionated words that is common in *Jews Without Money* and *Mich Hungert*.

Because of the passage of some twenty years, Enrique feigns a memory failure at the beginning of the novel: "Los años han borrado de mi cerebro los rasgos de casi todos los pequeños camaradas de aquella época" (*Sangre*, 17). The narrator is implying he will describe events that impressed him so much that other details are insignificant. This first chapter includes the most gory episodes of the novel. By having his narrator deny the conventional perfect memory that is his right as a storyteller, Guzmán hoped to convey an even greater illusion of reality.

17. Guzmán, "Plan de una novela," p. 44.

In a traditional sense, narrative distance is well defined in *La sangre y la esperanza*. Since Enrique-adult places Enrique-child in the key role, it is necessary to use the past tense instead of the present tense. Enrique is described most thoroughly and presented most clearly as both narrator and protagonist at the beginning of the novel, but letters are also used to aid character and plot development in *La sangre y la esperanza*.

There are inevitable limitations in first-person narration, but Guzmán was able to overcome the major ones. For example, there are difficulties in enabling the narrator to be present at all times and in all locations to observe all the action. Enrique, as an obscure little boy, is able to hide in corners, squeeze through a crowd for a close-up view, and overhear conversations his elders consider confidential. He is easily overlooked since he is a member of the family, or because he is supposed to be too young to understand what was being discussed. Nothing is entirely hidden from him except the birth of his brother. And the intensity of the love affair between Elena and Abel is substantiated in their letters as well as in the amorous scenes that Enrique witnesses from a hiding place on the staircase.

It is hard to say just how intelligent an observer a five-year-old or even an eight-year-old can be. As a child, Enrique is perhaps not quite as perceptive as a narrator should be (though this has never been a problem in the evaluation of *Lazarillo de Tormes*). What he does not fully understand, however, Enrique repeats without comment. The reader is eventually able to interpret it, although an unskilled reader may need two or three readings of the novel to comprehend all of Guzmán's intricate insinuations, such as Enrique's hints of Elena's lost virginity. Because Enrique relays to the reader certain information which he as narrator is not yet capable of understanding, Guzmán the author is more visible behind the narrator than he was in *Los hombres obscuros*. Nevertheless, Guzmán's insistence on objectivity was undoubtedly strengthened by his inclusion of a little boy as narrator. The reading public remembers Enrique better than it does Pablo.

In spite of obvious weaknesses in the use of a child as narrator, there were also definite technical advantages for Guzmán. First, the convention of a perfect memory in the narrator, often present in fiction in the form of a gentlemen's agreement between the reader and the creator, was used extensively by Guzmán (in spite of

Enrique's attempt shown above to negate it). Second, the author was able to structure the life of his hero around his own autobiography. This adds credibility to the development of the protagonist. Third, as he wrote the book, the writer was able to refer to other child-narrators as models for his own protagonist. There are many important child protagonists in Chilean literature.

Those pieces of information that Guzmán could not convey directly through Enrique, he conveyed indirectly, or through letters. A good example of indirect information is Enrique's vision of the scene where Angélica has been raped by her mother's alcoholic lover. Not really comprehending the seriousness of the situation, he observes the blood and realizes a few days later that Angélica has never returned. Only the reader comprehends the full impact of the scene. Later, when Enrique witnesses the rape of Antonieta, he understands a little better what must have happened to Angélica.

Other than those chapters of La sangre y la esperanza and "Los trece meses del año" which were published as "short stories," the only story Guzmán wrote in the first person is "El pan bajo la bota." Since the protagonist is Enrique Quilodrán and his mother and father are Guillermo and Laura, the story appears to be an attempted beginning of a sequel to La sangre y la esperanza, promised by the author when that novel was a success. However, Ester Panay insists that "El pan bajo la bota" is not a frustrated attempt at a sequel, that it is a short story and nothing more.

The Enrique of the story is no longer innocent, nor is he as convincing a character in the few finished pages of "Los trece meses del año," since Guzmán finds it too easy to have him voice protests that he would never have uttered before:

> El guardia se mantuvo impertérrito. Yo hubiera llorado. Mas la entereza de mi padre me daba coraje. Cerré un instante los párpados y me tragué el odio. Sí, el odio, el horrible odio que, aun en los pueblos libres, germina contra la buena voluntad de los hombres limpios. (El pan bajo la bota, 35)

Though his protest appears mild, it is much more than the Enrique of the novel would have expressed. Enrique's frequent tears are excusable in the novel, for he is an innocent child, but as he becomes older and goes to work, his crying is baffling. These tears seem to be an attempt by Guzmán to create a symbolism of humility rather than a means to create reality.

Letters

Guzmán's use of the letter has been mentioned previously in various contexts. In *Los hombres obscuros* he employs the letter as a frame around which he can show the ultimate development of Pablo. More than one critic, however, has not understood what Pablo means in his reply to his father's invitation or why he is so adamant in his refusal to return to the country and his family home. There are at least eight reasons why Pablo might intentionally insult his father by rejecting his invitation to return to the countryside.

1. Pablo has just been converted to Marxism; in fact, his letter, in part, is a document of his final conversion from a spectator of life to a worker-revolutionary ("Tengo por delante una bella y noble obra que realizar"). His father's letter, which seemingly antagonizes him, may help him make this final decision toward militancy.

2. He is attracted to others of his kind who are forced to live in the slum environment; he enjoys the company of the conventillo and especially the personality of the workers; and he has been unable to find this type of pleasing social environment anywhere else in Chile.

3. He has the hope of working, of eventually becoming a laborer; because of unemployment in the North, nowhere else in Chile is there a proletarian nucleus, and elsewhere he has been exploited or unemployed.

4. He has been exploited at home, apparently by his father, perhaps in some sort of farming venture:

> No tengo interés en acompañar en sus "Labores" a quien, en más de una triste ocasión me dio "muestras tan elocuentes" de sus "sentimientos paternales. . . ."
> Me resta agradecerle, como ya le agradecí personalmente en "aquella oportunidad," el poco de cultura que su "bondad" me proporcionó. Ahora me será muy útil. (*Hombres*, 206–7)

5. Fernando Alegría presents the picture that previous Chilean literature had painted of the capital:

> El patrón seducía a la joven campesina; ésta viajaba a Santiago y se internaba en alguna mala casa. . . . Surgía la imagen de una ciudad cruel y devoradora, construida sobre deleznables prejuicios; ciudad que perdía sus decorados de aldea, sus caballos . . . y se industrializaba llenándose

de sindicatos y factorías, de motores . . . de altos edificios y más altas injusticias.[18]

As has been shown, Guzmán stressed repeatedly that his fiction was realism; and his realist novel is the type of writing that Alegría emphasizes in this book, which bore the original title *Las fronteras del realismo*. Moreover, Guzmán's realism was the negation of Chile's criollismo. In this sense Pablo's letter is Guzmán's attempt to negate the criollistas' stereotyped conviction that the *aldea* (country village) was more beautiful than, and superior to, the capital. In short, the letter is an inversion of the traditional image of the countryside as portrayed by the criollistas, a rejection of rural political rule in central government, a challenge to the criollista depiction of dominance by brutal nature, a denial of the value of ecstatic contemplation of earthly beauty, and a reversal of the *menosprecio de cortes* theme.

6. The Generation of 1938 was anxious to characterize the "universal Chilean archetype," the roto, and to understand him as a proletarian being. By interpreting the roto's essence, the young writers felt, they could also define Chile's essence. Pablo's history is the same as the roto's. Historians felt that the roto had forsaken the land—where he had been exploited and starved as a peasant. His only hope for survival was to flee to the city, and rotos migrated there in droves. His plight in Santiago or Valparaíso was no better; yet the city continued to attract other rotos. In the capital they could be close to government officials, who might listen to their pleas, and they would be near the sites of future factories and industry.

In attempting to define Pablo, Guzmán is defining not only the roto but all of Latin America, for mass migration from the country to the cities is a problem that has plagued most Latin American nations during the twentieth century.

7. The previous six explanations are based on intuition, but there is still another interpretation that is easily documented. It would seem that Pablo's main reason for not wanting to return to the country and his father's home is based on the Marxist theory that the country itself does not produce proletarians—only the city does. The land produces the peasantry, an appendage of the bourgeoisie. This opinion was strongly and definitely reiterated by Trotsky, who stated that while the peasantry has *followed* revolutionary causes,

18. Fernando Alegría, *Literatura chilena del siglo XX* (Santiago: Empresa Editora Zig-Zag, 1967), p. 9.

it has never risen independently to achieve its own political aims.[19] Marx and Engels also insisted that peasants are "not revolutionary but conservative. Nay more, they are reactionary, for they try to roll back the wheel of history."[20]

Pablo has found the true proletariat only in the city. Apparently because of the bankruptcy of the nitrate industry, not even in the North can the proletarian be found; this is surprising, for the North gave birth to the Chilean workers as a class and to the Marxist parties in Chile. Pablo wants to remain close to his newly found comrades because his home situation was a bourgeois experience and was entirely unsatisfactory to him.

8. Another reason for Pablo's attitude became apparent when in an old box filled with newspaper clippings at Lucy's house I found in 1973 the rough draft of this letter, hand-written in Guzmán's favorite green ink. The letter had been drafted at the time Guzmán was revising *Los hombres obscuros* from "Un hombre, unos ojos negros y una perra lanuda," and it bore the arbitrary date of May 7, 1933. One key sentence by Pablo's father was soon deleted: "Estoy deberas [crossed out] de veras arrepentido de aquella mi violenta actitud para contigo." Another, by Pablo, was later revised: "Sería una crueldad de parte————que su *hijo de descuido con una guasa* y del 'hermano plebeyo'————el ir a amargarles———— en la burguesa paz campesina de que gozan" (lines indicate illegible omissions and the words in italics were replaced by the more abstract "hijo de ocasión"). And the third was a similar classist comment by Pablo: "Déjeme, pues, aquí, señor latifundista [crossed out] terrateniente . . ."

The rough draft of the letter further clarifies the personal and class differences that separated Pablo socially from his "father" and led him to respond in such a tone, even though his first reaction had been to tear the note to bits.

9. A final reason for his desire not to return is implicit in the letter; Pablo is a proletarian Cinderella. He has a stepmother and "hermanas" who do not appreciate his proletarian situation: "Además no quiero ensombrecer con mi presencia la tranquila vida de su esposa y 'hermanas.' Sería una crueldad de parte de su 'hijo de

19. Leon Trotsky, *Literature and Revolution* (Ann Arbor: University of Michigan Press, 1960), pp. 108–9 (see also p. 90).

20. Karl Marx and Friedrich Engels, *Communist Manifesto* (Chicago: Great Books of the Western World, 1952), p. 424.

ocasión' y del 'hermano plebeyo' el ir a amargarlas en la burguesa paz campesina de que gozan" (207). The alert reader becomes aware at the close of the novel that the Cinderella motif pervades the entire work. There was a party and dance that ended abruptly at midnight when the landlady came to break it up, but a fight dispersed the guests.

The element of Cinderella's shoes is represented in the actions of Pablo, who helps women doff and don them during his excessively long day; he shines shoes, repairs them, and observes them as their wearers walk past him from daybreak to dusk. His success, his living "happily ever after," is centered in the fact that he is able to reject the ordinary world of bourgeois exploitation to discover the saving element of work together with its strong proletarian camaraderie. This promise of Marxist hope transcends even physical love, for through unanimism, Pablo is able to withstand the loss of his temporal companion Inés, which is caused by the unthinking actions of the government. Human incomprehension is the central theme also of the later short stories "Perro ciego" and "La hora de la vida."

It is only through the letters in the novel that most of these hidden elements are fully developed.

The letters of Elena to Abel in *La sangre y la esperanza* have several functions. One of them is to characterize Elena more fully by showing her from a different point of view. The reader also sees the parents from a more mature vantage point. Enrique is characterized somewhat, but mention of him is brief. Most important is that the letters furnish information to the reader that Enrique would otherwise be unable to convey.

Third-Person Narrative

In his last novel and in eighteen short stories, Guzmán moves to a third-person narrator who is generally omniscient in his vision. None of the works show this narrator in any role in the story, and the narrator always remains unidentified.

The change to third-person point of view adds dimensions that were not available in the earlier works. The author is now free to work with space, to show changes of location, and to focus suddenly on different characters, things he had been unable to do in the time-structured autobiographical novels. Also, he is free to shift the narration or change narrative tempo, as in *La luz viene del mar*, when the narrator makes a verbal "still" of Virginia's walk along the beach, describing it almost as if it were motionless in time.

Very seldom does Guzmán vary from the pattern of the omniscient narrator who reads the thoughts of the characters (which he inserts in quotation marks to identify as internal monologue). His third-person narrator, like his first-person narrator, usually refrains from character judgments, apostrophes, or other interruptions; the action, the dialogue, and the story are allowed to define and develop the character for the reader.

In some of his third-person short stories, Guzmán experiments with different types of narrators. For example, in "Extramuros," he attempts a narrative based solely on external observation, but he finds it necessary to include a fragment of interior monologue in the minds of three of the characters. He begins in the present tense, as if he were actually present at the scene observing the four vagabonds and the cat around the fire; he summarizes or reviews the arrival of each, one by one, using the past tense; then he returns to the present for the surprising dénouement.

More than half of "Destello en la bruma" is narrated by telling; then, as in the majority of Guzmán's short stories, the characters solve the conflict in the plot for the reader through their own actions and dialogue. In the dramatic portion of the story, the narrator occasionally inserts the conscious thoughts that are unspoken on both sides of the argument between the drunkard mother and her illegitimately pregnant daughter.

In only one short story is the narrator less than omniscient. In "Rapsodia en luz mayor," the narrator seems to be unsure of what is going on in the mind of the character, even though elsewhere throughout the story he has omniscient powers of awareness:

> Ella tembló. No de frío. No. No era de frío que temblaba. Era de temor, *tal vez*. Hubiera lanzado ahora ese quejido de bestia herida que se desplazaba hacia el rincón más oculto de su pecho.[21]

Here the narrator is as limited as if he were the person being described, as if his point of view were that of the character, for even the character seems unsure of why she is shivering.

21. Nicomedes Guzmán, *Una moneda al río* (Godfrey, Ill.: Monticello College Press, 1954), p. 78, or *El pan bajo la bota* (Santiago: Empresa Editora Zig-Zag, 1960), p. 134.

In his last published short story, "La hora de la vida" (*Pan bajo la bota*, 169–87), Guzmán experimented more with new techniques than in his earlier works. The story contains many interior monologues presenting streams of consciousness in the mind of a poor old widow, and it is the first story in which the flashback is a major element.

In *La luz viene del mar* the omniscient narrator attempts to remain objective and invisible, but occasionally he stands out inadvertently: "El Huacho Fieroga, *labra que te labra*, cuchillo en mano, daba formas al barco que fabricaba para Fernando, el nieto" (142). The phrase "labra que te labra" belongs to a popular idiomatic structure like "mira que te mira" and "dale que te dale," which also appear in the novel. Although such phrases are common in colloquial Chilean speech, they tend to place the narrator in linguistic juxtaposition to the character; the reader can tell that the narrator is Chilean. The narrator also asks rhetorical questions on a few occasions:

> ¿Dónde el barco prisionero en la botella? ¿Dónde los instrumentales náuticos que el abuelo querido ya por toda la eternidad confiara a la custodia y a la veneración familiar? (*Luz*, 308)

In addition to such rhetorical interventions, the narrator imposes his own viewpoint at least once to make sure that the reader understands the implicit irony:

> Desde una muralla, encerrado en un marco de dudosa pintura, la Virgen del Perpetuo Socorro, con el niño en brazos *sonreía dulcemente, presenciando la escena.* Y, un Cristo sufría, enclavado en una cruz de yeso, *sin atender a nada* que no fuera su condenación sufriente de crucificado. (*Luz*, 314; my italics)

The irony comes from the fact that the narrator describes in minute detail the scenery of a room which he usually passes over. He not only points out the unobserving crucifix, a self-centered God on a cross of plaster, but also the Virgin, smiling approvingly over the scene of love that she is witnessing in the brothel. The women seem to have little comprehension of the significance the two images should have for them.[22] One of the characters in the novel states

22. When I spoke with Professor Eduardo Godoy Gallardo of the University of Chile about the irony of Guzmán's literary brothels, Godoy cautioned me that such situations were beyond my cultural awareness, and that they actually exist. I should emphasize that Guzmán has a penchant for irony, either because of his love of antithesis, or because of some impulse toward satiric

that the Northerner is so wrapped up in his own preoccupations that he has no time for his fellow beings, let alone for religion.

Finally, since the narrator is able to see inside the minds of the characters, on rare occasions he steps beyond his narrative boundaries to insert a comment on the psychological development of a character: "Pedro Andrade hubiera quierido poseer sus dos manos enteras [he had just cut off his hand] para frotarlas de gozo, como un niño, frente a la sola idea de ser dueño una vez más de Fresia." (*Luz*, 216) The narrator is too cautious; the subjunctive "hubiera," which Guzmán occasionally turns to in such instances, may cause a lack of confidence on the part of the reader, for it suggests that the narrator is inferring a psychological situation, and he is ordinarily omniscient.

For the most part, Guzmán's narrators do not inject the propaganda line that is commonly the contribution of the narrator in proletarian works. This freedom from bias has raised Guzmán's works above the level of the purely tendentious to an artistic plane. From *La sangre y la esperanza* on, Guzmán continually toned down and camouflaged the propaganda element in his work, so by the time he wrote *La luz viene del mar*, the narrator's tone of social commitment had been greatly disguised. In essence, Guzmán's narrator assumes the position of a fictional observer and not that of a proselytizer.

Evolution of Narrative Focus

Several different aspects of point of view were detailed at the beginning of this chapter. The attempt here will be to show just how successful Guzmán was in achieving what Henry James called the "problem of centre" or "focus" for his stories: "A beautiful infatuation this, always, I think, the intensity of the creative effort to get into the skin of the creature."[23]

Guzmán chooses an unusual approach in making a shoeshine boy the narrator of *Los hombres obscuros*, for, rather like that of Gregor Samsa, the protagonist of Franz Kafka's "Metamorphosis," who suddenly turns into a dung-beetle, Pablo's vision is from un-

---

caricature. The vision of the prostitute will be treated in this chapter and in Chapter 13.

23. Henry James, *Art of the Novel: Critical Prefaces*, ed. R. P. Blacknur (New York: Charles Scribner's Sons, 1962), p. 37.

derneath; he sees things from ground level. At first the reader cannot tell why the narrator's concentration is mostly on legs, and why he lives in a sensuous world of well-turned ankles, calves, knees, and thighs. After a few pages, the reader discovers that Pablo is a bootblack and sees that the author has introduced a significant proletarian perspective!

After the initial experimentation with technique and psychological levels in his first novel, Guzmán continued to show his narrative skill in *La sangre y la esperanza*. The narration is more Freudian, and Guzmán is more interested in indirect exposition. The point of view of the child-narrator, Enrique, is masterfully uniform and demonstrates the author's remarkable sensibility. In fact, Guzmán's works reveal his sensitive feeling for both children and animals.

The narrator's point of view becomes more remote with each of Guzmán's novels. It is first-person present in *Los hombres obscuros*. *La sangre y la esperanza* is also in the first person, but it is written like a memoir or autobiography; the protagonist is separated from the narrator and reader by the epic distance of some twenty years. Finally, in *La luz viene del mar* and in eighteen of his nineteen stories, there is experimentation with streams of consciousness since Guzmán's narrator assumes a position of omniscience; he is always anonymous, slightly removed in distance from the characters in order to maintain objectivity, and his narration is in the preterit. This narrative stance should not be taken to represent a cold and apathetic relationship of the author to his characters, but rather as Guzmán's attempt to be as objective as possible. Spatial alienation is a cause of social alienation in *La luz viene del mar*, and the objective narration typifies the remoteness of the desert. In such an environment it is appropriate for the poet to assume an Olympian view of the North and its inhabitants.

This final aloofness, as if the narrator were observing from an *atalaya* (which parallels Virginia's vantage point of the belfry), and the evolution of point of view in all Guzmán's fiction can best be understood through a concrete examination of one element that is common to all three novels: the prostitute. The various attitudes of the narrators toward prostitutes form an interesting basis for comparing the overall vision of the different narrators.

Pablo has close relationships with prostitutes; but they tend to offer only a superficial solution to his frustration, while his friendship with Inés is much more meaningful to him. When Pablo is frustrated because his romantic relationship with Inés does not allow him sexual satisfaction, he turns to the prostitutes of the conventillo. Yet such transitory involvements leave him with deeper anguish, as is shown in a scene where Inés rejects his caresses because of her declining health:

> —¡No, Pablo, yo encuentro tan humano esto! pero me hace mal. No debemos atormentarnos; es necesario que nos separemos. . .
>
>   *   *   *
>
> La beso una vez más en las manos, sobre la suavidad callosa de sus palmas trabajadoras.
> —¡Hasta luego! . . .
> Me quedo como un muerto de pie bajo la noche inquieta y pestañeante. Y, no sé por qué, *pienso con dolor en las rameras del suburbio.* (*Hombres*, 116–17; my italics)

During the self-imposed separation that follows this scene, the climate of the entire conventillo seems unbearably amorous to Pablo—even the cats on the roof make love. In his desperation Pablo visits a prostitute whom he had apparently frequented earlier. Guzmán attempts to reveal how youthful she is, like Pablo; she is an orphan, forced by poverty into prostitution, like most Chilean prostitutes. Her attempt to better her economic plight will be futile, however, for salvation is available only to proletarian characters who work. Like the naturalist novelists Zola and Edwards Bello, Guzmán seems to insinuate that prostitution is a way of life that is often inherited by the children raised in such conditions; he indicates that her infant is also in bed with the couple:

> No puedo más. Salgo. La pequeña Rebeca no ha traído a nadie esta noche a su cuarto. Y me recibe con su habitual y triste alegría abierta en el rostro en forma de sonrisa, que es dulce y tersa a fuerza de orfandad.
> —¡Al fin vienes, chiquillo! . . .
> Atranca la puerta y se desnuda.
> Su nene es una pequeña porción de vida que respira quedamente en el mismo miserable lecho en que nos acostamos. (*Hombres*, 135)

Through his portrayal of the prostitutes in each novel, Guzmán attempts to show that even though there is a superficial attraction, there is nothing glamorous in prostitution.

In *La sangre y la esperanza* the prostitute remains a mystery to young, innocent Enrique, and the point of view reflects this juvenile incomprehension. Although Enrique does not understand the social function of prostitutes, his friends do (65). He is partially awakened to the realities of the world outside the protection of his home when his friend Sergio Llanos explains how he contracted a venereal disease. Sergio confides to Enrique that late at night one of the prostitutes in his mother's brothel had "raped" him when he awoke to go to the toilet (98–99). A few minutes later Enrique has the opportunity to observe these streetwalkers when he passes Sergio's house. Later he sees them at the double funeral held for Sergio and the prostitute whom he murdered because she had infected him with syphilis; once again Guzmán is moralizing indirectly. Enrique reacts morally to the presence of the whores at the funeral and paints an animalistic image of them; he also observes in Sergio's mother (the madam) the same image that he sees in her dog. In contrast, Enrique's family is always optimistic, full of love.

The moral decision will not always be easy for Enrique. For example, in the third part of the novel, in which he is older, Enrique becomes interested over a period of several days in the conventillo prostitutes who appear so beautiful to him. His childlike attraction is quickly reversed, however; one evening after he has heard these women singing sensually, he observes one of them drunkenly stagger out on the landing, where she urinates and defecates:

> Las prostitutas de la pieza diez poseían una bella risa. Yo me iba de vez en cuando hasta el fondo de la galería, por sólo la conquista de un instante habitado por metales de su garganta.
>
> * * *
>
> Yo apenas las había visto alguna vez lejana, a distancia. Sabía que eran rubias. *Vi entonces competir al sol con sus cabelleras*. . . . Desde entonces . . me lancé a la caza del fruto de sus gargantas.
>
> * * *
>
> De pronto, una mujer que sale. No me vio. Estaba borracha. . . . Se alzó las polleras. . . . La vi encuclillarse. . . . Sonaron los orines sobre el entablado. Y algo más . . . diferente a su risa, desde luego. Pensé que aquello no podía ser. Pero, era realmente . . .
>
> ¡Sí, la muerte de una pequeña ilusión! (*Sangre*, 249–50; my italics)

Guzmán employs Gongoristic metaphors here to accent the irony of the harlot's bleached hair, which is brighter than the sun. Compare Guzmán's hyperbole with a strophe from Góngora's 1582 sonnet, number 228:

> Mientras por competir con tu cabello,
> oro bruñido el Sol relumbra en vano,

mientras con menosprecio en medio el llano
mira tu blanca frente al lilio bello. . . .[24]

Guzmán enjoys using baroque extremes like this one, as do other members of the Generation of '38.

Enrique's final disillusion with the prostitute is due to a basic human act, portrayed socrealistically, which offends him as it would any child. His childlike vision has finally been able to penetrate the paint of the prostitute; throughout the remainder of the novel neither she nor her criminal counterpart in society will have any further power over Enrique's decisions. He has started on the road to maturity.

In *La luz viene del mar* the narrator attempts to convey to the reader the overwhelming geographical vastness of the North, which causes both psychological and social alienation in its inhabitants. These social schisms result in the creation of prostitution. In the desert the prostitute is a buffer, a catalyst to ease human alienation; yet she is also cause and effect of other hostilities. A female is a luxury in the desert North; most women cannot survive in its hostile environment, so the prostitute becomes a necessity for the man of the North. Furthermore, the prostitute in Guzmán's North is a faithful counterpart of the alienated male laborer. The female opposite of a man without an eye (Cara de Pescado) is his mirrored reflection, "Teresa la Tuerta." For a man without a hand (Pedro Andrade), there is "La Coja," the girl who jumped under the streetcar on which Pedro was the motorman, losing her leg and his baby (a motif reminiscent of Edwards Bello's *El roto*).

The typical poor family finds it nearly impossible to survive in the decadent and destructive North. In *La luz viene del mar* few of the characters originate from or represent successful families or even family structures that are whole. (One exception, perhaps, is the minor character Eudocio.) The thesis of the novel is quite negative: the downfall of the nitrate-based economy of the North brought with it the downfall of the family. Therefore, the prostitute class, the lowest of society, is depicted as absurd; it is the most negative element in the decadent middle-class and proletarian world that at one time had been part of the great oligarchic nitrate empire. Just as the nitrate fields and their laborers are exploited, so are the women,

24. Luis de Góngora y Argote, *Obras completas* (Madrid: Aguilar, 1961), p. 447.

and especially the prostitute; she is the key to survival for the worker of the North, who would obviously explode without some feminine vent for his passions.[25]

Narrative Influence of Faulkner

The "neo-naturalistic" resemblance of Guzmán's short stories to William Faulkner's fiction has been pointed out elsewhere.[26] Interestingly, Faulkner's influence on Guzmán's novels has not been examined to date.

Faulkner is among the most widely imitated of the innovative twentieth-century artists. Guzmán's generation had easier access to Faulkner's works than to those of, say, Proust, Joyce, or Woolf, and—unlike many Americans—they viewed Faulkner as a socially committed writer.

Many critics feel that experiments in fiction during the twentieth century have been limited to portraying streams of consciousness in third-person novels and that such experimentation "has not created any completely new and generically original first-person narrative."[27] Romberg theorizes that third-person omniscient recording of stream of consciousness is only another manifestation of the author, since the character in the novel has no concern about how his thoughts might be communicated to the reader.

Romberg has neglected the shifting multiple first-person point of view introduced first by Faulkner, which one critic has termed "kaleidoscopically rapid," and which another has referred to as a carousel.[28] Romberg has also avoided Faulkner's more complicated major works in preference to two minor novels, *The Town* and *The Unvanquished*. In his references to these works, Romberg compares them to the *Briefwechselroman* of correspondence between two or more persons, which is not always considered to be a first-person novel.[29]

While critics for several decades have referred to Faulkner's re-

25. Further mention will be made of the development of the prostitute in Chapter 13.

26. John P. Dyson, "Los cuentos de Nicomedes Guzmán," *Atenea*, 404 (1964), 234.

27. Romberg, *Studies*, pp. 100–101.

28. Conrad Aiken, "William Faulkner: The novel as form," in Frederick J. Hoffman, ed., *William Faulkner: Three Decades of Criticism* (New York: Harcourt, Brace and World, 1963), p. 134, and John M. Ditsky, "Faulkner's Carousel: Point of View in *As I Lay Dying*," *Laurel Review*, 10 (1970), 74–85.

29. Romberg, *Studies*, pp. 46–47.

volving narrations, such as *The Sound and the Fury* and *As I Lay Dying*, merely as "stream-of-consciousness novels," there is no rationale for considering them to be entirely stream-of-consciousness or even third-person, nor can any voice in the novel be identified as that of a single narrator. The narrator is instead a plurality—the first person of several characters. If the author were noticeably present as an editor or collector of the various internal monologues, he would be obliged to reject many passages that repeat information previously communicated by a different point of view. Such repeated elements are often meaningful motifs or signposts of time, such as the multiple vision of the flood in *As I Lay Dying*, narrated by several characters.

The principal Faulkner novel to be dealt with in a study of Guzmán's use of point of view is *As I Lay Dying* (*Mientras yo agonizo*, 1930). A favorite book of Guzmán's, *As I Lay Dying* fascinated him and was the model for the parallel structure and the parallel characters in *La luz viene del mar*, as it was for Gabriel García Marquez's *La hojarasca* (1955). When I asked Ester Panay (Quilpué, Chile, 22 July 1971) if Faulkner's *Light in August* (*Luz de agosto*) had played any role in the structure of *La luz viene del mar*, she replied no, that Guzmán modeled his novel on Faulkner's *Mientras yo agonizo*, which he greatly admired and had in a Spanish translation in his personal library.

Just as there are varying levels of apparent madness in the Bundren family of *As I Lay Dying*, there are also intensities of another type of hostility and alienation in the men of *La luz viene del mar*. Although *As I Lay Dying* was Guzmán's model, there is an obvious difference between the two novels in point of view: Faulkner alternates first-person narrators to produce a circular point of view, whereas Guzmán maintains a third-person Olympian point of view but alternates protagonists and themes to create a circular impression.

Faulkner employs fifteen first-person narrators who relate a total of fifty-nine sections; in Guzmán's novel, nine characters or themes are developed in thirty-five chapters. Darl narrates more sections of *As I Lay Dying* (nineteen) than any other character; his little brother Vardaman narrates ten; the other characters have fewer chapters. Guzmán's chapters are longer; he focuses his novel on Virginia (ten chapters), and six chapters deal directly with labor problems ("En la brecha"). All the other chapters involve minor characters; like some of the minor narrators in *As I Lay Dying*, they appear in the spotlight only two or three times. The central point of view in *As I Lay Dying* is that of Addie Bundren, who is a corpse when she speaks in the middle of the book. In *La Luz viene del mar* Guzmán is attempting to depict a new panorama of the North from a new central focus, but the center of the novel is the brothel.

The influence of Faulkner's novel on the structure of *La Luz viene del mar* is obvious, and the fact that this influence has been substantiated by Ester Panay, who helped Guzmán structure his novel with her home town as background and her family as models, suggests a new approach to the interpretation of Guzmán's fiction.

It is possible that *As I Lay Dying* was also a model for the earlier *Los hombres obscuros*. It is one of the few novels that Guzmán read whose author is consistent in his use of the present tense. Faulkner's occasional use of the past tense is mainly for flashbacks (especially in the scenes surrounding the flood and fire), although his present tense usage slips into the historical present in the voices of one of two minor narrators. Such stylistic conscientiousness would have been noted by Guzmán who has been one of the greatest point-of-view experimenters in Chile.

Another characteristic Faulknerian device is mirrored in *Los hombres obscuros* (and in later fiction). In *As I Lay Dying* Darl has a poetic view of the world as well as clairvoyance. He describes his world with poetic images. This poetic expression caught the imagination of the Generation of 1938. It will be remembered that Guzmán included a poetic narrator as one voice of Pablo and that he was one of the first writers to use the poetic estampa. (The estampa was included in Godoy's manuscript of *Angurrientos*, but the novel was not published until after Guzmán's first novel.)

Thus when Romberg states that there were no innovations in the first-person novel because the third-person stream-of-consciousness novel has ruled the twentieth century, he misses the great innovative technique of the first-person narrative with multiple perspectives. The genre begins with Faulkner and includes Guzmán's four divisions of the one narrator of *Los hombres obscuros*, as well as Carlos Fuentes's brilliant portrayal of the "yo," the "ego," the "tú," and other perspectives in the dying Artemio Cruz. The multiple vision in Artemio Cruz points to Faulknerian influence, for the protagonist lies dying and is later a corpse with multiple voices.

Faulkner was also one of the first authors to add internal monologue to his first-person narration. In *As I Lay Dying* the narrators' stream-of-consciousness ramblings are intermingled with "vocalized" remarks to the reader. This interior monologue, which may be in the form of stream of consciousness (especially with Faulkner's endless-sentence style), is also generally in the immediate present tense, not past or historical present. In other works (*The Sound and The Fury*, for example) the external world is in the past while the internal world is in the present, but in *As I Lay Dying* the past is used principally for flashbacks, which appear especially in Addie Bundren's narration. Guzmán employs similar techniques in *Los hombres obscuros*. Flashbacks and internal monologues are used by both novelists to expand the present-tense narrators' comments, to add lyric passages, and to help characterize the protagonist and round him out.

Guzmán adds another narrative dimension when he shows Pablo's ego competing with his conscience. Faulkner was one of the few authors Guzmán had read who experimented similarly with various levels of narration, intermingling them in the same work.

With its rotating point of view, *As I Lay Dying* might be said to belong to a dramatic mode more than to a novelistic one. Romberg seems unsure of the classification of Faulkner's novels, as well as Schnitzler's *Leutnant Gustl* (1900), a first-person present novella with a point of view similar to that of *Los hombres obscuros*.

When one places *Los hombres obscuros* beside *As I Lay Dying*, new aspects of point of view become apparent. First it is obvious that Faulkner's innovative present-tense narrative spoken or thought by fifteen narrators is not really stream of consciousness as traditional criticism has suggested. Next it becomes apparent that the first-person novel in the immediate present tense is a rare form. Both Guzmán and Faulkner went wide of what were considered the limits of point of view.

Regardless of the narrator's stance or the tense that he uses, Guzmán strives to achieve his goal of artistically creating an illusion of reality through socrealist methods. After examining his entire output, we can conclude that he was much more successful in imitating reality with his first-person novels than he was with his later works. It appears that once he left first-person narrative he could not easily return to its youthful spontaneity. This is why, perhaps, "Los trece meses del año" was a futile and frustrated attempt to return to the point of view he had so capably mastered in his youth.

11

Time and Space

Time

Time has many functions in literature and can be interpreted in many ways. Time in a character's experience is a subjective matter; clock-time references may serve as narrative guideposts—or they may be purposely meaningless. According to Edwin Muir's study of the novel, time is implicit in the "dramatic novel," whereas the "character novel" or social novel involves action that is continuously repeated in space.[1] It should be recalled that Guzmán's work evolved from the novel structured on time to the novel structured on space (while in the proletarian novel of the United States, the opposite was generally true). Time in another sense, then, is history, biography, or autobiography. During the twentieth century, time has also been used as a way to develop a personage by offering deeper insight into his psyche. In this sense Freudian and existential novels are "temporal" works.

Time serves still another purpose for Nicomedes Guzmán. It is used to convey the impression that what is being narrated is real.

Duration of Composition

At the close of each of his novels, Guzmán details the time and location of its composition: "Santiago de Chile, primavera de 1937–otoño de 1938" (*Los hombres obscuros*, published July 1939); "Santiago (Chile), invierno 1940–invierno 1941" (*La sangre y la esperanza*, published December 1943); "Iquique-Santiago-Concepción–Punta Arenas, julio de 1948–enero de 1949" (*La luz viene del mar*, published August 1951).[2]

As he searched for a publisher, one or two years passed from the time his books were written until they were published. For *Los hombres obscuros* the search for a publisher required nine months;

1. Edwin Muir, *The Structure of the Novel* (New York: Harcourt, Brace and World, 1938), pp. 62–63.
2. The seasons given are for the Southern Hemisphere. Also, the orthography of the seasons and months has been standardized here, though Guzmán generally preferred to capitalize them.

then, because the printing press was so small and primitive, an additional six months were needed to print the novel.[3] Guzmán did some polishing of his works, but he seldom made any major changes; thus, once he had written a story, the only alterations he would allow— except for corrections of major structural or rhetorical errors—were the deletions of irrelevant paragraphs and a few word changes. His composition time of six months to a year is not very long, especially since he worked in various other capacities while he wrote.

Conceptual or Clock Time

Though it is often thought of as absolute, time itself is entirely relative; clock time is important primarily as a gauge for social obligations.

Only in his first novel does Guzmán attempt to establish a definite historical moment. This happens when he attaches the dates of May 7 and May 9, 193– (1933 in the rough draft) to the letters exchanged between Pablo and his father. These dates tend to make the novel into a sort of "chronicle," along with the present tense reportage.

The temporal span of the novel is not definite nor is it rhythmic; *Los hombres obscuros* describes the sporadic activity that takes place during seven or eight months. The narrative commences in the early Chilean spring (October, p. 63), when the mornings are brisk. As narrative time progresses, often irregularly, the seasons (not the months) advance. The narrator first metaphorically humanizes summer: "El verano distribuye su manifiesto en las mejillas tersas de las primeras cerezas" (97). Later the author's favorite season, autumn, is portrayed with a novel image:

> Silenciosamente el otoño regresa. Y tranqueando por las calles, se da a desgarrar los vestidos desteñidos de las acacias. Sobre las cosas cae como una llovizna de tristeza. Y los hombres del suburbio parece que se agobiaran bajo el peso de un inaudito cansancio. (*Hombres*, 187)

Finally the trees are naked and winter is approaching or has arrived (May). The novel's cyclical aspect, mentioned earlier, is supported by the revolving seasonal time, which completes a full cycle in the novel.

Clock time in certain parts of *Los hombres obscuros* is very noticeable because of the immediacy of the narrator's present-tense chronicle. The bells of the parish tell Pablo that it is Sunday morning

3. Oreste Plath, "Quién es quién en la literatura chilena: Nicomedes Guzmán," *La Nación* (Santiago), August 6, 1939.

or that it is suddenly nine o'clock at night, and then immediately ten. The landlady warns the guests at a birthday party to stop the noise and end the party, for it is twelve o'clock. Time is very proletarian, with traces of Futurism: "Las siete y media. La mañana se llena de gritos de fábricas" (137).

Mention should be made of the subchapter divisions in the novel, which often begin with an emphasis on the unaccounted-for time that has passed between paragraphs. For example, after Pablo meets Inés, time is mentioned repeatedly at the beginning of the following chapter like a stylized motif used to characterize Pablo's emotion:

> *Tres días han acontecido* desde que la encontrara. Ayer *al tiempo* le tocó remolienda y zandungueó por los tejados haciendo sonar sus claros zapatos de agua. Como siempre que el *tiempo* viene de fiesta, no trabajé . . .
> *Tres días han acontecido*. No la he vuelto a ver . . . (*Hombres*, 29; my italics)

Following temporal structure breaks like this one, the narrator of the novel often emphasizes time that had been severed in the narration: "Pasan dos días" (140); "Pasan quince días" (152); "Han acontecido tres largos días. Tres largos días como el tormento que me agarrota" (127). In this last shifting of time, Pablo has become emotionally involved with the slow passing of time, which is emphasized by the repetition of "tres largos días." The second clause is a sentence fragment; Guzmán employs these, on a limited scale, in order to add emphasis, to show emotion, or to depict time flying. For example, four fragments begin one of the chapter divisions: "Uno. Dos. Tres. Cuatro días. También ha muerto la madre de Robles" (200). Guzmán uses fragmentation sparingly throughout his writings not only to show emotion but also to indicate a change in rhythm.

In each human being and in each novel time has entirely different values. For example, time is a vague concept that is difficult to explain to a child. Yet Pablo arrives at a meaningful and concrete comparison: "En una semana han muerto siete personas en el conventillo" (190). A week is the amount of time it takes for typhus to exact its heavy toll of lives in the slums: seven deaths make a week.

Time stops in Pablo's mind when he is finally face to face with Inés. For the first time he is at her level and not shining her shoes. The moment before he kisses her, time is suspended (65). After they decide to stop seeing each other, their time is full of anguish; time itself is the cause of their torment. Once they decide to see each other again and agree to have sexual intercourse, time flies as it never did before. During those tormenting moments when Pablo is waiting for Inés, he discovers that time is a constant doing and undoing. It is so elongated, so eternalized, that it is virtually destroyed:

> Los días pasan. Y aunque mucho de nosotros va quedándose enredado entre sus pasos bien acompasados, todavía prevalecemos con la inquietud y el tormento a cuestas, a la expectativa de sensaciones y acontecimientos.
> Los días pasan. El hombre, en tanto, se dobla y se desdobla. Se trenza y se destrenza. Se integra y se desgarra.
> ¡He aquí la vida!
>
>   * * *
>
> ...La espera me desasosiega. El ánimo alterado me obliga a pasearme. Es como si los segundos se fueran quedando aplastados en mi ir y venir. Los momentos se me hacen infinitos. (Hombres, 155; my italics.)

It is at this point in the novel that the emotional Pablo begins the previously cited three-way dialogue with his conscience and his psyche. These three or four pairs of antitheses are exterior symbols of the anguished Pablo's interior psychological time; thus psychological time is opposed to clock time.

Time in La sangre y la esperanza is much more vague. First, the narrator has confessed that he is looking back in retrospect over some twenty years and remembering everything. The narrator also makes time vague on purpose; where Pablo's letters were dated, those of Elena are not.

Another example of this intentional destruction of time is Enrique's statement that in 1920, 1921, or 1922 he was eight years old. Certain of his age, for some reason Enrique is not sure of the year. The vagueness of time becomes a narrative motif:

> Era la vida. Era su rudeza. Y eran sus compensaciones.
> Y nosotros, los chiquillos de aquella época, éramos el tiempo en eterno juego, burlando esa vida que, de miserable, se hacía heroica. (Sangre, 15)

This main motif of time reappears at the close of Chapter 1: "Corría el año veinte. O el veintiuno. O el veintidós. Y era la vida. Y era su rudeza. Y eran sus alternativas." Actually these are two intertwined temporal leitmotifs: the repetition of the indefinite years (1920–

22) and the repetition of the phrase that opens the second paragraph of the novel: "Era la vida. . . ."

This is the only direct reference in the work to any specific year or to any calendar time (except for labor day, May 1). Seasons are the more obvious elements of time for a little boy to remember. The penetrating cold of the Chilean winter of Enrique's youth is vividly recalled even now that he is older. Like Pablo, Enrique also utilizes the seasons to stylize the slums:

> El otoño estaba a las puertas de aquel día con su rostro de mendigo enjuto y lánguido. Sus harapos tenían el color indefinido de las brumas. Pero en sus manos callosas brillaban las cálidas monedas de un sol desbordando en fuegos cordiales. (*Sangre*, 36)

Though the image of autumn as a beggar is unusual, the autumn days also weep rain, a more traditional image:

> Los días caían perezosos, con lágrimas de neblinas y de lluvias. El otoño se alzaba aún a la vera de la vida con el fatalismo doloroso de todos los abandonados. Y era como si en la voz de las campanas, precisa, para decir su palabra matutina, desperdigara a veces el otoño sus desamparados cantos de ciego sin lazarillo. (*Sangre*, 97)

Toward the end of the novel, the season of winter symbolizes the height of oppression, anguish, and disease:

> *Los días rodaron* con los ojos cerrados, famélicos, trágicos. La viruela y el tifus azotaban sin piedad *las horas de los hombres. El sol* andaba como un potro ciego, cabeceando contra los árboles y las murallas, perseguido obstinadamente por los tábanos de la bruma. (*Sangre*, 314; my italics)

Guzmán's favorite season, fall, is pictured as an old man. Winter is death itself. Spring, on the other hand, is a young woman and almost a symbol of biological time:

> La primavera, entonces, había llegado inútilmente para nosotros. Pero estaba, pero existía en las arterias de las horas, en la premura de los segundos, y era una briosa hembra para el galope gozoso del tiempo. (*Sangre*, 234)

Following this entrance of spring, the seasons fly for the reader. At the end of Part II it is spring (but Enrique is only four or five); as the narrator begins Part III, it is suddenly summer, but it is actually three or four years since the action on the previous page. The narrator has indicated no passage of time, except for mention of the season in passing: "El verano a nuestro alrededor llenaba el aire de calientes rumores. Las horas tostadas y terrosas piafaban a nuestro lado, como yeguas en celo" (238). Guzmán continues to give the impression that the time is fleeing, for after a few pages of Part III, the summer has rapidly passed, and autumn calls again at the doors of the city (258).

Since the narrator claims to be far removed from the time of the action of the novel, he usually refers only to the more general concepts of time, especially those that a child might understand: the seasons, morning, afternoon, sunset, dusk, night. Time is often vague—"esos días"—yet four-year-old Enrique is somehow able to recall that "two days went by" without his seeing Leontina (*Sangre*, 226). If the author is visible behind Enrique, it is when he refers to the four seasons:

> Rodaba el otoño. Y rodaban los días, al borde de mi infancia.
> El clima, trágico, rojo, sangriento, el clima con vísceras colgando . . . pesó dura y negramente en los estadios breves de mi corazón. (*Sangre*, 277)

Time "rolls" by also in another metaphor (actually an estampa), where time is compared to a vendor's cart: "Los días pasaban como carretas cargadas de pesadumbre, crujiendo, quejándose sordamente por las calles del barrio" (*Sangre*, 33). An exact historical moment is specified only once in the novel, at the beginning of Chapter 5, "May Day," the day of the Chicago Martyrs:

> En esa madrugada no sonó la sirena del depósito tranviario. *Eran ya las ocho.* Y el silencio parecía haberse constituido soberano del día. Era la fiesta del trabajo. Y había "paro general." Apenas sonaron un rato las campanas de Andacollo. (*Sangre*, 76)

The bells, or lack of them, the work stoppage, the ideology all indicate that this is May 1. But is it 1920, 1921, or 1922? In its preciseness, the description is also vague—it is *any* year, a typical proletarian holiday—and the occasion is vivid in Enrique's memory. Such a holiday alters the normal rhythm of a child's life.

When he first becomes aware of time, the four-year-old Enrique sees it stop or hide: "La guagua dormía. El tiempo creo que se ocultaba bajo los catres como un ladrón arrepentido." Later, the days fall: "Varios días cayeron como pesadas piedras, trizando las turbias pozas del tiempo." Toward the end of the novel, however, as Enrique matures, time becomes more meaningful to him with all its impending psychological and moral implications: "Y sentía que el tiempo era un potro infernal pateando todos mis segundos" (283). This chapter, "Fantasmas," is filled with psychological phantoms that surge from the unconscious of the sexually inexperienced narrator:

> Los fantasmas, arrastrando en el aire sus más oscuras balas, emergieron al borde del *tiempo,* moviendo sus sigilosas patas de extrañas serpientes.
> ¿A la luz de cuántos días uno termina por encontrarse a sí mismo? A la luz de ningún día. (*Sangre,* 286)

Here the author emerges rather obviously from behind his little-boy protagonist. Time is also related to perception in Enrique. Exterior stimuli obstruct his concentration, so that his psyche becomes a vague eternity of confusion:

> Quería concentrarme en la realidad de todo. Pero, como desde el fin de los años, el aullido de los perros me aserraba el sentimiento. (*Sangre,* 287)

Even though Enrique ultimately arrives at some conclusion regarding time, it is always difficult to distinguish young Enrique's awareness of time from the mature concept that the older narrator might be imposing.

Although *La luz viene del mar* is dominated by space, time makes itself felt in different ways. The novel mentions no year, no seasons, and no dates, except for the historic December 21, 1907, when the Communist hero Emilio Recabarren organized a strike in Iquique that was extinguished at the Santa María school, where two thousand striking workers were massacred by soldiers (*Luz,* 192–203). This shocking past event was witnessed by some of the heroes of the novel when they were young men.

In his novel of the North, Guzmán attempts to show the seasons of the year as abstract, indefinite:

> La tierra, a su vez, que durante las cuatro estaciones no definidas sino por los rebenques del sol, los quejidos del frío y la humedad de las camanchacas, compartía como los borricos de la hermandad humana . . . Lo que las fuerzas telúricas acumularon por meses era absorbido por las presencias humanas. (*Luz,* 277–78)

In this novel Guzmán hopes to create an eternalized time; thus he avoids mention of clock time, which is also vague in the minds of the protagonists: "Cholakys había adquirido tal sentido del tiempo, que todo le era lejano y añejo en seguida de las más inmediatas experiencias" (*Luz*, 120).

The author "detains" time when Virginia goes swimming in the ocean and walking along the beach. Though the time that she spends at the water is brief, just a portion of an afternoon, Guzmán extends the scene through several chapters which are alternated in turn with other episodes, so that it appears to the reader that Virginia has made several trips to the beach. It is not until the end of the novel, when Virginia explains to her mother that she is going again to the beach and recalls in her own mind actions of the previous day, that it suddenly becomes apparent that the narrative time in the novel (not including flashbacks and the historical episodes) has been only twenty-four hours (*Luz*, 324).

Time in *La luz viene del mar* is psychological:

> —Bien, Rolando, pase, que se está mojando ahí . . . —dispuso Sofía después de pensar por horas en breves segundos. (*Luz*, 74)

In the mature works time also becomes physiological, much as the seasons were in his city novels: "El tiempo forjaba *anillos de acero* indestructible en el alma y en las *células* de Eudocio." The unusual image of concentric circles of steel emphasizes the angurrientista image of concentric time, tying Guzmán to his generation in one more way. Also unusual is the emphasis on "células," a new word in Guzmán's novels which becomes a symbol in his mature works (see p. 262) and is used freely in "Los trece meses del año," his unfinished novel.

In the North, the traditional values of time are unimportant. For example, time in the North is measured in sex endurance—the amount of time a man can endure without a woman, or two days of constant orgy (*Luz*, 228). The city of Iquique is an island or an oasis; the laborer who is away from the city, whether on the sea or in the mines and desert, has to withstand exile from women.

Where women do exist, in the city brothels, time is entirely inverted—day is night and night is day:

> La media noche era un día meridiano en la casa de La Siete Dedos. Un día invadido de luz y de música, aposentado en medio del salón. (*Luz*, 242)

Time seems actually to stand still in the North—just like the noonday sun, which seems to pause at its zenith. Time offers no progress or development in a decadent society. Even man does not change. Guzmán attempts to depict all of his northern men as static, seemingly parallel beings (except for the visiting labor hero, Ceferino López, and El Pirata Cholakys, the Greek sailor).

The most individual among the many similar men is the "romantic thinker," Lorenzo Carmona. He is nicknamed "La Reliquia de la Huella" in reference to his ancient pickup truck, which allows him the freedom and the means always to be on the go, to transport people and things, to share in his passengers' thoughts, and to enjoy a constant escape from the sands of the ocean. At times Carmona's "escape" is ironic, for it is only from the sands of the beach to the sands of the desert; or it is only an escape in his own mind, or an intent probe into the thoughts of those he is carrying in his ancient truck. His characterization is one of the briefest in the novel (only two chapters—"Un corazón soñador detenido en el tiempo"). Yet Carmona appears in many scenes, since he is the link between several flashbacks and the present (Virginia's birth, El Huacho Fieroga's past, and the abduction and near massacre of a group of laborers). He connects the characters and themes of the novel. Because his mind is always involved with time, his consciousness is important in the narration, although the novel is not told from his point of view:

> Pero él era el mismo, *como el tiempo*, siempre un corazón soñador detenido en el tiempo.
> Alguna vez distante—y esto se le venía al recuerdo al pasar junto a la caseta que rememoraba la presencia en espíritu de un buen camarada asesinado por luchas comunes—. . . se durmió y soñó con la "Pampa del Tamarugal." (*Luz*, 92–93)

The North changes one's perspectives. Time, even remote time, is interpreted by the narrator, by Carmona, and by other characters in terms of space: "El tiempo revuelto y el tiempo apasible, la vida misma se historiaban en maderas y campanas" (*Luz*, 58).

Guzmán suspends time; he also symbolically traps time in a bottle. Virginia receives two bottles, each of which contains both temporal and emotional memorabilia in an unchanging state. Ester Panay still has the two bottles that inspired this motif. One is an ancient bottle of sand patterned in beautiful swirls of colors, an artisan craft of the old North of Chile. The other is a bottle with an old frigate inside, an heirloom from her Greek progenitors. Like its real-life model, the first bottle Virginia receives is filled with silicate. She had asked Carmona to bring it to her from Eudocio, her boyfriend, in exchange for one she was sending to him through Carmona, containing sand from the beach. She keeps Eudocio's bottle of nitrate for a while even though it had been filled by Carmona and not by Eudocio as she had requested. Later she rejects it entirely as a symbol of Eudocio (and the desert), because he had not been faithful to her. Virginia discards the sand as easily as she discards Eudocio, but he leaves a scar on her soul. Then she replaces the bottle of sand with the ship in a bottle presented to her by her Greek grandfather.

At the end of the novel time and space are fused in metaphors and symbols:

> El tiempo trastrocado en sal y yodo regresado a los orígenes de la sangre y de la savia. . .
> Es decir, Virginia, como en pesadillas superpuestas, como en sueños de espinosos orígenes, arrancando al árbol la sabiduria que le dio la tierra y que maduró el mar . . . (*Luz*, 310)

By juxtaposing the North and the beginning of time, Guzmán accomplishes a fusion of the desert, the ocean, and time.

Paradoxically, Guzmán usually treats time metaphorically, not "realistically," even though we associate him with socialist realism. He hopes that by stylizing time he can make it a permanent reality, a more meaningful part of his prose:

> El tiempo pone en juego sus recios músculos. Las horas se alucinan en la esperanza del triunfo. (*Hombres*, 141)

> Afuera . . . la calle parecía más ancha. El sol pateaba los ámbitos, desencadenando su instinto de espeso oro. No había otoño en aquel momento. . . . El mediodía lucía el pecho robustamente azul de un cielo puro, sin nubes, sin brumas. (*Sangre*, 324)

> Sobre el tiempo la luz pasa como una ráfaga en renovada y eterna permanencia. No valen las sombras. Todo se hace epidermis desnuda al contacto de la luz. (*Luz*, 273)

As Guzmán's narrative abilities evolved, his presentation of time and space became more stylized, and time became increasingly important in his expression.

Space

Guzmán placed a major emphasis on space, but this element re-
quires no detailed analysis. *Los hombres obscuros* never leaves the
conventillo except for the amorous episode at the hotel. The author
is intent on portraying the slums—beautiful to him in spite of
their misery—through the eyes of Pablo, a stranger to the area.

La sangre y la esperanza offers a more complete vision of Guzmán's microcosm, the Santiago suburbs: schools, shacks, slums,
streets, stores; sidewalks, stairways, and stairwells; saloons and
stews. Seldom does culture appear in this setting. The proletarian
reality is one of work—no parks or pleasure. Only on May Day
or payday does the worker get to rest or socialize, or to know
his neighborhood as something other than oppression.

In the second part of the novel, Enrique becomes awesomely
aware of space the first time he leaves the protection of the conventillo with his mother to go to his father's hospital in the city.

La luz viene del mar was Guzmán's most ambitious attempt to
portray space as a Chilean reality. It shows a world of dusty roads
and deserts; beaches, boats, and docks; Virginia's humble home in
the northern slums; and the decadent society in the business district of Iquique and in the houses of prostitution. Although in this
desolate region the men are inexorably drawn toward the city,
they desire to flee once they have arrived. Some seek to return to
the sea, others to the hills, where they are exploited along with
the minerals of that region. Virginia, the embodiment of a feminine
mystique in this rude masculine world, often escapes to the beach
or to her bell tower.

John P. Dyson states that "time and space in Guzmán's short
stories are indefinite." This, he feels, gives his stories more uni-
versality, for the city of their setting remains unnamed.[4]

Because of the limited perspective of the narrator, space in the
earlier novels was limited to the actual location occupied by the
protagonists at the moment of action, usually the conventillo. The
spatial context of the short stories is also traditional and limited.
In all of Guzmán's fiction, however, space is viewed with a poetic
eye, as in the estampa. The author's poetic attitude toward the en-

4. John P. Dyson, "Los cuentos de Nicomedes Guzmán," *Atenea*, 404
(1964), 247.

vironment becomes increasingly more intense until it reaches its climax in *La luz viene del mar*. Not only is the structure of this novel spatial (thus depicting defects of society), but the entire focus of the novel is on the natural environment.

The estampa in each episode of Guzmán's fiction establishes the tone and fuses time and space. Indeed, the estampa stops time and motion, and it stylizes space. At the beginning of a chapter or episode it sets the scene and makes the reader anxious for the action that follows. At the conclusion of the chapter, it causes us to inspect the original motion and to try to discern its pattern. Thus in a way the estampa becomes the controlling metaphor of Guzmán's work and its influence pervades the poetic prose of the entire generation.

Guzmán's elaborate metaphorical language is not a means of avoiding the realities of time and space; rather the author is placing himself within the cold, destructive reality of misery. By using poetic imagery, he is attempting a dialectic transformation of that valuable but abominable world. This attempt to communicate proletarian space and time leads toward a paradoxical climax: Guzmán's language will destroy his world at the same time that it exalts it. Thus his manner of expression, albeit baroque, is not evasive; rather it is a magical device that will exorcise the evils of illegitimacy, poverty, and death and raise the writer's environment into the realm of dignity.

12

The Proletarian Hero
Characterization and Social Conflict

Characterization is a major problem for all authors, but especially the proletarian writer. Classical authors were able to create monumental heroes out of familiar gods and kings. Even bourgeois novels have made the proletarian into a hero of sorts. But how does a proletarian novelist in a capitalist country create a collective hero without either compromising artistic merit or violating the goals of his ideology? And how can that particular work, once published, reach and appeal to a majority of the people, especially if propagandizing is the main goal? There are no simple answers to these questions, which have been of great concern to leftists everywhere.

The ordinary reader demands that the author label his characters as good or bad and that he make these qualities easily identifiable. In revolutionary literature, the establishment becomes the antagonist. Traditional values are inverted, and the reader finds that the corner policeman is usually the bad man. This may be unconvincing unless his characterization is masterfully accomplished. Also, if the proletarian hero fights for goals that are not easily understandable or agreeable (in spite of the fact that they may be collective), he will not be attractive to the average reader, who usually dislikes the excess propaganda present in most radical literature. Thus, unless the socrealist artist is cautious, the popularity of his book will be minimal.

It has been repeated here that Guzmán's constant endeavor was to create "objective literature." In such writing, the reader's opinion of a character will be based largely on the speech and action of the personage: "A story will be successful only when the characters are dramatized—shown speaking and acting as in a drama. If we are really to believe in the selfishness of a character, we must see him acting selfishly."[1] In this way the reader can draw his own conclusions as to the consistency and plausibility of the character.

Nicomedes Guzmán seems to have solved successfully many of the major problems of creating a collective hero in his first two

1. Laurence Perrine, *Literature: Structure, Sound and Sense* (New York: Harcourt, Brace and World, 1970), p. 68.

novels by working with a first-person narrator; in his last novel, *La luz viene del mar*, he tried to expand his concepts and experiment with new techniques. Hope for a better life for the obscure proletarian is made universal and eternal by the author's extraordinary ability to create characters who have overcome pessimism. These characters, who have noble souls but workingmen's goals, are contrasted to the stoic, apathetic Chileans, who have resigned themselves to social and economic oppression.

Since in the fiction of Guzmán characterization and motivation are intensified by social conflict, an attempt will be made in this chapter to interpret the interrelationship of these elements.

First-Person Narrator-Protagonist

The role of the narrator was examined at some length in Chapter 10; however, because the first-person narrator is also a character, he must be studied from the standpoint of characterization. In this chapter the delineation of the protagonists will be examined as well as their evolution from their literary antecedents.

As we have said before, Nicomedes Guzmán's preference for a "realistic" protagonist in his earlier novels grew out of his desire to choose a character whom the reading public would accept and approve. He was a young man when he wrote *Los hombres obscuros*; therefore, it is natural that he should have chosen a young hero. Pablo—a humble type characterized like the other shoeshine boys in Guzmán's later works "Perro ciego," Animita," "El pan bajo la bota," and "Los trece meses del año"—is an apathetic protagonist, created as an underdog or *hombre obscuro*. He has been pushed around most of his life, but after seeking his fortune in the North without success and living in an *albergue* (one of the welfare tenements set up in Santiago for the unemployed by churches and the government), he finally discovers his ideal element in the proletarian environment of Santiago's slums. Because of his growth and his newly established ideals, his development is convincing and acceptable to the reader.

Guzmán had learned much from his experience with *Los hombres obscuros*, so in *La sangre y la esperanza* he turned from the limited "blow-by-blow" narration to fictionalized autobiography, which provided room for more action. The young novelist had also discovered that a younger and less prejudiced protagonist than Pablo would be even more credible to the reader. Like Mike Gold, who observed his nephew, Guzmán had live models to work with in his brothers and his children. The lives of these children and the additional use of literary models (Gorky, Gold, Fink, and others examined in this chapter) led to the creation of Guzmán's greatest figure, the child narrator, Enrique.

The child as protagonist-narrator of the modern novel has its origin in the Spanish picaresque novel, commencing with *Lazarillo de Tormes*. The narrator of the *Lazarillo* obtains the sympathy of the reader through a point of view similar to that of Enrique. Nicomedes was aware that *Lazarillo* depicted a decadent society, and he produces a similar panorama of Chilean corruptions. Although his works differ from the anonymous sixteenth-century masterpiece in intensity and irony, Guzmán's technique and purpose are similar to those of the author of *Lazarillo*. The reader will almost invariably side with an innocent boy-narrator.

The first-person child-narrator has been unusually popular in proletarian literature. Edward Dahlberg's *Bottom Dogs* and Michael Gold's *Jews Without Money* (which surprisingly sold eleven printings its first year), both first-person novels about chidren, are among the American proletarian novels that Guzmán knew well through Ercilla translations. Michael Gold, who lived several years in Spanish America evading the 1917–18 draft, and D. H. Lawrence, who wrote *The Feathered Serpent* in Mexico, were well known and popular, but the most widely translated and best-known novelist in Latin America was Waldo Frank, president of the League of American Writers and a Marxist darling of the Hispanic world because of his wide travels in Latin America and his extremely perceptive essays on Hispanic and American cultures.

Another proletarian-child novel that Guzmán read and used is Georg Fink's *Mich Hungert*, the immensely popular pseudo-autobiography of a little boy growing up in Berlin during World War I. Guzmán was indebted to this work for structure and ideas, but he created a more polished and artistic novel than Fink's or Gold's.

An influential earlier work of this type is Maxim Gorky's *Childhood* (1913). Though this book is a true autobiography, it was imitated by novelists like Fink, Gold, and Guzmán. In *Childhood*, the protagonist first becomes aware of reality at his father's death when he is four years old. Fink, Gold, Sepúlveda Leyton, and Guzmán pinpointed their heroes' first awareness of poignant but shocking reality (hunger or beatings) at the age of four.

Nevertheless, it should be pointed out that one Chilean reviewer criticized the first-person point of view of *La sangre y la esperanza* as not being "correct" in Chile.[2] For this reason I have stressed the innovative success of Guzmán's autobiographical novel of the slums.

Child-Protagonist Antecedents

Novels and short stories in which children are major characters have had little success in Spanish America; there have been few best-selling childhood novels in either the first or the third person. Even the patriarch of the genre, Mexican picaresque fiction, has produced few novels of this kind in 150 years (Pito Pérez is more adolescent than child). But in Chilean literature the genre has become something of a tradition. Significant innovations in the picaresque genre in Spanish America have been made by Manuel Rojas and Eduardo Barrios, according to Fernando Alegría.[3] Guzmán was impressed by Barrios's psychological technique, and he may have been influenced by Barrios's first-person point of view, common to most of his earlier works, and his central focus through a child, especially in *El niño que enloqueció de amor*.

A child-protagonist novel which may have indirectly influenced Guzmán is Pedro Prado's *Alsino*, a variation on the theme of Icarus. Alsino begins as a peasant boy who develops a humpback when he falls while attempting to soar out of a tree.

There are some minor similarities between Alsino and Enrique. Both are from poor families, but Alsino and his brother were abandoned by unloving and unconcerned parents. They are improperly cared for by their grandmother, who has to work as well as look after the boys. She cannot supervise them as a guardian should, and it is during their unsupervised play that they attempt to fly and twice fall to the ground instead of gliding away. In the second fall

2. Luis Meléndez, "*La sangre y la esperanza*, Novela de Nicomedes Guzmán," *El Mercurio* (Santiago), February 23, 1944.

3. Fernando Alegría, *Historia de la novela hispanoamericana* (Mexico City: Ediciones de Andrea, 1965), pp. 19–20.

Alsino injures his back so seriously that he becomes hunchbacked. Wings later emerge from his hump, bestowing on Alsino the power of flight that all men desire.

Enrique Quilodrán is much less idealistic than Alsino, but at an early age he also seeks his independence; like Pedro Prado's protagonist, he is a potential vagabond before his final commitment to work (see *Sangre*, 171–72). Parental discipline and example keep Enrique from erring; he chooses to emulate his father and become a laborer.

The first Chilean critical interpretations of the *modernista* (ivory-tower) novel *Alsino* were somewhat myopic; the novel was initially classified as a social work (in articles in *Atenea* and later by Arriagada and Goldsack).[4] But the social theme in *Alsino* is overshadowed by that of transcendence, a desire to rise above the banality of earthly existence. Since Nicomedes Guzmán preferred social literature, he considered *Un juez rural*, not *Alsino*, to be Prado's "most realist work with naturalist workmanship." Nevertheless he admired *Alsino* and called it "un poema novelesco de elevada imaginación, pero de un simbolismo maravilloso y ejemplar" ("Miniatura," 25). Apparently Guzmán did not feel that the exotic theme was an excessively exaggerated element in *Alsino*; moreover, eroticism, so important to twentieth-century Latin American literature, is another element in *Alsino* that Guzmán always referred to as "realism."

Tradition has it that Prado developed the plot of *Alsino* while telling bedside stories to his children about a hunchback who frequently passed their house. But *Alsino* transcends the simple fable, and it is not allegory or didacticism.

One of the novel's greatest attributes is its sensitivity in dealing with the subject matter of children. Here is where Prado and Guzmán are kindred spirits, for they share this sensitivity.

More influential on Guzmán is Joaquín Edwards Bello's *El roto* (1920; definitive edition 1927; evolved from a preliminary work, *La cuna de Esmeraldo*, 1918). It is the first Chilean novel to focus on a child protagonist in an impoverished or degenerate surrounding. Even though the novel takes place in the slums, the environment is not truly proletarian, for the setting is a house of prostitution and the characters are from the *Lumpenproletariat*. Also,

4. Alegría, *Historia*, p. 138.

Esmeraldo, the protagonist, is only a "roto in embryo." More important for Guzmán, though, was Esmeraldo's role as a delinquent in a drama of poverty:

> Como análisis de un ambiente, *El roto* es ya una novela definitiva en Chile. Su crudeza es el trasunto de una realidad amarga y muy chilena. Desde el punto de vista psicológico, el tipo que nos ofrece Edwards Bello no es propiamente el *roto*. Lejos de esto, es un retrato profundo del delincuente. *El roto*, más que por su personaje fundamental, vale por su fondo, por el escenario que nos expone a los ojos y al sentimiento, por el espectáculo de lacerante miseria que nos denuncia. Es una especie de advertencia en que nuestros novelistas insisten, luego en variada forma. ("Miniatura," 25)

El roto instituted a new genre in Chile, the story of the boy of the slums, the *palomilla* novel.

The last of the four Chilean novels with children as protagonists is a first-person palomilla novel, *Hijuna* (1934) by Carlos Sepúlveda Leyton. *Hijuna* affected Guzman's first novels more directly than did any of the other Chilean works; it especially influenced *La sangre y la esperanza*. There were many connections between Guzmán and Sepúlveda Leyton. Arnold Chapman points out their close ties: ". . . Hay semejanzas genéricas. Cada una recalca la pureza de animal joven el cabro; trata con amor los juegos de los muchachos; y sobre todo elogia la fortaleza anímica de los buenos."[5]

Many similarities are apparent in the writings of the two novelists. First, Guzmán was inspired by the conventillo setting of *Hijuna*. Several critics have mentioned this influence but have stressed only the criollista theme that Guzmán discovered in the conventillo literature of Alberto Romero, Manuel Rojas, González Vera, and others, as well as in the fiction of Sepúlveda Leyton. Second, Guzmán was so attracted by Sepúlveda's *Hijuna* that he included a dog, like Ñato, Hijuna's symbolic pet—his "brother"—in the manuscript novel "Un hombre, unos ojos negros y una perra lanuda." The dog would personify the anguish of the proletarian existence in the slums, reaching out of some dark alley, biting when one least expects it: "¡Ah, Vida, eres como la perra lanuda que vaga por el lado del mercado! Ahora, me estás mordiendo, mordiendo . . . Y yo te dejo. ¡Ya me lamerás! . . ." (18). Third, Guzmán's

5. [George] Arnold Chapman, "Perspectiva de la novela de la ciudad en Chile," in Arturo Torres-Ríoseco, ed., *La novela iberoamericana* (Albuquerque: University of New Mexico Press, 1952), p. 200.

innovation, the estampa, seems to be inspired by Sepúlveda's ecstatic vision of the conventillo, his own "picture postcard." Fourth, a girl, Lucía (also called Lucy) a symbolic, ideal little girl grows up with Hijuna. He observes her, prim and spotless, dressed in a beautiful white pinafore. She becomes a proletarian princess in the stories the school teacher, Sr. Arriaza, tells Hijuna's school class (suggesting the Cinderella motif Guzmán would use later), and her music and personality lift others around her psychologically out of the slums and make her father's business successful. Hijuna converts her in his dreams into a mother image since he is an orphan. Because this heroine bore the same name as Lucía (Lucy) Vásquez, Guzmán identified in one more way with Sepúlveda's novel when he was courting his wife and writing his first proletarian novel. A fifth prominent influence of *Hijuna* on Guzmán is its concern with the oppressive, deterministic environment of the slums. The child-heroes of both novelists must choose between good and evil, even though both are surrounded only by social evils.

Guzmán admired Sepúlveda because he was one of the first writers to "venture to portray Chilean reality" through harsh or obscene language, as is shown in the title *Hijuna*. His use of vulgarities undoubtedly encouraged Guzmán to include similar elements in his socrealist novels in order to portray the harsh milieu of the slums. He also saw in Sepúlveda's works a prose style he hoped to emulate: "Es un poeta de la prosa, un narrador preciso, pintoresco y a la vez crudo" ("Miniatura," 27).

Finally, Guzmán felt that the use of the child in literature helped to portray a "heroic life":

> Es toda la obra como un trozo de Chile. . . . Y es que Sepúlveda Leyton, profesor y padre de muchos hijos en Linares, al incorporar su nombre a nuestras letras incorporó, también, *la verdad de su heroica vida de chiquillo chileno* junto con la existencia de un mundo real.[6]

Sepúlveda Leyton, a teacher, was president of the teachers' union, the Asociación Nacional de Profesores de Chile. He was jailed and dismissed from his teaching position because of his political activities, though he was more a revolutionary in temperament than in doctrine. As a primitive novelist, Sepúlveda worked with many innovative techniques. Guzmán felt *Hijuna* was "the first authentic novel of the Chilean people":

6. Nicomedes Guzmán, "Carlos Sepúlveda Leyton, novelista del pueblo," *Atenea*, 189 (March 1941), 357.

Pasan por ella chiquillos, obreros, lavanderas, viejos rateros, vagabundos, prostitutas, guardianes y hasta corredores pedestres dando
vueltas a la elipse del Parque Cousiño. El extramuro sur de Santiago se
encuentra *alegremente, tristemente, chilenamente* logrado a plumazos
breves y precisos, de nerviosa significación.[7]

Had he not wanted to place strong emphasis on the three adverbs
I have italicized, Guzmán would have written "alegre, triste, chilenamente" (this last adverb draws attention because it is unusual).
These three adverbs summarize Guzmán's concept of literature and
socialist realism; they present a clue to his character development
as well as to the antithetical realist structure of his novels. He ar-
ranges the three elements, "happy, sad, Chilean," as the thesis,
antithesis, and synthesis of dialectic materialism: the Chilean proletarian faces misery on one side and joy on the other. A nationally
imposed fatalism forces him to partake of both. In short, Guzmán
foreshadowed in his 1941 *Atenea* article on Sepúlveda Leyton the
key to the structure and characterization of *La sangre y la esperanza*:
to be happy, partaking of brief moments of satisfaction, and to be
sad, forced to participate in the bitter, was to be Chilean and proletarian. As a mathematical formula it would read: *alegría + tristeza
= lo chileno*, or *sangre + esperanza = lo chileno*. The aristocrat
or bourgeois is not truly Chilean, for he does not know real sadness
and therefore cannot experience true happiness. The proletarian
child, who learns to experience both happiness and sadness and who
is represented by the novelist's heroic creation, is the only person
who can become a true Chilean. This formula also contains the
essence of Guzmán's realism.

The author recalls nostalgic memories whenever a proletarian
childhood is transposed to fiction:

Se goza con la novela de Sepúlveda admirando la jocunda libertad de
la infancia que en ella vive. Hay honda y ubérrima emoción en las
páginas dedicadas al juego del volantín y a otros tantos juegos.[8]

In a later passage of his article, when mentioning Sepúlveda's third
novel of the cycle, *Camarada*, Guzmán insists that the child is the
true (and most valuable) witness to social atrocities:

... La infancia chilena, descalza y haraposa, parece levantarse sin
llantos, fríamente, estoicamente, desde su hambre para crucificar a

---

7. Guzmán, "Sepúlveda Leyton," p. 358.
8. Guzmán, "Sepúlveda Leyton," p. 359.

toda una sociedad en su dolor. . . . Hay escenas de sangrante patetismo, como aquella de los chicos hambrientos que corren bajo la lluvia tras el perro que huye llevando en el hocico un trozo de pan.[9]

Guzmán clarifies his own works for a future reading public through his interpretations of the cyclical novels of Sepúlveda Leyton, whom he compares with admiration to the "cruel and formidable Russian writer, Nevierov, author of 'La ciudad de la abundancia.' "

As stated earlier in this chapter, another Russian who inspired Guzmán, and apparently Sepúlveda Leyton as well, was Maxim Gorky, the narrator awakened to reality in *Childhood* at four years of age through the death of his father. "Teddy" (Theodore), the narrator of Fink's *Mich Hungert*, is also four years old at the time of his first awakening to reality; he says, "I'm hungry," as he begs for drinking money for his father. Mikey, the narrator of *Jews Without Money*, awakens to life on the day before his fifth birthday through a hard spanking; Guzmán's Enrique has beatings when he is about four, but he is awakened to brutal reality more through hunger. Sepúlveda Leyton's narrator, Juan de Dios, explains at a similar age that his "good mother" (actually a stepmother) made him laugh because of her gestures when she spanked him. At the close of that same first chapter of *Hijuna*, his mother promises to save him the anguish and pain of an unfair whipping if he will just yell out as if he were being beaten. Hijuna does not understand as she flails the bed telling him under her breath to scream, so his mother becomes frustrated and begins to thump the boy with the stick, in the most humorous spanking scene of these child-hero novels.

La sangre y la esperanza differs, of course, from these novels in its concentric structure, used to de-emphasize time. In the above-mentioned novels, the boys awaken to life's reality at four years of age, and the rest of their development is traced chronologically.

Several other novels with child-heroes exerted some influence on Guzmán. The autobiographical novels of González Vera have not been mentioned here, because in *Vidas mínimas* the protagonist is an adolescent like Pablo in *Los hombres obscuros*. And though González Vera's *Alhué* contains reminiscences about the narrator's life as a child, it is a different type of literature, basically criollista. Also, it is doubtful that Guzmán read *Alhué*, since he does not refer

9. Guzmán, "Sepúlveda Leyton," p. 360.

to it in his comprehensive "Miniatura histórico-informativa de las letras chilenas."

Although Guzmán stated that the novel *Palomilla brava* (1923), by Víctor Domingo Silva, was an attempt to "interpret the Chilean roto," this novel seems to be outside the genre, too much a Horatio Alger (bourgeois) success story. Alberto Romero inspired Guzmán more than did Silva: ". . . Se adentra en los más trascendentales problemas del pueblo y expone su angustia con una sensibilidad que es la del propio hombre popular" ("Miniatura," 25). And Romero's second novel, *La mala estrella de Perucho González* (1937), includes many motifs that also appear in *La sangre y la esperanza.*

Guzmán referred to all of these authors—Barrios, Prado, Edwards Bello, Sepúlveda Leyton, González Vera, Silva, and Romero—as social novelists, and he grouped them in two basic tendencies or schools: "otros novelistas sociales" (about 1920) and "reafirmación de nuestra novela social" (about 1930) ("Miniatura," 25, 27).

My attempt here has not been to give a detailed analysis of Guzmán's sources, but rather to show that a Chilean tradition was just beginning in the twenty-year period of the young writer's childhood. First, the child appeared in the novel as a protagonist; soon afterward, the main figure was a boy—a palomilla—in the Santiago slums. This tradition will serve as a basis for further elucidation of Guzmán's child protagonists.

The Child Protagonist in Guzmán's Fiction

Guzmán's novels were the culmination of the new genre, for he artistically portrayed his child protagonists in credible stories:

> Tocante a la autenticidad de lo vivido, la súbita explosión del pasado inmediato recordado en los ojos de un niño pobre, donde la realidad supera toda ficción intencionada y demostrativa, Nicomedes Guzmán ha superado a todos sus antecesores llevando el género a la perfección y creando sus mejores reglamentos . . . Y del libro fluye una vida sin reparos, como una respiración necesaria y trágica.[10]

Enrique's narrative is entirely candid; he exposes his own weaknesses rather than disguise them as a traditional autobiographical narrator might attempt to do in an effort to make himself look better. The following passage from the novel exemplifies Enrique's

10. Fernando Uriarte, "*La sangre y la esperanza* (Orbe), por Nicomedes Guzmán," *Atenea*, 223 (June 1944), 91.

honesty and his way of making metaphors of his sensations. He feels lowered to the animal level after Antonieta attempts to seduce him in the toilet:

> Y salí como un diminuto bruto, olisqueando en las sombras, lo mismo que un perro ciego. Me sentí tan pobre cosa ... tan pisoteado escarabajo, que hubiera arrancado al límite del infinito a golpearme el desgraciado corazón contra el semblante de un lucero calcinado. (*Sangre*, 286)

The reader is left with little doubt about Enrique's final development, since he ultimately chooses to go to work to support his family.

> En *La sangre y la esperanza*, el pequeño héroe quedó como en el remanso de la abnegación cuando entregó los pequeños dineros ganados a su madre. Esta es la rúbrica de aquella *porción de cuadros*, como quiera llamársela.[11]

Guzmán's lack of emphasis on characterization can be seen in this quotation, for he considered his novels to be a collection of *cuadros*, or episodes. In general, socialist narrations are flawed in viewing all fictional characters as average; thus major roles go to flat, stereotyped characters since characterization is not considered important.

In later works—"El pan bajo la bota" or the three published chapters of "Los trece meses del año"—Enrique is not so clearly developed. Undoubtedly part of this lack of characterization is due to the brevity of the episodes; in addition, "El pan bajo la bota" is too thematic, too much of an attempt by the author to show an incident of injustice, and thus does not allow full character development.

Guzmán said little about his plans for Enrique's characterization in "Los trece meses del año," except that through some sort of inversion Enrique would become the exemplar for his father, who had been his ideal in *La sangre y la esperanza*. The author also hoped to create in Enrique a religious crisis which would involve him in a deep personal conflict:

> Laura, la madre, se dice católica. Pero es una católica al estilo de la mayoría de los católicos de Chile, y seguramente de América. Se persigna cuando lo cree conveniente, pero no va a misa.
>
> Sin embargo, sus hijos han hecho la primera comunión, al igual que fueron bautizados, y al igual que fueron al catecismo. Y por aquí

11. Nicomedes Guzmán, "Plan de una novela: *Los trece meses del año*," *Cultura*, 96 (1964), 50–51. Further references to the "Plan" will be in the text.

anda la quiebra de la fe de Enrique Quilodrán, pequeño pero avizor.

En el plano retrospectivo de la novela se proyectan varias circunstancias dentro de una atmófera [*sic*] de sensaciones, en que participan lo mismo el asunto religioso como la comprobación de las diferencias sociales. ("Plan," 50–51)

The writer, now older, admitted humbly that Enrique, his own creation synthesized from both Chilean and proletarian models, had become a prototype, a significant figure in Chilean literature: "Enrique Quilodrán . . . acaso represente a un prototipo infantil" ("Plan," 46). Guzmán realized the potential of the personage that he had created in his second novel; his mistake, perhaps, was in attempting to exploit Enrique further. Yet he wanted to expand his work to a three-volume cyclical novel, thus portraying the continued development of Enrique and creating an ongoing character, like Studs Lonigan.

Virginia in *La luz viene del mar* is the female counterpart of the novelist's youthful prototype, Enrique, except that she is not a narrator. She is the child protagonist at the threshold of adolescence. As her name implies, she is a virgin, but perhaps in a more spiritual than physical sense, for the narrator hints at sexual assaults on her:

> Todo esto era tan distinto a aquella vez, en tiempo ya casi lejano para su adolescencia,—¡qué pequeña estaba todavía[!]—en que otro muchacho la asaltó violentamente, allá, en "Santa Rosa de Huara." (*Luz*, 45)

> —¡Qué hiciste, Lucio!—exclamó Virginia, doloridos los muslos en que unas gotas de sangre seca recogían la piel y la pegaban a los calzones que le regalara Andrea. —¿Qué hiciste? . . .

* * *

> ¡Hice lo que tenía que hacer! . . . —exclamó Lucio, ceñudo, amurrado, casi fiero— ¡Si no te salvo, no habría pasado lo que pasó! . . . (*Luz*, 326–27)

Guzmán emphasizes the cyclical aspect of the novel by repeating Virginia's question, "¿Qué hiciste?" in each of these scenes. In the first, Eudocio finds her asleep on the beach and kisses her. She is startled and asks him what he has done; it also recalls to her a sexual attack she suffered as a little girl in the desert mining village. Later, she asks Lucio why he saved her from a suicidal drowning and why he raped her. The last dialogue is the key to Virginia's characterization, according to a one-page outline of Part III that I discovered among Guzmán's papers. It hinted of a central theme in the novel, leading to Virginia's entry to womanhood through her physical and emotional maturation, and her rape by Lucio was symbolic of her final sexual maturation. It is not clear in the outline that Virginia intended to die: "Virginia se va hacia su mar. Se desnuda y se lanza al agua." Lucio (as well as his mother), however, was evidently de-emphasized, for neither he nor his mother is developed as Guzmán originally proposed:

> Lucio que ha salido a bogar, desesperado por lo que le ha ocurrido a la Peta, su madre, con el chino Lam, la salva, pero deslumbrado por la desnuda belleza de la niña [Virginia], la desvirga en el bote.
>
> Virginia regresa a la casa desesperada. Le cuenta lo ocurrido a la madre. Llega Lucio a verla. Pero ella le deja, al atardecer, para refugiarse en la torre de su infancia.
>
> Aquí, junto a los sonidos sordos de las campanas, observa como el mar se levanta, y se arrodilla, arrepentido, de haber sido el cómplice de su conversión en mujer. Sobre el Alto de Molle se levanta una luna grandota y dorada en los momentos en que Virginia regresa a su casa.

Guzmán's last novel has been confusing to the critics, as they have been unaware of several facets of Virginia's complicated characterization. The model for Virginia was the author's second wife, Ester Panay, a capable short story writer herself, who related many stories to her husband about her childhood in the North. She accompanied him on his trip through northern Chile in 1948 and introduced him to many of the neighborhood haunts of her youth. One such place, which Ester used for escape, was the steeple of the San Gerardo Church in Iquique.

Virginia's greatest development takes place when she finally abandons her youthful romantic world—symbolized in her adolescent crush on Eudocio—and is forced to confront a world of reality. Part of this final maturing is shown in her rejection of the hypocrisy of the real world, which causes her to attempt suicide. Nevertheless, in the end she is forced to accept the deterministic world of the north. Unlike Pablo and Enrique, she is deprived of her free agency.

Virginia combines symbolically the two northern regional forces, the desert and the sea. She is the descendant of saltpeter miners and of seamen. The ocean and the nitrate plains both attract her; the desert sand in Eudocio's bottle, the beach sand in her bottle, and the ship in her grandfather's bottle all become synecdoches of the elements that make up her two personal climates. She observes both the desert and the sea from the steeple of the San Gerardo Church, which helps establish the Olympian point of view of the novel. As Virginia looks out over the city and the country, she creates her own world ("Virginia y su mundo"), a microcosm of the North, a synthesis of the sand and sea of Iquique.

Pablo, in *Los hombres obscuros*, is older than Virginia, so he is not a child; but neither is he really an adult. His self-characterization, like Enrique's, offers several difficulties, since a first-person narrator cannot portray himself objectively. He can adequately describe objects lying within his field of vision, but he cannot depict himself from the outside, although Pablo occasionally allows the reader to see him from other people's points of view. Yet we do see inside his mind, and, unlike many social characters, Pablo says little about his physical appearance. He analyzes his inner being rather systematically, but if he wants to give details of his physical attributes, "paint the external picture of himself, then he must look at himself in a mirror."[12] Since only one mirror is mentioned in the novel, much of our knowledge of Pablo's appearance and outward personality comes from the dialogue of other characters. Pablo could have some difficulty depicting his own objectivity, but he is so cautious a narrator that the reader retains the impression that his behavior has been objective. The fact that Pablo has a beard is revealed indirectly by Inés:

> —¡Me hacen daño tus barbas! . . . —dice alegremente.
> Las castigaremos . . . —digo, riendo y besándola. (*Hombres*, 169)

Pablo volunteers freely his various thoughts, sensations, and emotions in streams of consciousness; in addition, several psychological levels of narration compete with each other and more completely define Pablo's internal conflicts (as we saw in Chapter 10), as do the letters at the end of *Los hombres obscuros*.

In the short story "Una perra y algunos vagabundos," published in *La carne iluminada* (1945), a pregnant dog is the main protagonist that unites all the episodes of the story, but a group of children also appears. One, "La Guagua Rita" ("Baby Rita"), is poignantly characterized; she is a "tender" orphan, living in a world of promiscuity, where the children must flee the police to survive. In spite of her

---

12. Bertil Romberg, *Studies in the Narrative Technique of the First-Person Novel* (Stockholm: Almqvist and Wiksell, 1962), p. 59.

immature years, the tiny girl knows much about life. When the bitch, which has been abandoned like the children, begins to give birth to her pups, Rita announces with authority that the first female of the litter will be hers. Enough males are born for each of the boys to have one, but the only female, Rita's pup, dies as soon as it is born. At that moment of tragedy for Rita, the police interrupt the Christmas Eve birth scene, firing their weapons at the children as they escape; yet little Rita is oblivious to everything, even to her comrades' voices urging her to flee:

> —¡Rita, Rita!...
> Pero Rita no hacía sino sollozar, y su cuerpo se contraía como si también fuese a parir.
> —¡Rita, Rita!...
> Y ella, oyendo la voz, se mordía los dedillos de la diestra, cubierto entero el rostro mojado de lágrimas y por los cabellos sucios y abundantes.
>
> * * *
>
> ... Se decía que esa noche era Nochebuena y había nacido el Niño Dios, y por ello sonaban petardos y cornetas. (*Pan bajo la bota*, 152–53)

In his article "Los cuentos de Nicomedes Guzmán," John Dyson discusses style and other aspects of this story. A variation of Guzmán's theme of children at Christmas appears in "La ternura," from *Donde nace el alba*.

"Una perra y algunos vagabundos" was the first of several works that portrayed *el pelusa santiaguino*, the homeless waif living under the Mapocho River bridges. Such stories also pictured the plight of poor Chilean children who, unlike the richer ones, know no Christmas.

One of the first of these stories was Mariano Latorre's "Trapito sucio," about a poor little roto city girl at Christmas. In the words of the title, she is nothing more than a dirty rag.[13]

In addition to writing about children and adolescents himself, Guzmán attempted to inspire friends like Oscar Castro and Francisco Coloane to write novels about children.

> A menudo conversábamos sobre proyectos literarios. Me instaba a escribir una novela sobre Santiago cuyo bosquejo argumental y título

13. Benjamín Rojas Piña recently informed me that Mariano Latorre's "Trapito sucio" actually appeared in 1929 in some obscure literary periodical. However, when Latorre republished it in his anthology *Chile, país de rincones* (1946), it received much greater circulation.

se los había dado a conocer. Se llamaría "Mapocho Andino" y trataría sobre la vida de uno de los muchachitos que crecen junto al río. ¡Oiré a menudo su voz cordial preguntándome por el proyecto! Así era él. Se preocupaba de la obra ajena como de la propia.[14]

When Guzmán reintroduced the theme of the city child to Chilean literature, the time was ripe to develop it, and countless others have since written about poor and homeless children. One of the earliest such works was by Guzmán's close friend, the Argentine writer Bernardo Kordon, whose seldom-mentioned novel *Muerte en el valle* (1943), describes the pelusa vagrants living under the Mapocho bridges. Guzmán is a key figure in this popular genre. It is hoped that future studies—among them one that this writer has begun—will enumerate the many Chilean prose works with children as protagonists, including contemporary works by Jaime Valdivieso, others of the Generation of 1950, and younger writers.

The child-protagonist genre that begins with *La sangre y la esperanza* and "Una perra y algunos vagabundos" culminates in *Novela de Navidad* (1965), a *pelusa*-Christmas novel by Enrique Lafourcade. When I hinted in an interview with Lafourcade that "Una perra y algunos vagabundos" might have served as a source for his *Novela de Navidad*, he replied that the myth on which his novel is based originated in Dickens's *A Christmas Carol* (1843), with two other Dickens novels, *Oliver Twist* (1837–39) and *David Copperfield* (1849–50) as his secondary sources. Lafourcade insisted emphatically that he had not (and has not) read Guzmán's Christmas story. Lafourcade, however, is not entirely correct in asserting his ignorance of the novel, for he had chosen it for publication in his anthology of the Chilean short story. It cannot be proved but it is likely that Lafourcade read his good friend Guzmán's story with the same theme as his novel before *Novela de Navidad* was written.[15]

Russell Salmon refers to *Novela de Navidad* as the last in a long series of palomilla novels that begins with those studied in this chapter: *El roto, Palomilla brava, La mala estrella de Perucho González,* and *Hijuna,* the best one. Salmon studies the palomilla as a child roto who is still undeveloped, but is in his formative years.

14. Francisco Coloane, "Palabras de Francisco Coloane (Discurso fúnebre)," *Cultura,* 96 (1964), 14.

15. Enrique Lafourcade, *Antología del cuento chileno,* 3 vols. (Barcelona: Ediciones Acervo, 1969). Interviews with Lafourcade were at Salt Lake City, Utah, December 24, 1969, and at Denver, Colorado, the following week.

Also he calls the palomilla novel "one clear ramification of the picaresque novel in Chilean prose fiction." This type of fiction includes "Una perra y algunos vagabundos," but not Guzmán's novels, which, according to Salmon, are completely proletarian:

> Unlike the typical palomilla, or street urchin, Enriquillo Quilodrán experiences the healthy love of his parents for each other and for their children—"con su sinceridad anchamente proletaria."[16]

By creating a unique child prototype, Guzmán helped establish a type of literature in Chile that has in turn inspired a voluminous tradition of child-novels. Thus Guzmán's work, which had first evolved as a synthesis of all literature, both in and out of Chile, that depicted the proletarian child, became an inspiration to other writers who have continued this new Chilean tradition, which is nearly a folk-motif, especially when Christmas is involved. Most of the stories have been inspired by the ragged, dirty orphans and runaways who sang on trolleys, who once lived in gangs below the Mapocho bridges, and who stole anything to survive.

According to some sources, the pelusa had become a folk myth by 1970, and I have failed to discover his presence in Santiago (in the winter, at least); yet in large cities there will always be children like the malicious gangs I saw roaming the streets of Bogotá.

The child of the Santiago slums, narrowed by Guzmán into the proletarian child or the palomilla at Christmas, became a topic for numerous Chilean writers. They have continued the theme that Guzmán handled so sensitively and made so popular.

Adult Protagonists

Guzmán's presentation of adult protagonists evolves from direct to indirect in the course of his career. Direct presentation involves more telling, indirect more showing.[17] We can best understand the difference by briefly examining all the characters, both principal and secondary.

In *Los hombres obscuros*, Pablo's ability to reproduce dialogue other than his own is somewhat limited. He begins the novel by telling about his landlords, and most of the other characters are also

---

16. Russell Owen Salmon, "The Roto in Chilean Prose Fiction," Ph.D. Dissertation, Columbia University, 1969, pp. 223–24.

17. Perrine, *Literature*, p. 67.

presented directly by Pablo. The reader seldom sees the minor characters, except through the narrator's character summaries. The heroine, however, is presented as if through a camera eye. Inés speaks her own words; thus because he shows her, the narrator's development of the female protagonist is more realistic than the characterization of the many types that are described or explained (by telling) throughout the novel. When Inés speaks, for example, we have evidence of her moral sensitivity. The first-person present-tense subgenre lends itself to telling rather than showing, and similar weaknesses in characterization are noticeable in many such books, from one of the earliest novels of this class, Schnitzler's *Leutnant Gustl*, through the Chilean conventillo novels *Vidas mínimas* and *Hijuna*.

As Guzmán matured, he perfected his methods of characterization. Though many of the secondary figures were mere outlines in his first novel, in the second, *La sangre y la esperanza,* the author learned to characterize them through showing. The reader, as a result, becomes more involved in their development and remembers them longer than he does similar characters in *Los hombres obscuros*.

Because Enrique is an objective narrator, Elena's characterization and that of the parents is largely through their own speeches and actions. However, the narrator is inclined to help the reader whenever he wants to emphasize proletarian integrity; it is then that he leads his audience by the hand and says, "This is my good father, my saintly mother, who remain faithful and hardworking in spite of the social harassment they receive."

A reasonable balance between telling and showing is also achieved in *La luz viene del mar*. Virginia is clearly presented throughout the novel, but her final development is confusing to the reader because of the cyclical aspect of the narration. The other characters are somewhere between archetypes and stereotypes. Socialist critics might see these proletarian heroes as hardy miner and seaman archetypes, but the traditional critic is more apt to feel that they are stereotypes—static, two-dimensional figures. Of these working-class heroes, one of the most important in Ceferino López, the labor leader portrayed in the scenes or chapters entitled "En la brecha." The narrator says little about him directly; he is characterized indirectly by the speeches of those around him. Nevertheless, since he undergoes no psychological crisis, he is not fully developed in the novel and is a static "strike-poster" character.

Delineated as a fictional-historical figure, Ceferino López sometimes serves as a sub-narrator, as does Lorenzo Carmona.

Three of the male characters, Lorenzo Carmona ("La Reliquia de la Huella"), Cara de Pescado, and even "El Pirata Cholakys" are presented in parallel fashion by a historical summary of their past and their uniqueness. After their initial presentation by the narrator, the characters give further insight into their existence through their dialogues and actions. The fighter, Ricardo Figueroa ("El Huacho Fieroga"), could also be considered part of this group, because he is developed both by the narrator and by the commentaries of individuals like Lorenzo Carmona, who remember him for what he used to be—the region's greatest boxer. Yet he is more than a stereotype; the narrator probes deep into his consciousness to portray a unique insanity, which has been best explained by Mario Osses:

> Sobresalen algunos retratos. En primer lugar Huacho Fieroga (metátesis de Figueroa). "¿Quién podrá olvidarse de sus cinco jazmines?" . . . No es un perfil psicológico simple: ya en la vejez vive obsedido por el recuerdo de su padre, a quien hallaron muerto sobre un montón de huesos. Los pregones de los hueseros lo conturban. Piensa en que podrán vender la osamenta de su nuera y [nieto], y tiene que reprimir el impulso cada vez más imperioso de matarlos. Se recrimina más tarde, presa de remordimientos agudos. Es un caso de "fijación" infantil que Nicomedes explota con sabiduría, llevándolo a un punto donde se teme por el desborde. Nada sucede sin embargo, y el lector experimenta el alivio de que no ocurra una tragedia que en la pluma de un inexperto hubiera sido inevitable.[18]

Without a doubt this characterization is one of the most masterful in the book, for it recalls constantly to the mind of the reader the atrocities perpetrated in the slum environment where Fieroga's father was murdered. Fieroga recalls the death of his father and shakes, fearing he will murder his family whenever he hears the cry of the street vendor: "—¡Huesos, los huesos que venderrr! ¡errr!" This folk-poetry leitmotif, repeated throughout the theme sections entitled "Los cinco jazmines del Huacho Fieroga," creates intense suspense in the reader since the cry makes the old man temporarily insane.

A parallel character portrayed only through dialogue, though

---

18. Mario Osses, "Crítica literaria: *La luz viene del mar*, de Nicomedes Guzmán," *La Nación* (Santiago), July 5, 1953.

much of his history is told in his own words, is the tragic Pedro Andrade, who describes how he cut off his hand in order to be united with his lovely Fresia.

In his attempt to write a great spatial novel and to create parallel proletarian heroes, Guzmán has created a work similar in structure to a complicated drama played in a theater in the round. His stress on a revolving story results in a novel of types, interpolated episodes, and action repeated constantly in space.

Guzmán's short stories vary from one extreme—exemplified in "Destello en la bruma" or "Perro ciego" where nearly the entire story is direct characterization with little dialogue—to the other, exemplified in "La sagrada familia," where dialogue, flashback, and indirect characterization are predominant. When he wants to stress character, Guzmán turns to indirect characterization (showing); when theme is more important, the narrator controls the characterization directly (telling). In most of his stories action and dialogue make up the last half or three-quarters of the story. This structure picks up the pace of the narration, adds motivation, and helps develop the character intimately and objectively, making him a living entity in the mind of the reader.

Female Protagonists

The characterization of women was difficult for Guzmán. Although his first heroine, Inés, has been likened to Lucía, Inés is usually spoken of as "too romantic" to be a convincing factory worker. The mothers in his novels are shallow; Virginia's mother, Sofía, protagonist of the episodes in La luz viene del mar entitled "huracanes y estrellas," is little more than a stereotyped proletarian woman and mother, like Laura, Enrique's mother. Guzmán appears to have had the same problem with the characterization of Elena and Virginia.

Elena, the heroine of La sangre y la esperanza, has been referred to by critics as a romantic stereotype; Guzmán, however, conceived her as an archetypal figure of hope. The author's own sister Elena served as a model for the child-Elena of Part II of the novel, but the real-life model was little more than a shell, an excuse for further character development. Guzmán's son clarifies the situation: "Ingresó [Guzmán] junto con mi tía Elena (que murió muy niña, pero que la imaginación del novelista la transformó en personaje de su mejor producción) a una escuela ubicada en Cumming. . . ." Besides the younger Elena, there is a mature Elena in the novel who falls in love with the married poet. For the model of this older Elena, Guzmán may have chosen Lena, the working-girl aunt who lived with the Gold family for a time in *Jews Without Money*. The two characters have similar names: Lena (Gold) and Elena (Guzmán).

Elena is a convincing sister-type in *La sangre y la esperanza*, but Enrique also attempts to transform her into a mother image. Not only does he view her as a potential mother (later she is an expectant mother), but he converts her through Freudian associations and metaphors into the universal mother figure despite her lack of a husband (see p. 167).

Elena represents proletarian hope through her pregnancy, and she is definitely romantic in the mind of Enrique. The tendency toward romanticism (especially in heroines like Inés, Elena, and Virginia) is a common weakness in the radical writer who, as a rebel, takes on many characteristics of the nineteenth-century romantic revolutionary, both in his literature and in his life. Occasionally the protagonist also manifests such Promethean tendencies. For example, Virginia's romantic sentiments lead her to frustration and a desire to destroy herself. This self-destructive attitude is seen in Guzmán himself, and in Che Guevara, especially in his correspondence. These and other romantic aspects of the Marxist revolutionary have been studied by numerous North American and English critics. One theme that has been examined, for instance, is the cult of the child as noble savage, of which Enrique Quilodrán is a good example.

The first-person narration in Guzmán's first two novels tends to limit the development of the women. Of all Guzmán's female characters, only Virginia shows a definite psychological development (though it is difficult for the reader to grasp). Much of her maturation is portrayed through interior monologues.

The young novelist undoubtedly realized some of his limitations in portraying the feminine psyche. It should not have been beyond his capabilities to create more meaningful female characters, but in his first two novels he was deterred by his ideological tendency to subordinate character portrayal to thematic expression. For example, Guzmán confesses in his "Plan de una novela" that he is lost as to how he might best characterize Elena in the sequel:

Pero aquí en la novela también se halla Elena . . . Hay que hacer algo con ella. En *La sangre y la esperanza* representa propiamente la esperanza. Va a tener un hijo, siendo soltera. Lo tiene . . .

No sabemos hasta ahora qué vamos a hacer con Elena . . . Hay que encauzar su vida . . . Como ella representa la esperanza, tendrá que ser una heroína superior, como lo son naturalmente la abuela y la madre, y el mismo padre y los dirigentes obreros. ("Plan," 50)

Not only was Elena to continue as a mother image for Enrique, Guzmán also had other plans for her; she was to take over as the mother in the home after the death of Laura: "Tendrá mucho que ver como apoyo moral en estos momentos dramáticamente afectivos de la pequeña familia" (p. 47). It would appear that where characterization is subservient to thematic expression—as here where Elena represents the theme of hope—Guzmán was unable to create a new fully rounded character and achieve a convincing level of reality at the same time.

The Proletarian Hero

As long as the ideology of socialist realism confronts the novelist with the necessity of depicting a hero who represents a collective society (or a segment of society), the creation of a fully developed, three-dimensional protagonist will be a problem. The author's emphasis on collectivity too often converts the hero and heroine into symbols of the average proletarian. In the proletarian literature of the United States, this intent of leveling humanity produced characters that in many cases were little better than the stereotyped images often found in the pages of the *Daily Worker*.

Some of these difficulties with characterization are evaluated by the late Yerko Moretić in his outstanding essay on contemporary socialist realism. Moretić, a promising Marxist critic and member of the Chilean Generation of 1950, feels that no human or nation is one hundred percent hero at every moment. The optimism of socialist realism does not account for frustration and individual or collective failures. Novelists must strive to create meaningful heroes; any literature that falsifies or fails to show multiple facets of personality will fall short of the expected mark of socialist realism.[19]

19. Yerko Moretić and Carlos Orellana, eds., *El nuevo cuento realista chileno* (Santiago: Editorial Universitaria, 1962), p. 23. The seventy-page preface by Moretic, "El realismo y el relato chileno," is an attempt to examine recent Chilean short stories through dialectic-materialist criticism.

Though he followed guidelines like these to some extent, Guzmán chose not to follow strict Marxist tradition. His and Juan Godoy's techniques parallel those of the Russian Association of Proletarian Writers, the major Soviet literary group from 1928 to 1932. Guzmán reasoned that the simple, realistic portrayal of a "heroic proletarian life," such as his own, produced a hero. Through the protagonist-narrator, Pablo, the proletarian world was seen for the first time objectively, as though through the eyes of a camera, yet with human emotions. Enrique was as great a proletarian creation as any of his Marxist predecessors. Enrique's father, Guillermo Quilodrán, tends to be a flat type, as does Laura, the mother, though some critics acclaimed their originality: "En el fondo preside la madre, creación y estudio difícil de igualar en nuestra literatura. . . ."[20] The father shows some development, especially in his attitude toward Elena's ill-fated romance, but the mother changes little and has few opportunities to act.

The parallel proletarian types (quasi heroes) in *La luz viene del mar*—the miners, stevedores, and sailors—are reflections of the great North. These working-class figures embody in their collective consciousness the history of the nitrate North. Mario Osses refers to them as Ortegan existential heroes:

> Cada ser humano es él y su circunstancia. Respetando verdad tan notoria, Guzmán sitúa a sus héroes en el cuadro que recortan sus inquietudes preferenciales. No contento con esta manera de cifrarlos psicológica y socialmente, los caracteriza a menudo con un apodo. Cuando ha pasado mucho tiempo se recuerdan los grupos de asociaciones tangenciales: el nombre varias veces repetido de cada capítulo y el remoquete operan de consuno y anclan en la memoria con notable firmeza.[21]

In this sense, each of these heroes has found his niche in the decadent, mining-oriented society of Iquique and represents his own particular environment.

Basilio Cholakys, known as "El Griego" or "El Pirata," is the strongest and most admirable of these heroes. He was created with the help of Ester Panay, whose Greek grandfather was the model for him. A giant of a man, Cholakys in all his majesty is like the sun—his golden earring is compared to the sun—or he is like a refraction of the sun on the crystal sea. His vitality is eternal: "Le

20. Uriarte, "*La sangre y la esperanza*," p. 92.
21. Osses, "Crítica literaria."

gustaba a El Griego atraer, quizá sugestionar a las mujeres, que harto le removían los instintos aún, a pesar de la edad" (*Luz*, 109). Though the narrator occasionally portrays him as satanic, he radiates a tenderness that endears him to the reader. El Chino Lin reveres him, almost mystically: "le admiraba como a un dios" (*Luz*, 173). This mythical being attracts women through his cosmic strength, but the contrasting "tender" side of his personality makes him weep at a cradle song. Basilio's complex character comprises elements of the proletarian culture of the port where he lived and of the Hellenic culture of his youth (he retains nationality both in Chile and in Greece). His many-sided personality also symbolizes the temperamental nature of the ocean.

The other heroes in *La luz viene del mar* are more attached to the land. Cara de Pescado is a stevedore; "El Huacho Fieroga" is a creation of the city and the nitrate mines. Lorenzo Carmona evokes the sea, the city, and the desert. His remarkable memory marks the passage of time by the constant comings and goings of his pickup truck. Each hero reflects a different aspect of the North.

A major element in the motivation of Guzmán's protagonists is social conflict. Pablo's ultimate decision is to overcome impending defeat through work and revolution. Enrique decides to work to support his family. Yet the protagonists undergo major psychological conflicts and maturation as well. The heroes in Guzmán's fiction are molded by conscious and subconscious contradictions which are further conditioned by an unjust social environment. In order to bring such conflicts to the surface, the author delves deep into the mind of each protagonist. Guzmán liked to show both sides of the proletarian personality. Pablo struggles with the cave man in his veins; Enrique grows up to confront the harsh and shocking realities of the world; Virginia is deceived by the evil in her friends. Each of the characters can be seen striving to understand his own existence. But most often, the author seeks a collective understanding of existence. Each character is an individual, yet he must achieve harmony with the world as a whole and within his own soul. As the author examines each character's mind, he hopes to discover new dialectic qualities such as dedication, loyalty, "ternura," a will to work, or a desire to better one's environment through revolution—by sacrificing one's life, if necessary.

13

Minor Characters: The Mock Pastoral

Nicomedes Guzmán was masterful in his creation of minor figures. The discussion of major characters in Chapter 12 mentioned his early tendency to present characters directly through the narrator's eyes, giving them little chance to speak or act for themselves. As the young author gained experience, he realized that such superficial presentations are easily forgotten by the reader. He saw regretfully that his early characters, such as the landlords, Inés's father, Yolanda, the vagabonds, and others were little more than outlines.

Guzmán's most colorful minor creation, Evaristo, in *Los hombres obscuros*, is a hardy proletarian type whose "filthy" mouth spews forth the vulgar language of the slum and whose breath reeks of garlic and alcohol. More than half the words in the novel that the critics have referred to as "tainted" are spoken by Evaristo, who characterizes himself through dialogue.

The young author must have realized his success in creating the character of Evaristo, because a similar character, Tío Bernarbé, appears in his second novel.

The differences in the two novels between telling and showing as techniques of character portrayal can be seen by comparing the *cesantes* of the North that appear in each of the novels. There are four such vagabonds in *Los hombres obscuros*. The first, Coñopán, an Araucanian Indian, never speaks; he expresses himself only by playing his aboriginal musical instrument, the onomatopoetically named *trutruca* (sometimes *tutuca*), a long, hollow cane connected to a cow-horn bell:

> —Tru, tru, tru . . . Tru, tru, tru . . .
> La trutruca, en los labios del araucano,
> llora como una hembra sin macho. (*Hombres*, 101)

Like Coñopán, the other three cesantes are little more than excuses for the narrator to make comments. These three castoffs from society, who arrive from the bankrupt North with Coñopán, are a knife grinder named José María, a most unusual female tramp known as "La Gringa Pobre," and her son Raúl, a sexual deviate.

The narrator attempts to characterize these figures through telling only, a common fault in proletarian novels that try to include a panorama of human types. Union members and washerwomen participate in dialogues, but their roles in the novel are not important; they are included only because of their conversation about social injustice, which is reproduced by Pablo as indirect propaganda. This way the narrator presents the voices of other characters but still dwells on a socially important subject.

It is somewhat pointless to explain to the reader that José María was once a labor leader in the North or that he once worked with the founder of the Communist party, Recabarren, for one never hears from José María directly or sees him as a character in action. The same is true of the direct characterization of La Gringa Pobre, the clothes thief of the novel, whose son Raúl earns money as a male prostitute. Raúl is eventually caught in a toilet having relations with the daughter of the mayordoma, and both he and the girl are sent to jail.[1] Yet the reader is only told of all this; he sees none of it through showing.

The effect of direct characterization in *Los hombres obscuros* is a series of superficial character sketches; the cause is the author's attempt to introduce many proletarian types to create a panorama of the conventillo. In this sense, Guzmán's initial effort is much like Michael Gold's, and La Gringa Pobre is modeled after Mary Sugar Bum who appears briefly in Chapter 14 of *Jews Without Money*.

Most of the unique traits of Coñopán, José María, La Gringa Pobre, Raúl, and Gold's Mary are combined in *La sangre y la esperanza* into one of Guzmán's most singular creations, the vagabond Pan Candeal. Enrique first describes him as an animal (direct characterization): "De su labio inferior colgaba un hilo de baba que lo hacía asemejarse a los bueyes" (*Sangre*, 115). However, Enrique goes beyond simple telling, the weakness of the first novel. He reproduces Pan Candeal's Araucanian accent in dialogue; through the tramp's active participation in the narrative, he fixes the character in the reader's mind as a most peculiar creation (indirect characterization):

1. This motif is used again and is more thoroughly developed through dialogue in *La sangre y la esperanza*, where Antonieta is caught in the toilet with a boy; both Antonieta and the boy are sent to jail, where the judge makes them marry to save her "honor." Antonieta and Etelvina are two more of Guzmán's figures who seem to have their origin in Gold's *Jews Without Money*.

—¡Caraju!, ¿qué hago yo? ¿qué hago yo, aaah? . . . ¡No peguen ma, niños, no peguen ma! ¡Na hago yo! . . .

* * *

—¿Qué mira tú? ¿Qué mira? . . . ¿Querer pegar también? ¿Querer pegar? ¡Tú, niño bueno, no pega! ¡No pega niño bueno! (*Sangre*, 115–16)

This strange creature is tormented and teased by children in the same way that Mary Sugar Bum is harassed in *Jews Without Money*, and he unites similar traits that Guzmán had wanted to portray in the cesantes from the North in the first novel.

Little children in the first novel are only incidental characters, like shadows or a chorus in the conventillo. In *La luz viene del mar* children are more individualized, but they are still like stage props: Huacho Fieroga's tiny grandson seems to have been invented mostly as a potential victim of his insane grandfather, and Virginia's half-brother Segundo is little more than a name. The reader is bothered by Segundo's empty characterization; in fact, Virginia's dog plays a greater role than Segundo.

In the second novel, *La sangre y la esperanza*, children play minor but important roles as Enrique's companions. These children are convincing, but many of them die before we have seen much of them. The more important cabros in the novel are Zorobabel, his sister Angélica, Sergio Llanos, Leontina, and Mara (Marita), Tío Bernarbé's daughter. The first three come to tragic ends; Marita has great potential and appears regularly throughout the novel, but she is a very "flat" character whom the author fails to develop. Guzmán became aware of some of these flaws after the novel was published. In his "Plan de una novela" he wrote that the sequel should include characters like Zorobabel and his sister as companions for Enrique, to help him mature convincingly.

There are other important types in *La sangre y la esperanza*. The young poet, Abel Justiniano, is a revolutionary who plays an essential role in the novel, but he is always in the background because of his illicit relationship with Elena. Abel also represents the proletarian artist, and for this reason, or perhaps others, he calls Guzmán to mind.

The novel also includes teachers and doctors, evolved from similar characters in novels by Gold, Sepúlveda Leyton, and others. Guzmán's attitude toward these characters was often different from that of his predecessors, producing more believable characters. For example, Sepúlveda Leyton's characters (in *La fábrica*) and Michael Gold's express a negative attitude toward school: "School is a jail for children. One's crime is youth, and the jailers punish one for it. I hated school at first; I missed the street" (*Jews Without Money*, 22). Georg Fink was somewhat more optimistic:

> There was one thing that compensated me for everything else—school.
> I think this sounds queer. Was not school an institution for punishment, for education by force and was not the pupil the trembling slave of old dried-up misanthropes?[2]

Guzmán did not attack the institution of education; he saw school as optimism and hope for the youth. Thus it is a major decision on Enrique's part to quit school and go to work. However, society is to blame for the quality of education: "Los maestros también enseñan a ser hipócritas" (*Sangre*, 142).

Enrique's elementary school teacher is close to his boys. He referees their soccer games after school and tries to educate and discipline them. He is a very human character. Enrique surprises him one day kissing another teacher in the classroom; later Enrique and Turnio see the two teachers slip into a cheap hotel:

> —¡Qué joder! —hablé, incrédulo, recordando la humildad del señor Carmona, sus pantalones deshilachados, sus zapatos torcidos, rubricando su pobreza de maestro proletario.
> —¡Se quieren y tienen que hacerlo! —explicó como un hombre mayor, Sergio Llanos—. ¡Todo el mundo tira, no debía haber más que camas! ¡Allá en la casa, todos los hombres y las mujeres no hacen más que eso! (*Sangre*, 99)

The embarrassment of the children at the fact that their teacher is poor and wears humble clothing originates with *Hijuna*: "Pero, entonces . . . queda a la vista de nosotros un parche vergonzoso en el trasero del maestro." The boys, embarrassed, giggle and confess at his insistence that they are making fun, "—Del parche en el poto. . . ."[3] Because Sepúlveda was a schoolteacher, his books interpret education relatively humanistically. In *Hijuna* three different types of teachers are delineated, as well as an ugly but hard-

2. Georg Fink, *Thirty-One Families Under Heaven*, translation of *Mich Hungert* by Lillie C. Hummel (New York: Liveright Publishing Corp., 1931), p. 89.

3. Carlos Sepúlveda Leyton, *Hijuna: Novela* (Santiago: Austral, 1962), pp. 133–34.

working principal. *Hijuna* also deals with the irony of the government's having built a school without having enough money for teachers' salaries; the principal sits in his office alone all day while the boys on the street cheer their continued freedom from education. In spite of the irony that pervades his work, it is Sepúlveda Leyton who seems to have influenced Guzmán's thinking most in this area.

Whereas Michael Gold contrasts two doctors,[4] the rich, plump bourgeois physician who has no time for the proletarian, and the thin, poor, overworked doctor who dedicates his sad life to the poor, Guzmán depicts an almost-proletarian physician who works for the betterment of the poor, not for money. An ideal socialist, the doctor takes a May Day evening off from his duties to join in song and festivities with the Quilodrán family in the conventillo.

Nor is the priest in the novel a stereotyped or buorgeois figure. Padre Carmelo is a hero of the poor. He ignores Doña Párame's confession that she loves him, which leads to her attempted suicide; moreover, in "Los trece meses del año," the author planned to involve this same priest with one of the women who taught catechism, while Doña Párame would look on in patience ("Plan," 51). Doña Párame, an older woman, is a most interesting minor character. Though she is a reformed prostitute, she is also a *beata* who seeks donations for the church. It is rumored that syphilis or some other physical disability has left her unable to maintain her balance at times; she gained her name from the command she bellows at the first person to come by after she falls: "¡Párame!" ("Stand me up!").

A more static minor character is Enrique's grandmother, a stereotype, perhaps a folk type. In the 1942 manuscript of the novel, the grandmother's role was expanded in the third part, where she is introduced. The added paragraphs seem to indicate that she had been removed from the first part of the novel in an earlier draft because Guzmán discovered that she was very empty and would have more impact at the end. In "Los trece meses del año," the grandmother was to become an invalid. Also, in one published chapter, she gets lost, and the family is humiliated when Enrique finds her begging on the streets. Guzmán's generational colleagues talk of this episode as one of the most humorous in his writings.

4. Michael Gold, *Jews Without Money* (New York: Avon Books, 1968), Chap. 17, "Two Doctors."

As if she evolved from Doña Párame, a no less remarkable *beata* appears in *La luz viene del mar*; known as Tomasa or Tomasita, behind her back she is referred to as "La mensajera" because of her gift for gossip. She is the illegitimate daughter of a well-to-do Iquique family; yet her family refuses to recognize her except as their servant. The only person who ever showed love for her was an army officer who made her pregnant when she was young. She could have married him, but her family interfered, insisting that the soldier was a poor drunk. The real reason they objected, she claimed, was that the family did not want to lose her as a cook and servant. Now an old *beata*, Tomasa observes that her fiancé eventually became a military attaché; had her family not been hypocrites, she could have had a very different existence. She has become fanatically religious; yet she keeps the body of her unborn son in a box:

> Mi pobre hijo que no alcanzó a ser sino un triste recuerdo muerto de unos cuantos momentos de verdadero amor, lo guardo en una cajita, entre algodones, como una lombriz seca . . . (*Luz*, 307)

She prays a great deal in her later life, not only for her apparently aborted son, but also for her family, symbols of the decadence of the nitrate empire of Iquique and the North:

> A veces, abro la cajita, y rezo. . . . Rezo por su alma, que nada supo del mundo, y rezo por mi pobre familia, que vive derrumbándose y derrumbándose, hasta caer en una miseria que sólo yo endulzo con mis rezos y mis postres . . .
> —Es increíble. . . . ¡Increíble! . . . ¡Ay, Tomasita! . . . —clamó dolorida, Sofía.
> —En lo increíble está siempre la verdad . . . Lo cierto es lo que he contado . . . (*Luz*, 307)

Tomasita echoes here the author's philosophy of socialist realism. Guzmán felt that socrealism and truth were both shocking. Tomasa's unbelievable story, together with her gossip about the unfaithfulness of Virginia's boyfriend, Eudocio, makes Virginia realize that she does not want a life like Tomasita's. Thus Tomasa's socrealist characterization leads to Virginia's maturation. Virginia's first intent is suicide, for she prefers no world to the hypocritical world of the North. However, after she is saved from drowning (and is raped), she returns to her tower to enter her cyclical world anew.

El Roto

Guzmán's characterization of such minor figures as Tomasita is masterful. One reason for his success in this area may be found in his acute powers of observation. He often turned to a real-life model—a street vendor, a historical personage, or someone whom he had known personally—to create the character. The vendor especially was a colorful figure; he added an extra dimension, for the crying of his wares was a sound of poetry to the author:

> —¡Los pensamientos vendooooooooo!...
> Los vendedores ambulantes, como se ve, tenían un rudo pero un vital sentido tierno de las cosas.[5]

This was the cry that Guzmán's father used, according to his son, Oscar Vásquez Salazar, who explains in an article how his father would buy the whole basket of wares in order to converse with the roto and get to know him intimately:

> Era el invierno rudo con sus vientos y lluvias . . .
> Y como siempre llegó el motero gritando sus mercancías al barrio:
> —Motemeiii pelaoooo el meii y calientitoooo.
> Un brazo a manera de gancho con el canasto colgando y con la otra mano columpiando el farol.
> —Eh . . . Hombre, ven aquí . . .
> Se acercaba a la puerta el motero:
> —¡Entre pues hombre! . . .
> —No jefe. Cuántas "cachás" de mote quiere. Diga no más jefe.
> —Pero no sea tonto hombre . . . Puchas el tipito para jodido. Pase, pase.
> —No jefe . . . No ve que tengo que vender todo esto pa' los cabros . . .
> —Mire. No sea güevas, hombre. Pase, le compro el mote, el canasto y todo . . .
> Entraba . . . Y allí alternaba algunas horas con el hombre. Trabajaba con el alma misma de nuestro hombre proletario, al calor de un trago de vino tinto. . . . Allí forjaba esa luz de ternura y reivindicacion espiritual del trabajador, allí captaba al motero para meterlo en la tremenda, cautivante y real verdad de sus escritos.[6]

Dyson lists the character types that appear in Guzmán's stories, mixtures of the proletarian and roto strains that inhabit the conventillo: "paralíticos, prostitutas, obreros, venedores callejos, y, a veces,

---

5. Oscar Vásquez Salazar, "Mi abuelo Nicomedes, el heladero ambulante," *El Siglo* (Santiago), May 21, 1967. See pp. 127–28, above, for Guzmán's philosophy of the "pregón" as "proletarian poetry."
6. Oscar Vásquez Salazar, "¡Así era mi padre!" *El Siglo*, June 26, 1966.

comerciantes o empleados de oficina menores." Added to this list are children, dogs, "lustrabotas," and "lavanderas."[7] In an *estampa*, after the arrest of the greatest *roto* of the novel, Pan Candeal, Guzmán makes the sun a resident of the *conventillo*: "El sol, roto grandioso, se descubría mostrando la espesa y rubia pelambre de su pecho." Finally, Guzmán also employs the term *roto* in a pejorative sense: "—¡Parte luego, roto sinvergüenza . . . !" (*Sangre*, 44). The *roto's* rebellious spirit becomes the soul of the typical Chilean in Guzmán's works, but the class that will provide Chile's salvation is the proletarian mass. Nevertheless there is something about the *roto* that entices the author to explore the thoughts and idiosyncrasies of the type, whether in his most lofty or his most banal expression. The *roto* is symbolic of "upright manliness," of true life. He incorporates the true essence of contemporary Chilean identity, especially in the light of his close relationship to the proletariat.

The Prostitutes: A Mock Pastoral

In Guzmán's short stories prostitutes play quite ordinary roles (a confused, poverty-stricken mother; a reformed-prostitute wife), but in the novels, as was shown in Chapter 10, they often convey an element of irony. Some of the female types in *La luz viene del mar* are very similar to the absurd whores in Valle-Inclán's *Tirano Banderas*. In the light of this notable irony in Guzmán's fiction, a new interpretation of Part II of *La luz viene del mar* would appear to be necessary. As a basis for this explanation it is essential to acknowledge William Empson's idea that proletarian literature is fundamentally a form of the pastoral novel:

> Proletarian literature usually has a suggestion of pastoral, a puzzling form which looks proletarian but isn't. . . . I think good proletarian art is usually Covert Pastoral.
>
> * * *
>
> The essential trick of the old pastoral, which was felt to imply a beautiful relation between rich and poor, was to make simple people express strong feelings . . . in learned and fashionable language. . . .[8]

In his study *La novela pastoril española*, Juan Bautista Avalle-Arce disagrees with Empson. Following the same logic that I used in

7. John P. Dyson, "Los cuentos de Nicomedes Guzmán," *Atenea*, 404 (1964), 231, 247.

8. William Empson, *Some Versions of Pastoral* (New York: New Directions Paperbooks, 1968), pp. 6, 11.

Chapter 7 in contrasting criollismo and realism, Avalle-Arce insists on an ideological opposition between the two types of novel: "Los pastores, en una palabra, son tradicionalistas; el proletario, revolucionario."[9] It is interesting to note that after 1950, the year he was editing *La luz viene del mar*, Guzmán continually became more criollista, less realist, abandoning the revolution for tradition.

Empson, one of England's leading critics, suggests several ways that basic elements of the pastoral novel have been used in proletarian literature. For example, by alternating proletarian prose with another version of pastoral (stories of children in a paradisiacal environment), several authors have created works of the child-cult genre, centering on the noble savage child. Other writers have created the pathetic criminal hero and the sacrificial tragic hero. While Guzmán's early novels were of the first type, *La luz viene del mar* represents the second two: "The realistic sort of pastoral (the sort touched by mock-pastoral) also gives a natural expression for a sense of social injustice."[10]

It is this "mock-pastoral" that becomes a point of departure for a study of the brothel scenes in *La luz viene del mar*. These ironic scenes might be seen as parodies of a sixteenth-century Spanish pastoral novel like Montemayor's *La Diana*.

Guzmán was intuitively aware of the similarity between the pastoral and the proletarian novel. In the unpublished manuscript of his first novel, "Un hombre, unos ojos negros y una perra lanuda" (1937), he referred to the need to work in pastoral terms: "¡Trabajo! . . . ¡Palabra mágica, me suenas a la voz dulcificada de todos los martillos del mundo, *a la égloga campesina* de todas las hoces del mundo rumoreando al ras de los trigales! . . ." (105).

The traditional pastoral begins with an "eclogue," an idyllic description. Guzmán begins *La luz viene del mar* with an estampa invoking a bucolic setting; but irony becomes apparent when the paradise for the proletarian men in the novel turns out to be the brothels of La Siete Dedos or the Palacio de Cristal, where men like El Chino Lin spend their free afternoons in a haven of opium and women. As in a pastoral romance, Lin longs for Fresia, the prostitute, but cannot have her, even though he wants to marry her (cf. *Luz*, 37).

9. Juan Bautista Avalle-Arce, *La novela pastoril española* (Madrid: Revista de Occidente, 1959), p. 7.

10. Empson, *Pastoral*, p. 17.

Still in the anticipatory first part ("climate") of the novel, Basilio surprises everyone in the house of La Siete Dedos when he picks up the violin and plays a haunting melody of his childhood. It is not clear at the time whether the tune is classical, romantic, or popular. Later the author implies through the chapter headings "Canción de cuna" that it was a cradle song (*Luz*, 116–17). This reminder of his youth (the *ubi sunt* motif of the pastoral) causes the powerful Basilio to break into tears. Once he has sung his song and put down the instrument, he refuses to play for the others who have been attracted by his lament and his music and beg him to continue.

A principal trait of pastoral fiction was to alternate prose with poetry. Intermixed with the narration of Guzmán's pastoral episodes are songs and poems, estampas, and extraneous love intrigues. Though the novel as a whole is structured around Virginia, the mock-pastoral is set in the house of prostitution, where Guzmán grotesquely inverts space and time. The traditional pastoral begins at dawn and concludes at dusk. Guzmán commences the actions of the mock-pastoral at sunset, ending the episode suddenly and tragically at sunrise. Nevertheless, the novel itself begins with a poetic description of the northern daybreak and closes with the oncoming shadows of night.

The second "clima" of the novel ("Anclas de la noche") is the central part of the mock-pastoral. Pedro Andrade comes down out of the mountains like a "pastor peregrino," explaining his love conflicts to Lorenzo Carmona, in whose truck he is riding. The story seems to have begun *in medias res,* a typical sixteenth-century device. Pedro loves Fresia, but she does not love him. He is frustrated because she keeps running away with someone else. To complicate matters, Melania loves him, but he does not respond to her love. He can only be satisfied when finally he wins Fresia, who has become a prostitute, by chasing her from one end of Chile to the other (*Luz*, 218).

The house of prostitution is also an idyllic paradise for Eudocio, Virginia's boyfriend. He has escaped to the brothel from the desert with another man's bride, whom he has seduced. In this illicit bed Eudocio finds a fleshly paradise with Clementina Huit, his oriental beauty:

> La existencia se concentraba aquí en el lecho, dulce y cálida, entera de pasión que se preparaba para desencadenarse. (*Luz*, 224)

In a lush Renaissance metaphor, Clementina herself is a marvelous landscape—an exotic isle—and Eudocio the naked Hispanic *conquistador*: "Eudocio tenía la certeza de haber descubierto hasto lo más misterioso y secreto de sus selvas, sus savias, sus tesoros" (*Luz*, 226). The exotic oriental tone is heightened through the alliteration of *s* sounds in this passage. Note also the alliteration of *s* and *c* in the following sentence:

> Lo único que vivía fijo en su pensamiento, en sus huesos y en sus carnes, era confirmar el descubrimiento de aquella isla misteriosa y exótica que le pareció la china, y comprobar en su intimidad misma la belleza, la espesura y el sabor de sus selvas, de sus savias, de sus tesoros." (*Luz*, 227)

Later in the novel, we learn through Tomasa, the gossip, that Clementina has been exiled to her oriental homeland by her Chinese husband. Such poetic justice, characteristic of Spanish Golden Age literature, is further fulfilled in Eudocio's loss of his job. Eudocio's unfaithfulness causes Virginia to attempt suicide. Virginia also overhears Tomasa gossip that El Chino Lin, the other oriental in the novel, hanged himself because, the reader is told, Fresia, who spurned so many men, has called him "a dirty old man."

Fresia herself, who rejects the courting gestures of both Lin and Andrade, suffers from an intense passion for the Greek, Basilio, whom she "loves" for his masculinity and virility. When Cholakys rejects and insults her, she tries to stab him, but he grips her arm and laughs at her satanically.

The climax of this section occurs when Andrade bleeds to death while making love to Fresia, with whom he has been reconciled again after Basilio ridiculed her. In an ironic mock-pastoral orgy, several minor characters weep as they make love to one another because they are not in the arms of their beloved. The prostitutes all gather around the bloody scene of Andrade's death in an absurd chorus:

> Las mujeres hacían coro a los aullidos de Fresia y algunas comenzaron a desmayarse. (*Luz*, 267)

At first the women howl like a pack of animals, then the male voices join in and they all begin to sing a protestant hymn (two of the four verses have been cited above on p. 129):

> Por siempre, ¡oh, víctima de amor!,
> poder de sangre retendrá,

> y allá en el templo del Señor,
> salvado el fiel al fin será. (*Luz*, 270)

The author exaggerates the irony with baroque metaphors; the approaching dawn is reflected in the tender, weeping faces of the characters in the chorus:

> Y todos, densas las cabezas de humores de alcohol, hicieron coro de cristales y diamantes, los ojos devorados por las lágrimas. Los rostros eran finos y acendrados manantiales en donde la alborada quería eternizar el brillo de las estrellas que se derrumbaban encima de las brumosas lontananzas marítimas.
>
> > "Después que la corriente vi
> > de pura sangre enrojecer,
> > tu amor fue ejemplo para mí
> > y por los siglos lo ha de ser." (*Luz*, 270)

By juxtaposing a gospel hymn with the prose of the story, the narrator goes to the extreme of confusing the sacrifice of Christ with this ironic death of a proletarian.

Basilio, who has been accompanying the grotesque figures of the chorus "que se adosaban a los acordes que El Pirata arrancaba a las cuerdas," hurls his violin against the wall, smashing it and putting an end to the second part of the novel.

> Los ecos del himno se aquietaron y fueron como resabios de inciensos largo tiempo ha quemados en las comarcas avasalladoras del amor. (*Luz*, 270)

The bloody death of Andrade has broken the peace of the bucolic *beatus ille*:

> Eudocio esperó un momento propicio. Y cuando un carabinero despedía de la casa a un grupo de intrusos trasnochados, arrastró a la calle a Clementina. Se perdieron, *roto el idilio maravilloso*, en la esquina próxima, perseguidos aún por un alarido trágico. (*Luz*, 268; my italics)

The ironic weeping of unrequited love, the author's insistence on the brothel as an idyll, the *carpe diem* theme, and the motifs that are used in an inverted sense all substantiate the thesis that Guzmán is parodying the pastoral novel. Each character is busy rejecting one suitor and courting someone else. Even the grotesque figures in the novel, those who have suffered physical mutilation, become involved in love triangles: Teresa la Tuerta rejects one-eyed Cara de Pescado, so he makes love to Melania (La Coja), even though she continues to weep for Andrade, who has just cut off his hand to buy Fresia her freedom. (In the original manuscript Melania was both "tuerta" and "coja," but she evolved into two personages.)

Guzmán also planned to compound the love-conflict of the novel with racial problems, but some of the situations were eliminated from the plot as the novel was polished. In the final version of the novel, Lin claims race prejudice: "¡Las chilenas no quelel chinos! . . . Ellas buscan amoles entle chilenos, nala má . . ." (*Luz*, 178). This conflict was inspired by *Jews Without Money*, where a blind prostitute, Masha, earns the nickname "Sweetheart of the Yellow Cholera" by sleeping with a Chinese laundryman, unaware that he belongs to another race. Guzmán eliminated a social-love conflict between La Peta (Lucio's mother) and Lam, an oriental, who never appear in the final version of the novel. Except for the racial problems claimed by Lin, Gold's depictions of racial prejudice (and any such problems Guzmán may have observed in the North) have become class prejudice in *La luz viene del mar*.

The mock-pastoral takes on an existential aspect in Tomasa's summary of the pastoral episode's final outcome:

> —Ve usted, señora, este es un pueblo donde las gentes viven de sí mismas, arañando en sus propias cosas . . . (*Luz*, 309)

Tomasa is echoing the words of existentialist critics who have attempted to interpret the pastoral genre of literature as an illustration of man's narrow vision of the world, his inability to even help himself because he cannot see beyond his own nose. Tomasa insists that the Chilean of the North is too "ensimismado" to see beyond his own difficulties. As in the pastoral novel, each character weeps because of his own anguish but does little to solve his problems or to help others overcome theirs:

> Aquí sólo se entiende la lucha con la lucha . . . y la sangre con la sangre . . . En cuanto a las personas, puede ser el amor con el desengaño . . ., o la vida con la muerte . . . (*Luz*, 309)

The criminal hero can criticize society, because he is an outsider. Moreover, his point of view is a source of irony directed against both the hero and the society. The traditional pastoral, which was not ironic, attempted to reflect the society of the time, according to Empson, who says that the reader "was made to mirror in himself more completely the effective elements of the society he lived in."[11] In Guzmán's mock-pastoral, the society is not faithfully mirrored but rather is distorted; in place of a faithful or idealized reflection, the effect Guzmán seeks is the twisted image of the *esperpento*. Thus even though the critics have been bothered by the socrealist language and the degrading element of the brothel in *La luz viene del mar*, its obvious intent is to invert the real world. In addition, definite influences of the creator of the esperpento, Valle-Inclán, appear in the novel. There is an effeminate, absurd figure, El Yerba Luisa, of the same type that originates in *Tirano Banderas*; and an unusual phrase that Valle-Inclán uses to depict a mock-hero in comic relief dancing alone in a brothel is also echoed in Guzmán's pages: "Ensayó unos pasos de vals" (*Luz*, 261). Both Valle-Inclán and Guzmán accentuate the animal feelings of the man who wants to bark in the brothel: "Cara de Pescado tuvo deseos de ladrar, más, de rugir" (312).

Other motifs derived from Valle-Inclán appear in earlier Guzmán novels. In *Los hombres obscuros* there is a puppet-like character, who suddenly realizes that her appearance in a doorway draws attention to her farcical non-human state (*Hombres*, 50); in the same novel, the image "nariz de ombligo" (*Hombres*, 107) is derived from Valle-Inclán.

Using stylized irony to portray the exaggerated absurdity of existence in the decadent, bankrupt North, the author has created a sort of esperpento, a mock-pastoral, where the drunks and prostitutes weep copiously over unrequited love. Another mock-pastoral aspect of *La luz viene del mar* can be seen in the author's selection of character names like Basilio, Rolando, Lucio, Eulogio, Eliodoro, and Eudocio, which are not common in Chile and which give an archaic, neo-Baroque flavor to the work. Guzmán eliminated from the manuscript the name Narciso, which is even more suggestive of pastoral fiction, and Romualdo became Cara de Pescado, indicating animal traits typical of the esperpento. The surname of Basilio was changed from Sepúlveda to Cholakys, a Greek name. Fresia, the lovely prostitute, has the same name as the wife of Capolicán, the Araucanian Indian chief, protagonist of Pedro de Oña's *Arauco domado* (1596). It is possible that a sensual scene where Fresia bathes with Capolicán in a beautiful setting was the

11. Empson, *Pastoral*, p. 12.

inspiration for the nude bloodbath episode in *La luz viene del mar*.

The novel also contains musical elements. One of the repeating theme-chapter headings in the novel, for example, originally carried the title "Preludio," which usually indicates an introductory musical section. Later this title was changed to "Alborada," and it finally evolved in the manuscripts to its final version, "En la brecha," a Communist song. "La música de la miseria" was changed to "Los mastiles del día."

Guzmán also stylized light and sound during this period into musical terms, in his only short story set in the North, "Rapsodia en luz mayor." Like a musical rhapsody, this story is an emotional but informal contrapuntal composition. *La luz viene del mar*, a novel, is a major composition, structured around antitheses suggested in a paragraph from "Rapsodia en luz mayor":

> Golpeaba allí la luz. Era una luz grande, enorme, como un moscardón infinito que zumbara y acezara incesantemente en los aires. . . . Y es que la Pampa en cuerpo entero es bullicio. La vida y la muerte tienen allí su caja de resonancia. El trabajo y el amor. El canto del mar y el huracán hirsuto de las montañas. La sonrisa y la lágrima" (*La carne iluminada*, 23).

If "Rapsodia" is a minor composition, a "rhapsody of light in major key," *La luz viene del mar* is a major composition, using variations of themes, inversions, counterpoint, and a proletarian chorus. Even though proletarian elements predominate at times, Guzmán's chosen instruments for his pastoral symphony were light, colors, sounds; the ocean, mountains, and desert; poetry and rhythm. His style exaggerated image and counterpoint; his participants were pastoral characters placed ironically in the northern desert, not in a green pasture radiating peace and beauty.

In the characterization of minor figures such as the roto and the prostitute, we can trace a major evolution in Guzmán's fiction. At first his proletarian figures are little more than strike-poster figures. Later they become flesh-and-blood personages. Finally, in *La luz viene del mar*, minor characters join the protagonists in a tragic proletarian mock-pastoral to demonstrate the severe deterioration of the once-great Chilean nitrate empire. Whereas the traditional pastoral represents perfect man living in a perfect state, the proletarian novel presents the communist state as an ideal. In the traditional pastoral persons of importance in the community are lightly disguised as shepherds; *La luz viene del mar* also discloses the identity of certain heroes, but they are as common men: laborers, miners, union leaders, washerwomen, and the like. Only when these figures are shown in contact with the *Lumpen*—that is to say, with the prostitutes—does the novel become an esperpento, an inverted pastoral novel mocking an unjust society. Thus the novel is a judgment of "guilty" against the social decadence of the North, an economically and morally bankrupt society where the bourgeoisie will be totally annihilated in the end.

14

Synthesis of a Proletarian Style
Tradition and Innovation

Style is a very personal aspect of writing. Many writers, like Guzmán, have labored most of their careers to evolve a unique, poetic or compact manner of expression, which eventually becomes the trademark of their art. Guzmán's very poetic style is not extremely different from that established with Juan Godoy's *Angurrientos* and shared by all his generational colleagues. However, Guzmán, who began as a poet, also influenced his fellow writers with his stylistic innovations.

Diction

A writer's choice of words, or diction, is a major component of his style. Guzmán often emphasizes popular words—*chilenismos* or *americanismos*, which will be considered "regionalisms" here. Archaic words appeal to him, but erudite terms do not, because he is searching for words with poetic significance or popular appeal. Many of his terms are unknown to readers in other Spanish American countries, and even to many Chileans, let alone to North American readers who have gained their knowledge of Spanish through textbooks. Guzmán realized the limitations his vocabulary placed on his reading public after the Argentine edition of *La sangre y la esperanza* was planned, so a vocabulary was placed at the end of the novel which has been republished with subsequent editions. The generational tendency toward regionalisms and popular expressions is illustrated by the fact that Godoy's *Angurrientos* and Guzmán's generational anthology, *Nuevos cuentistas chilenos*, as well as the regionalistic *Autorretrato de Chile*, also include glossaries. Besides the glossary in later editions of *La sangre y la esperanza*, Guzmán footnotes many uncommon terms. On page 21 *consejo* is footnoted as *sede gremial*. And the world following *consejo*, *compañeros*, was first *compinches* in the manuscript, then *cama-radas*, and finally compañeros in the first edition. Guzmán's word selection will be examined here with special emphasis on regionalisms, *modismos,* and neologisms unfamiliar to the universal Spanish speaking public.

From the common Quechua term for an infant, *guagua,* to the obscenities spoken by Evaristo and Tío Bernarbé, Guzmán chooses words that he feels will portray Chilean reality through language.

Los hombres obscuros includes few words that could be termed *chilenismos,* but in the vocabulary at the end of *La sangre y la esperanza,* Guzmán lists seventy-six regionalisms or specialized words that appear in the novel. The term *regionalism* as used here signifies a word that has acquired a new derivation or retains an archaic meaning in relation to the Spanish language as used elsewhere. The glossaries of Guzmán's works are my main source for this discussion besides reviews and articles on his works that have pointed out unusual usage. Guzmán could have added about twenty-five more items to his glossaries—clarifications of words like *pololear* (to flirt, to date, to "go steady," to make love) or *cresta* (an obscenity, from a rooster's comb), which are not known to many readers.

An example of how Guzmán attempted to portray Chilean reality through diction can be seen in his use of the word *tirar* and its derivations. First, in *La sangre y la esperanza* the noun *tira* is used according to Guzmán's glossary definition in its South American sense of "detective" (Argentina, Chile, Colombia). Next Guzmán includes in his dialogues the Chilean colloquial expression *al tiro,* meaning "quickly," "immediately." Finally, *tirar* is employed in the colloquial sense of having sexual intercourse:

> —¡Dicen que se metió a la pieza de la loca Rita, y le vio el *poto* a la Antonieta!
> ¡Qué *miéchica* —chilló, pateando, su hermano—, qué le iba a ver el poto, no más! . . . ¡Se la tiró, se la tiró! . . . (*Sangre,* 104)

This quotation includes other vulgarities, "poto" and "miéchica," which are excellent examples of Guzmán's preference for words of the *pueblo.*[1] Note the similar colloquial expressions in a cradle song from *Hombres,* p. 17:

> Hace tuto, guagua,
> que viene la vaca

1. See Francisco J. Santamaría, *Diccionario general de americanismos,* 3 vols. (México: Robredo, 1942). Henceforth referred to as Santamaría.

a comerte el poto
porque tiene caca.

In *Los hombres obscuros* Guzmán utilizes several Americanisms. *Paco* is the colloquial expression for "cop" in much of Spanish America, but in Chile it has been extended specifically to the *carabineros*, the national police force. *Chancho* is the most common word for "pig" in Spanish America. In extension it is often applied in Guzmán's prose for someone who is "piggish," and in the feminine in Chile it also means "slut."[2] *Hacer la chancha* is idiomatic in Bolivia, Colombia, and Chile in the sense that Guzmán uses it: "to play hooky."

Localisms in *Los hombres obscuros* that are more limited in their dissemination are *zandungear*, "to dance," and *colorín* which is preferred in Chile to *pelirrojo*. *Remolienda* (from *remoler*) is used by by the narrator in place of *fiesta*; it is a drinking party, almost an orgy, but without sex.

Other words illustrate Guzmán's specialized proletarian vocabulary. The term *serruchos* as he uses it refers to labor "scabs," strike breakers or workers who do not observe a picket line. *Serrucho* (also a trolley inspector in Chile) is ordinarily employed in Chile to mean a person who vilifies another in order to undercut him at his job and get his position. Santamaría adds an additional usage: *serrucho* is used for *ramera*. The name of the musical instrument, *trutruca*, is Araucanian (see above, p. 222). In Santamaría it is spelled *tutuca*.

In his vocabulary at the conclusion of *La sangre y la esperanza*, Guzmán lists many words which were too specialized to be familiar to the general reading public. Several of these words were archaisms used in an attempt to recreate a setting of the 1920s. *Chaucha*, for example, is a coin no longer in use, but the idiom "not to be worth a chaucha" (of very little value) has remained meaningful. Occasionally Guzmán lists as a Chilean idiom a word which has universal acceptance. One example is *moquear*, "to snivel"; another is *finado*, "a corpse."

In his glossary Guzmán implies that his frequently used word for a boy, *cabro*, refers only to an adolescent. However, Juan Co-

2. Edwin B. Williams, *The Bantam New College Spanish and English Dictionary* (New York: Bantam Books, 1968). Guzmán uses it in this sense in *Hombres*, p. 175.

rominas indicates that *cabro* is Chilean for *muchacho*; actually then, it is equal to the English *kid*.[3] *Chimbirocas* is a vulgarism for "prostitutes," according to Guzmán, and *ñato* ("guy") or *ñata* ("gal") can be endearing in one tone of voice or insulting in another.

The author acknowledges that three of his words come from English: *yoque* from "jockey," *chute* from "shoot," a hard kick (actually a shot on goal in soccer), and *overol* (an Americanism) from the proletarian clothing "overalls." *Chita* is an interjection that Guzmán cites as signifying "desagrado, desilusión, amargura, o sorpresa." Although this meaning may have been derived from Spanish usages of the word, it is not likely. It appears to parallel *chute* in its evolution, in that it suggests the same violent feeling as the English ejaculation, "shit!"

Some of the author's terms are so limited that they mean little to the present-day middle-class Chilean. Such is the case with *tamaña*, a child's obscene gesture. Literally "sign of the eggs," it has little meaning outside Santiago. Other terms not clarified in the glossary are *poto* or *traste*, both provincialisms for "butt" or "rump."

It has been pointed out in previous chapters how the obscenities and vulgarities in the dialogue of the first novels shocked both the critics and the reading public. The two most offensive words in these novels are *cabrona* and *huevón*.[4] According to Santamaría *cabrón* means "pimp" in Chile. As Guzmán changes it to the feminine, *cabrona* implies "madam"—a mother who prostitutes her daughter (*Hombres*, 175). *Huevón* may imply stupidity, but more generally it describes someone who is animal-like, over-sexed, and extremely lazy because of huge testicles. Since the word was considered obscene, Guzmán spelled it "güevón" in the early editions in order to avoid complications. In later editions he chose to use the correct spelling.

Obscene words and harsh colloquial speech were both employed to portray the slums realistically and record the speech of the types who lived there. Evaristo is the character who corrupts the language the most in *Los hombres obscuros*:

3. Joan [Juan] Corominas, *Breve diccionario etimológico de la lengua castellana* (Madrid: Gredos, 1967). Henceforth referred to as Corominas.
4. This term in print offended several of the early critics. See Januario

—Oiga, amigo, ¿sabe?, estoy celebrando mi santo con *tamboreo* y *güifa* [pounding and shouting]. . . . Hay victrola para los que quieren bailar agarraos . . .
Larga una carcajada estruendosa, olor a vino y cebolla, y me invita:
—Pase, amigo . . . ¡Está *regüena* la fiestoca. . . . (*Hombres,* 38)

It is also Evaristo who employs most of the vulgar or obscene words in the first novel: *carajo, fregar, joder, mierda, puta,* and the epithet, *maricón.* Chileans differ in their definitions of some of these terms and the degree of their coarseness. Some feel they are only vulgar; others consider them to be obscenities in Chile as they are in many Spanish-speaking regions.

In the second novel the boy companions of Enrique have the most vulgar language and slang:

—¿Qué, te reís hijo'e puta? . . . (*Sangre,* 62)

—No le hagai caso a ese pendejo . . . Es una porquería . . . —me habló Llanos. (*Sangre,* 98)

The changes Guzmán made in his manuscripts and in the corrected editions of his books were primarily in diction. Once a work was written he made no structural changes, but on occasions he would change words or eliminate paragraphs. An example of deletion of this type is the highly rhetorical paragraph at the end of Chapter 2 of *Los hombres obscuros* which was omitted after the third edition. Several alterations can be seen in a comparison of manuscript page 35 and the corresponding printed page of *La sangre y la esperanza.*[5] For example, in the following sentence Guzmán deleted *mierda* and substituted *carajo* in the manuscript itself, but neither *mierda* nor *carajo* appears in any of the published editions:

—¡Ah, trayendo mujeres aquí, [carajo,] trayendo mujeres, ah! . . . (*Sangre* 56)

In addition, between manuscript and book *clamaba* becomes *exclamaba, titán* is changed to *bestia,* and *y tiritaba* becomes *temblando.* Though *carajo* was deleted from the above sentence, it was

Espinosa, "Nicomedes Guzmán y su libro *Los hombres obscuros,*" *Atenea,* 172 (October 1939), 110–11.
5. Page 35 of the MS corresponds to pp. 63–65 in the 1st and 2d eds., 55–57 in the Argentine ed., 56–57 in the Nascimento ed., 59–60 in the Zig-Zag ed., and 61–62 in the Quimantú editions.

added to another. Once the book was in print, however, few changes were made. One sentence that is eliminated after the third edition is "Y pensé: 'mamá.' " There are several possible reasons for the deletion. One is that Guzmán decided the sentence was too reminiscent of Gold's novel (cf. pp. 148–50, above), or too Freudian. Another, less likely reason is that a sentence was eliminated inadvertently by a typesetter, because "también" in the revised sentence makes little sense: "Y pensé también: 'Angélica.' "

Most of the changes that Guzmán made in his works involved vulgarities. He often changed *tetas* to *pechos*, or *mierda* to *miéchica*. In these instances, perhaps, the author does not want to use language too harsh for his character. It is in these instances that he turns to substitutes for vulgarities, which in their own way are even more provincial. *Pucha* often replaces *puta* in dialogues; *puto* is replaced by *pucho*, slang for "cigarette butt." Occasionally *caracho* is used in place of *carajo* (*caracho* refers to the aspect of one's face; and it is a shade of violet). Through such euphemisms as well as slang, the author is able to represent the natural talk of the conventillo.

In *La luz viene del mar*, Guzmán attempts to reflect the vocabulary of the North. There are references to fish, animals, and birds of the region, such as *gallinazo*, which generally means "buzzard" in South America, but in northern Chile and Peru is generic for any large bird. Vulgarities like *mecón* ("turd") represent the rough talk of the miners.

This has been only a minor sampling of the many colloquial or regional words which Guzmán selects to depict the popular speech of the masses. It is only natural that the author's preference for *modismos* has limited the popularity of his works in other countries where the reader may not be familiar with the expressions he uses. Guzmán had noble intentions. He hoped to produce a meaningful portrait of the Chilean proletarian during a three-decade period (1920–50) in order to make the soon-to-emerge proletarian culture as meaningful and accessible to the masses as possible. His art would elevate the common man and give heroic character to his folk language.

We can trace an evolution in another aspect of diction, the author's use of derivatives. Diminutives are occasionally formed in the traditional manner, by adding -*ito* suffixes to the word: for example, Elena becomes Elenita. Guzmán prefers, however, to employ words with the alternative diminutive ending *-illo*, which is popular in Chile: *chiquillos, escalerilla, carboncillo, putilla, pocillo, portillo*. The *-illo* diminutive may also convey a pejorative meaning, as may some of the suffixes explained in following paragraphs.

Only occasionally do other suffixes (such as *-oca*, as in *fiestoca*) appear in the first two novels. In *La luz viene del mar*, however, caricature becomes important. Objects become large, ugly, and distorted, and we see words like *gallinazo, trabajadorazo, barquichuelo, cabezuela, locuela, portezuela, salvajuelo, polluello de pájaro marino, ratonzuela* (the Chinese girl), *carretón, mascarón, vozarrón, gigantón, mecón,* and *lagrimones.* Marathon Montrose Ramsey points out that *-uelo* endings express contempt; they may or may not indicate smallness.[6] Derivatives indicating amplitude, magnitude, and repulsiveness are used in strategic locations to give the novel a tone of absurdity or add a pejorative inflection (see, for example, *Luz*, 294–95).

In the first two novels, few neologisms were used. The only apparent invented word in these two novels is the onomatopoetic *ñauquear*, meaning "to meow." In *La luz viene del mar*, however, Guzmán revealed a special talent for inventing words. One reviewer found at least eight neologisms in the novel: *tremeluciente, brotecer, hojecer, llagosos, zorrastrón, sebientos, zangolotear,* and *fauceando*.[7] Two words he cites as neologisms, *aparragado* and *amorriñada*, are seemingly common Chilean words.

The author's onomatopoetic words follow a definite pattern also. Although there are only four such imitative words in *Los hombres obscuros*, each sound is repeated in a trinary rhythm: "*tan, tan, tan*" (a bell); "*tru . . . tru . . . tru . . .*" (the trutruca); "*crac . . . crac . . . crac . . .*" (the sounds of Pablo's landlords making love); and "*pum . . . pum . . . pum . . .*" (police shots during a strike).

In *La sangre y la esperanza* this pattern is generally broken except when Enrique calls his dog with a "*¡pch, pch, pch! . . .*" (*Sangre*, 118), and Elena rocks a baby to sleep, humming "*Schss . . . Schss . . . Schss . . .*" in both trinary and binary patterns (*Sangre*, 183–84). Also, the words imitating noises are more innovative: "*¡Pafff!*" (watermelon rinds thrown as children's bombs into the water);

6. Marathon Montrose Ramsey, *A Textbook of Modern Spanish*, revised by Robert K. Spaulding (New York: Holt, 1956), p. 629.

7. Cedomil Goić, "*La luz viene del mar, novela*, por Nicomedes Guzmán," *Atenea*, 324 (June 1952), 538.

"¡Papúuuu! . . . ¡Papúuuu! . . ." (an ambulance siren). Except for laughter (generally *ja, ja, ja* in all of his narrations), only rarely does the narrator revert to the trinary pattern so prevalent in the first novel. The sound of a spanking is *"¡chas! ¡chas! ¡chas!"* Enrique recalls a song that his mother sang so his sister could dance to its rhythm:

> Tínguilin, tínguilin,
> tínguilin, ton . . . *(Sangre,* 225)

The author's most artful use of onomatopoeia is to be found in his short story, "Extramuros," where sounds weave a leitmotif in neo-Baroque counterpoint. The rain drips on the ash-covered coals, giving off two different sounds, and the cat meows intermittently: *"¡Afff! . . . ¡Afff! . . . Ñau. . . . Pfff, pfff."* Guzmán even attempts to intensify and diversify sounds with punctuation and italics.

In his later short stories and in his last novel, the author places less emphasis on his onomatopoetic words. They are not set out in triplets or italics as they were in earlier works. This does not mean that they are any less suggestive; rather they are less obvious, more a part of the narration. In *La luz viene del mar* Carmona's pickup-truck motor overheats, producing a *sisear,* and later it begins to howl *(aullar)* as it humanly tries to communicate its total incapacity. *Guaaa* and *ulular* are used in the novel much like the traditional onomatopoetic words in the following paragraph cited by Dyson:

> Y, abierto el portalón, salimos todos como una bandada de extraños pájaros a los cuales hubiesen cortado las alas, en medio de un crujir de canastos, sonajera de tachos y rechinar de ruedas.[8]

Onomatopoeia is replaced by poetic expression in the later works, for the narrator prefers to describe sounds rather than create them:

> La vida de Tomasita tendría desde este instante la significación de las campanas de San Gerardo, que, por más que tocaran y tocaran, guardaban en aglutamiento melodioso, sólo la sonoridad secreta y onomatopéyica de la vida en la simple florescencia de sus metálicas pieles mordidas por los verdes vegetales de la herrumbre, olor a mar, a camanchacas, a soles secos, a melancólicos atardeceres. *(Luz,* 309)

In this instance the author prefers to strengthen his prose with alliteration and only refer to onomatopoeia. In the first novel the

8. John P. Dyson, "Los cuentos de Nicomedes Guzmán," *Atenea,* 404 (1964), p. 248. Quoted from "El pan bajo la bota," *El pan bajo la bota,* p. 35.

intent was different, for the narrator was like a tape recorder, attempting to capture all the sounds of the *conventillo*.

Guzmán makes frequent use of alliteration. Dyson gives several examples of alliteration in the short stories, and he discusses another phenomenon mentioned earlier in this work, Guzmán's frequent repetition of certain words or phrases.[9]

The elements of Guzmán's diction harmoniously combine popular expression—a reflection of the newly born Chilean proletarian culture—and poetic expression. His poetic expression is gained through onomatopoeia and through Baroque embellishments—archaisms and archaic syntax, which will be examined in the next section.

Though in his first two novels Guzmán shows a preference for -*illo* diminutives, in his last novel his relationship to reality is less intimate, for he uses words ending in -*azo*, -*uela*, -*ón*, suffixes that generally connote animosity instead of endearment.

Finally, Guzmán's desire to reflect the underlying linguistic norms of his people by including regionalisms for their popular values also leads him to create neologisms in the guise of *chilenismos*. This attempt to express "reality" faithfully is a socrealist technique whereby the novelist repeats the vulgarities and obscenities of his proletarian and subproletarian types because of their outstanding shock value.

Syntax

Through syntax Guzmán attempts to reflect popular thinking and to echo the language of the masses. Except in dialogue, Guzmán's sentence structure generally follows traditional norms. There are two slight deviations: archaic syntax and fragmentation.

The entire Generation of 1938 experimented with archaic expressions and a Baroque style. Guzmán indulged in neo-Baroque imagery and excessive use of enclitic verb forms. In the beginnings of his novels, when his narrators emphasize clarity in their presentation, few pronouns are joined enclitically to verb forms other than the more commonly accepted unions (with present participles, infinitives, and imperatives). In *Los hombres obscuros* Pablo uses few enclitics. In the first two chapters of *La sangre y la esperanza* there are apparently only two or three like "Y largóse a 'cuncu-

9. Dyson, "Los cuentos de Nicomedes Guzmán."

near.' " Although such unions of verb and pronoun do not usually appear in dialogue, they do appear in the narrative, especially in Guzmán's essays where he affects a rhetorical tone. The author's autobiography contains more enclitic structures than any of his other works. Enclisis in some forms is avoided in many Spanish speaking areas because of its archaic aspect. Guzmán even violates the accepted Chilean rules of enclisis:

> Con los modos indicativo y potencial, los pronombres van generalmente en proclisis, es decir, antepuestos al verbo: "Nosotros lo vimos." "El me escribió." Pero *pueden* igualmente ir en *enclisis*, es decir, pospuestos, siempre que el verbo sea la primera palabra de la frase, siga inmediatamente a una oración subordinada o cláusula absoluta, o esté empleado con valor de imperativo.[10]

Violations of this norm can be seen in the following sentences: "Los alientos tornábanse blancas volutas en el aire helando" (*Sangre*, 151); "Los urgentes menesteres hogareños obligáronme a enfrentarme a la visión de un mundo en mucho espantable, desconcertante y, sin embargo, ejemplarizador" (*Una moneda al río*, 7).

An archaism that Guzmán frequently employs is the use of the conjunction *mas* instead of *pero*, especially where contemporary usage would prefer *pero*: "Mas esta sombra que le abrumaba y la insistencia de Fernandito, por permanecer a su lado o entre sus piernas."

Guzmán also has a peculiar manner of combining an adverb and a possessive pronoun:

> Es el rostro de un agente. *Detrás suyo* hay dos carabineros chatos y fornidos. (*Hombres*, 137)

> Aunque las malas lenguas no dan tregua a su palabrería, y aunque *alrededor nuestro* se crean historias inverosímiles, hemos aprendido a encastillarnos dentro de nosotros mismos. . . . (*Hombres*, 173)

Guzmán was in accord with the spirit of his generation when he used archaic words and constructions (*famélico* in place of *hambriento*, for example, or *fenecida* for *muerta*). Often such terms have multiple meanings that the contemporary words do not have, and they allow for a style that is frequently neo-Baroque, both in diction and syntax.

10. Julio Meza T., *Gramática castellana del siglo XX. Curso general para la enseñanza en los colegios secundarios y en las escuelas normales* (Santiago: Editorial Nascimento, 1955), pp. 265–66.

As was mentioned in Chapter 11, whenever Guzmán inserts a sentence fragment—a clause, phrase, or single word in the place of what would ordinarily be a complete sentence in the narrative—he does so to increase the tempo of the story: "Las nueve. Las diez."

Fragmentation in syntax also represents the rapid thinking of the narrator-protagonist during a strike: "Palos, peñascazos. Disparos. Balance: uno, dos muertos. Varios heridos" (*Hombres*, 141). The author does not use these incomplete sentences to excess; rather he saves them for rapid action or for scenes of emotion. A good example of this depiction of rapid action can be found in Enrique's first excursion outside the familiar world of the conventillo. Not only is the tempo increased, but there are too many things in his new world for him to be able to comprehend them all in just a brief glance:

> Corredores. Jardines. Patios friolentos de árboles.
> Uno. Dos. Tres pabellones.
> Aquí, Sala "San Juan."
> Camas. Enfermos. Visitas. Monjas. Y, por sobre todo, el espeso, obstinado y fastidioso olor a medicina, a clínica. Quejidos. Palabras acezantes. Lágrimas.
> Cama ll. ***
> —¡Papacito!... ¡Papacito!... (*Sangre*, 214)

In this Whitmanesque poetic vision of a child's first visit to the hospital, each single word conveys an image except for the child-captivating odor of medicine, which is given the emphasis of two lines. The reader is able to identify with the child jerked along by his mother as he attempts to contemplate the strange new scene.

Fragmentation has become an important and meaningful element in Guzmán's narrative technique. Besides adding time, tempo, and emotion, it adds a poetical characteristic with its brief images and short phrases.

Adjectives

An author's use of adjectives reflects his sensibility. Here we will examine Guzmán's innovative patterns in the use of adjectives and attempt to define the tone of his writing.

Single Adjectives

The adjectives in Guzmán's works are often taxed to the very limits of their capabilities. In the following example, one adjective extends its semantic values to modify three nouns: "Mis manos se encuentran ya palpando la suavidad, el calor y la dureza *vírgenes* de sus pequeños pechos" (*Hombres*, 165). *Vírgenes* must stretch the reader's imagination through transformation as it modifies *suavidad, calor,* and *dureza.* On another occasion the author extends to the adjective "virgin" a quality that is only symbolic:

—¡Soñaba, ay, no sé qué! —continuó, restregándose los ojos con los dedos *olor a sexo virgen*—. ¡Los sueños se olvidan al momento de soñarlos! (*Luz*, 274)

Occasionally the adjectives are used in unusual combinations: "Su diestra convida de su *obrera* suavidad a mi rostro" ([*sic*] *Hombres*, 150). Or the image of death is extended to an unusual combination: the metal in a bullet is "metal mortífero."

Through adjectives the author often focuses on putrid odors, sounds, and abnormalities in the conventillo. A common socrealist image in all three novels is *dentadura cariada.*

Several of the neologisms in *La luz viene del mar* are adjectives: *zorrastrón, tremeluciente, llagosos,* and *sebientos.*

In *La luz viene del mar* Guzmán achieved his greatest innovations with adjectives as can be demonstrated in the progressive complication of the adjective "blue." *Azul* sufficed for the first novels; but in his last, his preference is for *azulenco* (*Luz*, 15), compounded in "La claridad *azulenco-rojiza* trepaba por los ramajes del cielo . . ." (*Luz*, 95), and later, "Los ojos abrazaban la cabeza del conductor, enredada ya entre las láminas *lechiazulencas* que aleteaban en el foco de las linternas" (97). This limited example demonstrates Guzmán's evolution of an innovative poetic expression.

Double Adjectives

Where a single adjective will suffice, Guzmán does not add the embellishment of the double adjective unless he definitely feels that it is warranted. Sometimes he exaggerates Gongoristically: "Los dientes *albos y parejos*, dientes de conchuelas niñas, son, en medio de su risa, como instrumentos de gorjeo" (*Luz*, 17). Or a pairing of adjectives begins and ends a sentence to give balance: "*Hermosa* y *pulida* la mañana colmada de luz *aurífera* y *cuprífera*" (*Luz*, 15). Here two popular adjectives at the opening of the sentence contrast with two latinate adjectives at the end.

Most of Guzmán's literary universe rests on antithesis. Counterbalancing adjectives are often paired to show two faces of the same coin:

> Y todo fue un conjunto *grotesco* y *conmovedor* de voces *distintas* y *angustiadas*, que se adosaban a los acordes que El Pirata arrancaba a las cuerdas. (*Luz*, 269)

The first pair of adjectives is antithetical: a "grotesque" chorus ordinarily would impart disgust, but here it is "moving." The second pair emphasizes the contrast between the girls ("voces distintas") and between this spontaneous chorus and an orthodox choir, which would not sing with such personal anguish. The second pair also reverses the order of the first; "angustiadas" is related to "grotesco," while "distintas" emphasizes "conmovedor."

Since excessive pairing of adjectives tends to tire the reader, Guzmán treated this device with caution, but he used it where necessary to produce contrast, emphasis, or Baroque embellishment.

Triple Adjectives

Though he does not use it as frequently as double or single adjectivation, the multiple adjective is Guzmán's great strength. In his early works he used this device only to round out the noun in three small steps: "Las ropas de cama las devolvieron todas *manchadas, quemadas* y *hediondas* a desinfectantes" (*Hombres*, 192). Each new adjective augments the original image only slightly, in a progressively negative sense.

Later each additional adjective begins to add different values to the noun and to add contrast: "Su muslo era *suave, caliente, duro*" (*Sangre*, 199). While the images of the adjectives are those of touch, *suave* and *duro* are antithetical. Undoubtedly the narrator hoped to convey the idea to his audience that little Leontina's flesh was capable of being both soft and hard. The Spanish implies a double meaning which may be conveyed in English as "velvety and firm," or "soft and hard."

During this middle period of the author's productivity, the trio of adjectives was commonly linked without the conjunction "y." This pattern is especially prevalent in the short stories written during the early 1940s:

No fue menester que echara afuera un pecho, puesto que ambos estaban desbordándose por sobre el escote de la pulgueada camisa, *grandotes, abundosos, brunos.* . . .

Había en el cuartucho un olor profundo a leche, a sebo quemado; o quizá si perseverara en el aire un hálito de vida estelar *ciega, desatentada, fenecida.* ("Rapsodia en luz mayor," *Una moneda al río,* 62)

The adjectival trio is used by the omniscient narrator in this passage to characterize a social type, to depict a personage in spatial terms. The unusual image of the first paragraph also caught the attention of John Dyson, who discovered that the very same three modifiers are repeated:

". . . *grandes* pechos siempre *grávidos, rebosantes*" (pág. 44); "y seguidamente, con la pequeña llorona en la falda, echó al aire uno de los *sabrosos, grandotes y brunos* pechos" (pág. 57).[11]

This ternary motif repeats itself like a short melody or like an erotic triad harmony in Guzmán's "Rapsodia en luz mayor."

In *La luz viene del mar,* where there are many triple adjectives, the most common pattern is a return to the simple augmentation of the original value of the noun with each succeeding adjective, whether it be on an ascending or descending scale of intensification: "rosadilla, tostada, arenosa" (*Luz,* 45), "blancos, reverberantes, enceguecedores" (*Luz,* 193), and "temblorosa, mágico e inquietante" (*Luz,* 281). While the first two examples increase in intensification, the last describes a generally decreasing state of motion and emotion, which the narrator observes in Virginia's eyes whenever she undergoes "momentos de *inquietud,* de *asombro* o de *ternura.*" The narrator clarifies the three adjectives with the three nouns at the end of the sentence: *tembloroso—inquietud; mágico—asombro; inquietante—ternura.*

Guzmán returns to the more common use of the conjunction with three adjectives in his final novel, but he still appears to prefer asyndeton.

One of the author's most artistic elaborations, seen in his short stories and last novel, is the addition of a further modifier to the last adjective of a series. For example, the final adjective is expanded by a short prepositional phrase that adds a plastic image or metaphor: "Carcajadas circulares, triangulares, rodeadas de aristas" (*Luz,* 235).

11. Dyson, "Los cuentos de Nicomedes Guzmán," p. 238; references by Dyson are to "Rapsodia en luz mayor," in *La carne iluminada.*

Multiple Adjectives

In some of his later works, Guzmán experimented with combinations of four or more adjectives:

> Pero, se estaba allí, sin moverse, *erguido, digno, pálido, limpio,* varón sin mancha, luchando en esa lucha sorda, pero grande y eterna de la conciencia contra el corazón. ("Aún quedan madreselvas," *Una moneda al río,* 39)

Besides the four adjectives, the sentence contains additional phrases and elements with adjectival values.

La luz viene del mar was written at the height of the author's concentration on style, and it contains numerous strings of adjectives: "Desnudez *estoica, tranquila, pura, libre*"; "el tamarugo *gigantón, gesticulante, heroico y profundo*"; "vio alejarse a los hombres, *airada, sorda* y *odiosa, perdida* lo mismo que un pájaro ciego en los ramajes de la amargura."

Guzmán's ultimate effort in adjectivation is Andrade's death scene in the brothel, which is not a sentence but a sentence fragment:

> Y encima de la cama, entre sábanas que apozaban inmensas cantidades de gelatina roja y humeante, Pedro Andrade, *desnudo* también, *desencajado,* huido de ánimos, *pálido, transparente, fenecido, rígido* el chongo de brazo, en el que se enredaba aún una tira de venda cárdena. (*Luz,* 267)

The stylistic intensification of death is heightened even further in the novel by the erotic scene that precedes it. Each of the adjectives adds a supplementary image of death and intensifies the mock-pastoral tragedy. There is also an implicit absurdity in Andrade's nakedness before the world; moreover, the adjectives here intensify progressively down to the last, *rígido,* which through its two implications (death and stiffness) focuses on the arm stub—the absurd and meaningless cause of Andrade's death.

Guzmán's use of multiple adjectives in his later works can be attributed in part to his change to a third-person point of view. In his early works, with their boy narrators, such flowery language would be unreal. Also, in much of the later narration, the characters are stereotypes or proletarian stock characters. The poetic enumeration of their qualities and descriptions of the scenery are thus justified, for the author's intent is to characterize in superficial, rather than penetrating, terms.

Imagery

In literature an image conveys a psychological message: "The only way that ideas can be transmitted or preserved is by their transformation into pictures, models, words (most of which are arbitrary symbols), or other symbols."[12] Generally, Guzmán has a message, which he often conveys through an image, always insistent that imagery be faithful to life, truth, and reality, a concept proposed by Gorky.[13]

Although socialist realism makes use of images that have previously been avoided because they are offensive, Guzmán's writings also contain moving scenes and images of an artistic nature. Repulsive images have a purpose; the socrealists argue that they stand for elements that have been imposed on the lower segment of society by a dominating class. An author like Guzmán shows contrast in his works, because he is obligated to portray certain offensive scenes and situations, but at the same time he evokes antithetical elements of beauty emanating from the proletarian class. This last selection betrays his great sensitivity, an important factor in Guzmán's personality.

Though his imagery often portrays the oppressive determinism of the conventillo in all its squalor and filth, Guzmán also creates plastic images as fine as any in Chilean prose:

> Hunde sus manos en las lavazas.
> Las lágrimas aflorando en sus pestañas,
> reflejan, en miniatura, la llama
> nerviosa de la vela. (*Hombres*, 123)

Contrast is a key to understanding Guzmán's imagery and his fiction.[14] Here the poverty-stricken washerwoman who has to work by candlelight into the late hours is contrasted to the beauty of the

---

12. Mary McDermott Shideler, *The Theology of Romantic Love: A Study in the Writings of Charles Williams* (Grand Rapids, Mich.: William B. Eerdmans Publishing Co., 1966), p. 15.

13. Maxim Gorky at the 1934 All-Union Congress of Soviet Writers, quoted by William Empson, *Some Versions of Pastoral* (New York: New Directions Paperbacks, 1968), p. 17.

14. In outlining a brief article I was commissioned to write synthesizing discoveries of my first year's research on Guzmán, "Nicomedes Guzmán y el espejo doble del conventillo," *Revista de los sábados* (Santiago), August 21, 1971, Luis Sánchez Latorre suggested that emphasis be placed on this antithetical aspect of Guzmán's *Weltanschauung*.

candle flame reflected in the accumulating tears suspended from her eyelashes.

Other candle images have been pointed out earlier in this book. There is a dramatic image of Pablo's landlady reflected esperpenti-cally by candlelight on the sheet that hangs across their tiny room, dividing Pablo's area from the family's. See page 131 of the Zig-Zag editions of the novel for an artist's sketch of a similar scene.

Images can be grouped according to the sense that perceives them. Thus it is possible to speak not only of visual images but also of images of sound, odor, taste, and touch.

The narrator's visual images are occasionally altered by their passage through his psyche, where they are augmented by free association:

> Me quedo mirando cabrillear las letras del libro. Se me ocurre que, de improviso, cobran vida. Las veo danzar como mujeres desnudas, que provocan dulce y terriblemente. ¡Ah bellas e incitantes hembras danzando al ritmo caliente de mi sangre! (*Hombres*, 134)

Though Pablo is trying to read, he is so sexually aroused by the conventillo's night sounds that even the letters on the page of a book become dancing nudes.

As was mentioned in the preceding section, adjectives generally incorporate an image into the narration. These images become very striking, especially when each additional adjective adds visual qualities or when the image is augmented through a simile:

> Las manos *enflaquecidas, transparentes, nervudas* y *venosas*, aparecían en el extremo deshilachado de las mangas, como los ramajes podados de quizá que extraños arbustos. ("Aún quedan madreselvas," *Una moneda al río*, 30)

Auditory images also serve an important function in Guzmán's novels, and Dyson cites odors and sounds as favorite motifs in his short stories.[15] When Pablo and Inés leave the hotel in *Los hombres obscuros* after experiencing intercourse, they are suddenly bombarded with sounds:

> Un borracho orina junto a un poste, *entonando* una cueca. A lo lejos, *se oye rechinar* un tranvía girando en una curva. Tras una puerta, *ladra* furiosamente *un perro*. (*Hombres*, 170)

15. Dyson, "Los cuentos de Nicomedes Guzmán," pp. 234, 238, 247.

The young couple's experience of sex has made them more aware of their surroundings and of their own existence. A honking horn is also repeated as a motif throughout this episode.

A unique image that Guzmán employs frequently, almost as a motif in the first two novels and in many of his stories, is the sound of urine ringing like a tambourine against a floor or a basin:

> Los orines arrancan sonidos de pandereta al fondo de la bacinica. (*Hombres*, 69)

> Después, el tiesto sonó como una pandereta bajo el chorro de los orines. ("Destello en la bruma," *Una moneda al río*, 92)

This exaggeration of the unusual, which some readers may find obscene, is a major part of Guzmán's socialist-realist imagery, and it draws attention to the poverty of the conventillo. Yet more orthodox images are also to be found in his writing:

> De súbito los hombres callaron. Apenas se impuso un:
> —¡Schsss! . . . —suave como rasguido de viento en las alas de un gallinazo.
> Las velas que apresuráronse a apagar los hombres dejaron en el aire un *olor* profundo a velorio. En la cueva ligeramente horadada, los calicheros se tendieron, fino y firme el oído alargado hacia las distancias.
> Ni un ruido más allá de la sinfonía azul y profunda del silencio. (*Luz*, 22)

Here, besides sounds, and the synesthesia of the last paragraph, reference is made to odor. Occasionally odors are nostalgic, but sometimes they are nothing more than an excuse to metaphorize the slums: "Parpadeaban las luces del depósito. Había un *olor húmedo* a sombra. *Olor a invierno* apercancado. *Olor a charca* sin estrellas" (*Sangre*, 143).

More often than not, Guzmán's proletarian odors are those of urine and decay. Evaristo, it will be remembered, spews from his mouth offensive obscenities and evil-smelling odors: "Larga una carcajada estruendosa, *olor a vino y cebolla* . . ." Occasionally the author compounds the images:

> *Alientos alcohólicos.* . . . Y sobre todo, el *hálito* atosigante, y, sin embargo, agradable, tónico, del alquitrán en ebullición. ¡Y la *fragancia* de los troncos de eucalipto que se doblegan enteros entre las muelas de las llamas! ("Extramuros," *Una moneda al río*, 85)

The "teeth of the fire," is also an interesting and innovative image. Odors and flavors are often mixed. Enrique Quilodrán cannot stomach the odor or flavor of a soup his mother has made out of putrid leftovers. The social implication is important, and the author stresses the gravity of the family's situation by explaining that the spoiled soup makes both Elena and little Enrique vomit. At times these images may offend the sensitive reader. Yet because of Guzmán's desire to remain faithful to reality, he often exaggerates it through shocking images. A sickly woman being asked to drink fresh donkey milk exclaims:

> —No, mamá. No me da lo mismo. Tibia parece que tuviera gusto a pasto malo, olor a orines . . . No sé . . . Ni fría la tomaría . . . ¡Ay, si no estuviera enferma. ("Leche de burra," *Pan bajo la bota,* 100)

This story is filled with various odor images, each with its own symbolism. The situation has symbolic implications as well. The woman who sells the milk is having an affair with the sick woman's husband; later she entices him to run away with her, and the sick woman's mother adds a final blow when she confesses that she too was in love with her son-in-law.

A tactile image memorably executed in *La sangre y la esperanza* also unites two contiguous episodes. In the first, Enrique is taken from his family's flat and placed in bed with little Marita. In the second, he is allowed to return to his family's room, from which he had been banished because his mother was delivering a baby:

> A mí me acostaron con Mara . . .
> —¡Estás calientito! . . . Y se puso a tocarme. Yo palpé también sus muslos. Sus carnes eran tibias, apretadas.
> —¡No acá! . . . —me susurró ella, y se desabrochó el calzón.
> La felicidad de nuestras manos era felicidad, también, de nuestros pequeños corazones. (*Sangre,* 108)

> El chiquillo era feo, rojo, arrugado . . . . No me gustó mi hermano. Pero toqué ligeramente su rostro. Era terso. Acudió a mi mano la misma sensación de terciopelo que me produjo el contacto del pequeño sexo de Mara. (*Sangre,* 109)

Through the images Enrique associates psychologically two experiences he is too young to understand: the birth of the baby and the female sex organ, which is the origin of life.

This motif of hiding birth from a boy seems to have its origin in

Víctor Domingo Silva's *Palomilla brava*.[16] In this novel the parents send Papelucho to the house of Torres, the shoemaker, who helps him change his life in a brief interview; when Papelucho returns to his proletarian home, his parents attempt to deceive him (as do the parents of Enrique and Hijuna): "Te ha llegado un hermanito de las Uropas."

Psychological imagery takes the reader inside a character's mind. Pablo's thoughts run in streams of consciousness when he is waiting for Inés (*Hombres*, 155–58); from the depths of his psyche come images that pertain to a concrete world, although some are surrealistically distorted. Pablo is also startled when he comes across his own image staring back at him in a mirror:

> Me levanto. Enciendo luz. Tengo la cabeza como desvanecida. Un espejo canalla me entrega a los ojos el ridículo de mi propia imagen. Mechas caídas sobre la frente. Ojos medio encapotados. Me agarro la cabeza. Busco asiento. Una terca angustia me aprieta la garganta. (*Hombres*, 166–67)

Pablo has just gotten out of bed after having had intercourse with Inés; he has given in to his animal instinct. The image he sees in the mirror is one of Guzmán's first attempts to illustrate the absurdity of human existence when it is outside of unanimist social effort. The method the author employs is like an esperpento. The mirror image also allows Pablo to describe himself to the reader, who has no opportunity to see him except through the mirror and the comment of other characters. His reactions to the reflection reveal elements in his character that the reader would otherwise miss.

Guzmán's imagery ranges from preciosity to shock. The precious image is often augmented through neo-Baroque metaphor; the harsh images are derived from socialist realism. Both reflect the style that is particular to Guzmán and his generation, and they illustrate contrast, a major characteristic of his writing.

Later in his career Guzmán discovered that his most striking images could be developed through the stream-of-consciousness of his omniscient narrators. This style evolved from his first novel, where several levels of the narrator's conscious mind were exposed; such free association was not possible in *La sangre y la esperanza*.

16. Víctor Domingo Silva, *Palomilla brava* (Santiago: Editorial Nascimento, 1923), pp. 36–41.

Closely related to the metaphor is the figurative language of synesthesia, in which several responses of the physical senses are blended into a single image (see the two examples cited on p. 255). Most of Guzmán's synesthesia appears in *La luz viene del mar*:

> Batíase flojamente la delgada cortina, en la que cerníase el *olor espeso* de la *luz*, trayendo algo así como una *fragancia* de sandía madura recién partida. . . . (*Luz*, 297)

The narrator has combined touch (*espeso*), odor (*olor*), and sight (*luz*).

One of the most artistic passages of the novel is also one of the most absurd; the contrast is typical of Guzmán. The scene presents a choir of prostitutes singing a Protestant hymn at the death of Andrade:

> Y todos, densas las cabezas de humores de alcohol, hicieron coro de cristales y diamantes, los ojos devorados por las lágrimas. Los rostros eran finos y acendrados manantiales en donde la alborada quería eternizar el brillo de las estrellas que se derrumbaban encima de las brumosas lontananzas marítimas. (*Luz*, 270)

The poet in Guzmán makes himself heard even when his narrative is focused on the degradation of society.

Metaphor

Even though metaphors have been pointed out throughout this study, Guzmán's use of them should be examined more closely. Generally, his metaphors humanize inanimate objects (the slums, the sun, the pampa, the sea) or of animals; some, however, dehumanize characters who allow their primitive instincts to overcome them. For the purpose of this study, no distinction will be made between metaphor and simile.

In the first two novels the conventillo is often compared to a person or given human qualities. On one occasion it is pictured as "extático en su actitud de viejo en cuclillas y de cara acongojada, en la imposibilidad de elevarse . . ." (*Hombres*, 18). The slum molds all its inhabitants. Not only is the conventillo humanized, so too are the sky, the sun, and even a cot:

Arriba, el cielo nos tiende su mano ancha y cordial de estrellas, su recia mano de verdadero camarada. Y por los ojos sentimos su contacto suave y rudo al mismo tiempo, lo sentimos como una bendición armoniosa del universo. (*Hombres*, 171)

El guardia paseábase como un patrón omnipotente. Sus bigotes ralos,

Much of this humanization occurs in Guzmán's estampas, which do not follow a predictable pattern until *La sangre y la esperanza*. At that time in the author's career, the suburbs, the animals, all the elements of the universe become the poor man's comrades and are humanized:

Los suburbios, bajo el otoño, frente a la mirada turbia del tiempo, arrugaban el ceño, estiraban su osamenta crujiente, abierto el pecho franco a las cabezadas locas de los días. (*Sangre*, 274)

Occasionally an inanimate object, such as the sun, is seen as a goat or as a colt:

Ya era tarde. El sol galopaba sobre el poniente con las rojas crines al viento, tiñendo de cobre la cabellera verde de un naranjo plantado junto a un corredor. (*Sangre*, 64)

In the novel of the North, the sun, the desert, and the ocean are humanized: "El sol golpea de repente su augusta cabeza contra el 'Alto del Molle,' estallando en estrépitos dorados" (*Luz*, 16). This humanization is reversed when "El Pirate Cholakys" is introduced:

Por los rostros de El Cara de Pescado, El Yerba Luisa, La Siete Dedos, Teresa la Tuerta, Arsenia y los extraños contertulios que había en el salón nacía un aura brumosa de sacarina melancolía. Los ojos azules de Cholakys se llenaban de estrellas fugaces, que iban transformándose lentamente en lágrimas. *El rostro barbado se convirtió en pampa o mar onduloso*, por cuya superficie rielaban dos caravanas de corales cristalinos, esplendentes. (*Luz*, 116)

Cholakys himself is a metaphor. He embodies both the ocean and the desert. The pampas, the sea, and the sun form a unity; they reign as a single collectivity in Iquique. And for one moment two tears roll down the pampas-like bearded face of the invincible Greek. In this image Cholakys has been depersonalized; he has become the pampas or the sea.

Generally, however, human characters are depersonalized by being compared to animals:

Ya se acercaba Melania. Arrastraba la muleta y, extendiendo la bandeja de níquel, semejaba un raro pajarraco malogrado que intentara emprender el vuelo mediante una sola ala. (*Luz*, 244)

In most of Guzmán's works this "animalization" is applied to someone who is not a proletarian, like a prostitute or a policeman, both of whom are compared to lap dogs in the novels: "El agente echa a caminar hacia adentro. Los carabineros le siguen como dos perros falderos" (*Hombres*, 137). Perhaps because the two carabineros are "lap dogs," the other dogs of the neighborhood dislike them and cause a ruckus (*Hombres*, 138–39).

In a very metaphorical chapter of *La sangre y la esperanza* (Part III, Chapter 4, "Fantasmas"), the first three of the eight sections that make up the chapter consist mainly of metaphorical expressions. The dream sequence that follows is the most surrealistic passage of Guzmán's fiction, aggregating metaphors of Enrique suffering bestial feelings. During this period of Guzmán's career it is the nonproletarian who is animalized:

El guardia paseábase como un patrón omnipotente. Sus bigotes ralos, de punta, clavaban el aire. Y sus ojos oblicuos, de caliente y filosa mirada, hacían ver en su semblante el rostro agrio de un *gato en celo*. Sus pasos golpeaban en la vereda *como los de un caballo desatentado*. (*Sangre*, 275)

The animal image portrays man in a state of awkward absurdity, as though in a farce, or occasionally a caricature.

Metaphor is an important element in Guzmán's writing. Because of his carefully worked style, many readers and critics have considered Guzmán to be more poet than fiction writer. His background as a poet is clearly discernible, even in his earliest novels.

Irony

Irony exists in a work when there is a difference between what is said and what is meant, or between a character's intention and his accomplishment.

We have seen examples of irony in the above sections on Guzmán's treatment of prostitutes, point of view, and the mock-pastoral. Irony is evident in such characters as Cara de Pescado, who cuts out his eye for a girl who was only joking and playing with his affection. It is more apparent in Pedro Andrade, who cuts off his arm to achieve his life's dream but then dies in his sleep. The scene in which the prostitutes mourn Andrade's death by singing a hymn about being washed in the blood of the Lord is both ironic and grotesque. They have left their beds and are standing around his corpse in a total state of undress. The scene is an ironic commentary on proletarian morality.

Though irony is more intense in the later works, it is also common in the early writings, especially when Guzmán attempts to show the proletarian state as ironic in contemporary society. In *Los hombres obscuros* a man is found slit from his throat to his belt; an observer lifts the dead youth's shirt and states, "¡No fue nada!" (*Hombres*, 54). When the mother of this murder victim comes on the scene by chance and has a heart attack from the shock, the police officer states that they will have to wait until the woman comes to her senses before they take her off to jail to interrogate her.

Similar examples of irony pervade the entire literary production of Nicomedes Guzmán; yet the reader often misses this essential element, especially in *La luz viene del mar*, which has not been understood completely because of a lack of critical interpretation of irony and similar elements.

Symbol

The symbol is a word, a sign, a figure of speech, or even a situation that the author uses by constant repetition or suggestion to convey a very personal feeling or idea.

In Guzmán's writings it is possible to consider *ternura* (examined in Chapter 9) as a personal symbol. Especially is this true in light of the constant repetition of the word, *ternura*. Other obvious symbols are light in *La luz viene del mar* and blood and hope in *La sangre y la esperanza*. The light of the sun is one symbol, another is the light of the stars, and still another is the light of a candle. Often such symbols are combined with *ternura* in metaphors to convey in concrete terms Guzmán's ideal of proletarian existence.

The conventillo is a symbol also, the greatest symbol of space in the microcosms of Pablo and Enrique. Space in *La luz viene del mar* is symbolized in terms of light. The desert, the sea, and the people that space creates are, in themselves, symbols of the great North. The sand in the two bottles exchanged between Virginia and Eudocio (actually it is Lorenzo Carmona) is also a symbol of both space and time. The bottles are also symbolic, and the exchange symbolizes Virginia's love for Eudocio.

Time in all the novels is symbolized by bells. In *Los hombres obscuros* they ring from an indefinite "parroquia cercana"; in *La sangre y la esperanza* they sound from Andacollo; in *La luz viene del mar* we hear the bells from the tower of San Gerardo, from which Virginia observes her symbolic world.

All of the cosmos is the ally of the proletarian class, and besides symbolizing time and space, it signifies a glorious future for the poor:

> La madrugada es como una inmensa flor que se abriera. Como el *símbolo* de una nueva vida que viniera al encuentro de los hombres. Y allá, bajo sus pétalos mojados por el rocío de las últimas estrellas, bajo la sinfonía discorde de los gallos ciudadanos, se va el maestro Mercedes. (*Hombres*, 113)

The greatest single symbol in Guzmán's prose and poetry is the Marxist emblem of "callused hands." Calluses are found in the sensitive hands of the laborer, but they are also an erotic symbol in the palms of the heroines, Inés and Elena.[17] At the end of *Los hombres obscuros*, Pablo raises his callused fist in victory, threatening the world with the prophecy of revolution by the workers. In his autobiography Guzmán praised the callused hands of his father.

Guzmán planned to name *La sangre y la esperanza* "Las manos rudas." The symbolism of the callused hands is obvious in the novel; and it is used to show the evolution of Enrique. When he comes home from work at the end of the novel and discovers that his hands are growing calluses, he and the reader realize that he has become an adult; he has matured and joined the labor force of the world.

In conclusion, it should be pointed out that Guzmán began to abandon the callused-hand symbol in his later works. He turned to an angurrientista symbol of individuality: "El tiempo forjaba *anillos de acero* indestructible en el alma y *en las células* de Eudocio." "Sus células totales erizábanse de una inquietud familiar—propia de la integridad de su espíritu—frente a esta posición sugestionante de objetos." (*Luz*, 303).

17. [George] Arnold Chapman, "Perspectiva de la novela de la ciudad en Chile," in Arturo Torres-Ríoseco, ed., *La novela iberoamericana* (Albuquerque: University of New Mexico Press, 1952), pp. 203, 211–12, n.3.

In his "Trece meses del año" the biological cells become a metaphor for time:

> Luego, el hombre y la verdad están en el tiempo, o sea en el átomo de los segundos, en la *célula* de los minutos, en el organismo dinámico de las horas, en el heroísmo de los meses, en la vitalidad de las estaciones, en la arruga de los años, en el temblor sufrido del pasado, del presente, del futuro . . . en la quintaescencia del infinito. (*Cultura*, 96 [1964], 53)

As Guzmán becomes more individualistic and more humanistic in the course of his writing career, the symbol of man's cells replaces the Marxist emblem of callused hands, which held such high importance for the author in his youth.

The tone or mood of Guzmán's works emerges from an analysis of the author's style, for in a sense, tone is the aggregate of all the stylistic devices: diction, syntax, imagery, metaphor, symbolism.

Though all of these elements may be used to suggest optimism, pessimism does, in fact, dominate the author's prose fiction. His novels shock the reader into thinking about social evils. Often the author places the most intense violence near the end or the beginning of the novel in order to impress the reader with his realism. He digs in the dirt of social injustices to uncover true human feelings. In all Guzmán's fiction, however, the more artistic, more traditional elements complement the raw realism, enriching it by means of antithesis, internal rhyme and rhythm, and complicated patterns of images and motifs.

15

Conclusion

A boyish-looking national figure during his triumphant years, a frail wisp of a man when he died at fifty, Nicomedes Guzmán was always a proletarian. Even when he had gained international fame as an author, he surprised people by his modesty, for he often dressed in working clothes, even overalls; his pockets stuffed with notes, addresses, and old sales slips, he carried a briefcase bulging with books. A dynamic and hard-working man, Guzmán rushed from his bed early every morning into a cold shower (even in winter), singing the Chilean national anthem as he washed. His workday was long and often complicated when he obligated himself to more than one employer in order to support his large, fragmented family. After a career of hundreds of lectures on socialist literature and proletarian culture, he gained a reputation as an unflagging promoter of popular culture.

His idealism and his honesty were both remarkable. Once, even though his family was almost penniless, he bought a whole cage of birds from a street vendor in order to set them free. Such impetuosity was due to his perpetually free spirit, which caused him to act as if his personage offered refuge to the spirit of the Chilean roto, and impelled him to seize opportunities as they arose. This same tendency eventually destroyed him, for he would work to excess, going for long periods without proper nourishment or sleep, and then, as if he were a true embodiment of *angurrientismo*, he indulged to excess in food, alcohol, and sex.

Beginning as a poet like the majority of his generation, Guzmán learned from Pablo Neruda the essentials of poetic expression. Neruda, Danke, Sepúlveda, Rojas, and perhaps Romero were his contemporary idols, and when he turned to the past for inspiration, he read over and over the works of Lillo, D'Halmar, Barrios, Pezoa Véliz, and Edwards Bello.

When Miguel Serrano involved his generation in a serious polemic, Guzmán intervened and introduced a generation of proletarian writers. Guzmán insisted that his generation must alter not only Chilean literature but the methods and the approach of literary criticism.

His generation blossomed in 1938; a few years later it suffered a disintegration in unity, leadership, and ideals. Guzmán had become the leading theoretician of the group and outlined for his comrade writers a blueprint for Chilean socialist realism which he felt would put an end to criollismo and focus public attention on unjust social conditions. With the defeat of the Popular Front's ideals of "pan, techo y abrigo," and the swing of public attention away from socialist realism, Guzmán and his generation turned to investigating folk elements, in another kind of search for a collective identity. As they altered the structure and themes of their fiction, many socrealists formed an alliance with their previous enemies, the criollistas.

Guzmán's fiction progresses from the autobiographical to the dramatic, from the first to the third-person, from the present tense to the preterit.

After he matured, Guzmán became aware of certain weaknesses in characterization in his first novel, for, imitating North American Marxists, his present-tense chronicle attempts to portray proletarian problems and poverty in the conventillo through a mere panorama of persons and types. Although his archetypal mock-heroes in *La luz viene del mar* are too fragmented to be complete, and though his techniques in that novel confused his readers, the major characters in his early novels that emerged from his own experience are masterful and have been hailed in Chile as his greatest contribution to literature. For example, as a tribute to Enrique in *La sangre y la esperanza* and "El pan bajo la bota," a Chilean literary review carries the name *Quilodrán*. Guzmán also made an intense effort to depict the roto and other minor types as realistically as possible searching into the minds of such popular figures in order to discover the identity of Chile. He reproduced their graphic language and described convincingly the horrible environment in which they were forced to live. William Faulkner influenced Guzmán profoundly, especially through his innovations in structure.

As Guzmán presented the deplorable social situations that class privilege had imposed on his people, he contrasted the realism of his setting and action with a poetic vision of his proletarian world. His plastic images are either socialist-realist or neo-Baroque, his symbols are most often Marxist, but his greatest contribution to the Spanish American novel is his estampa—the picture-postcard view of time, space, light, and society—which becomes a characteristic device in his works and in the novels of other members of his generation, causing Guzmán to be remembered as one of Chile's most lyrical novelists. In his writings Guzmán exhibited a deep sense of reality and a profound sympathy with the downtrodden and oppressed. He invested the lowliest person in his works with a redeeming spark of hope for a better life. In Guzmán's philosophy, society, not the individual, was the villain.

Selected Bibliography

Works by Nicomedes Guzmán

Literary

La ceniza y el sueño. Poemas. Santiago: Talleres Gráficos de Ferrario, 1938.

———. 2d ed. Introductions by Pablo Neruda, Angel Cruchaga Santa María, and Juvencio Valle. Santiago: Ediciones del Grupo Fuego de la Poesía, 1960.

Los hombres obscuros. Novela. Preface by Jacobo Danke. Frontispiece by Alhué. Santiago: Ediciones Yunque, 1939. 2d ed., 1939.

———. 3d ed. Preface by Jacobo Danke [a new preface, same for all subsequent editions]. Frontispiece by Enrique Cornejo (Penike); zinc engravings by Carlos Hermosilla Álvarez. Santiago: Editorial Cultura, 1943.

———. 4th ed. Frontispiece by Gustavo Carrasco Délano; engravings by Carlos Hermosilla Álvarez. Santiago: Empresa Editora Zig-Zag, 1946.

———. 5th and 6th eds. Frontispiece and illustrations by Pedro Olmos. Santiago: Empresa Editora Zig-Zag, 1961, 1964.

La sangre y la esperanza. Barrio Mapocho. Novela. Vignettes by Carlos Hermosilla Álvarez. Santiago: Editorial Orbe, 1943. 2d ed. 1944.

———. 3d ed. Preface by Ricardo A. Latcham [appears in all subsequent editions]. Vignettes by Carlos Hermosilla Álvarez. Buenos Aires: Siglo Veinte, 1947.

———. 4th and 5th eds. Santiago: Editorial Nascimento, 1952, 1957.

———. 6th, 7th, and 8th eds. Santiago: Empresa Editora Zig-Zag, 1964, 1966, 1968.

———. 9th and 10th eds. Santiago: Quimantú [state-owned successor to Zig-Zag], 1971 (2 vols.), 1972 (1 vol.).

Donde nace el alba. Novelas breves. Santiago: Editorial Orbe, 1944.

La carne iluminada. Pequeñas narraciones. Linoleum engravings by Aníbal and Lautaro Alvial. Ediciones Amura. Santiago: Editorial Cultura, 1945.

"Una moneda al río." In *El cuento chileno.* Santiago: Editorial Nascimento, 1948. This was an offprint of *Atenea* 279–80 (1948).

"Coin in the River," translated by Paul J. Cooke. *Amigos* (Godfrey, Illinois), 3 (1950), 14–27.

La luz viene del mar. Novela. Illustrations by Enrique Lihn and Osvaldo Loyola. Ediciones Aconcagua. Santiago: Editorial Cultura, 1951.

———. 2d ed. Santiago: Empresa Editora Zig-Zag, 1963.

Leche de burra. Pequeña novela. Santiago: Ediciones Renovación, March 1953. A small pocket book, 2 x 3 inches, 55 pp. in the monthly series Antología Autores Actuales.

Una moneda al río y otros cuentos. Drawings by Osvaldo Loyola. Godfrey, Illinois: Monticello College Press, 1954. Includes edited version of "Pequeñas notas autobiográficas."

El pan bajo la bota. Preface by Fernando Santiván. Santiago: Empresa Editora Zig-Zag, 1960; reprinted 1963.
"La poruña." *Atenea*, 394 (1961), 138–51. Chapter 2 of *Los trece meses del año*.
"Algo de su autobiografía," "Plan de una novela: *Los trece meses del año*," and "*Los trece meses del año, novela*." *Cultura*, 96 (1964), 42–57. The "Plan," and the "Novela," or first chapter of the novel, are posthumous.

Critical

"Carlos Sepúlveda Leyton, novelista del pueblo." *Atenea*, 189 (March, 1941), 354–61.
"Miniatura histórico-informativa de las letras chilenas." In *Catálogo general de obras de autores nacionales*, pp. 15–30. Santiago: Editorial Cultura, 1946. Guzmán also inserted several one-page features on writers like Gabriela Mistral throughout the *Catálogo*.
"Encuentro emocional con Chile," *Atenea*, 380–81 (1958), 77–88. Speech given at the Primer Encuentro.

Editorial

Nuevos cuentistas chilenos. Antología. Selection, prologue, and notes by Nicomedes Guzmán. Santiago: Editorial Cultura, 1941.
Antología de Baldomero Lillo. Santiago: Empresa Editora Zig-Zag, 1955; 2d ed. 1965; 3d ed. 1969; 4th ed. 1970.
Antología de Carlos Pezoa Véliz (Poesía y Prosa). Selection, prologue and notes by Nicomedes Guzmán. Santiago: Empresa Editora Zig-Zag, 1957.
Antología de Carlos Pezoa Véliz (Poesía y Prosa). Selection, prologue mán. Santiago: Empresa Editora Zig-Zag, 1957; 2d ed. 1966, paperback.
Antología de cuentos [de] Marta Brunet. Selection, prologue, notes, and bibliography by Nicomedes Guzmán. Santiago: Empresa Editora Zig-Zag, 1962; 2d ed. 1970; 3d ed. 1971.
Antología de cuentos chilenos. Santiago: Editorial Nascimento, 1969. Posthumous.
Colección La Honda (Santiago: Editorial Cultura):
 1. Coloane, Francisco A. *Golfo de penas*. 1945.
 2. Norero, Raul. *Sinfonía en piedra*. 1945.
 3. Lomboy, Reinaldo. *Ventarrón*. 1945.
 4. Bahamonde, Mario. *Pampa volcada*. 1945.
 5. Castro Z., Oscar. *Comarca de jazmín*. 1945.
 6. Valenzuela Donoso, Guillermo. *Por el ancho camino del mar*. 1946.
 7. Drago, Gonzalo. *Una casa junto al río*. 1946.
 8. Donoso, Juan. *Tierra en celo*. 1946.
 9. Tangol, Nicasio. *Las bodas del grillo*. 1946.
 10. Castro, Baltazar. *Sewell*. 1946.
 11. Sabella, Andrés. *Sobre la Biblia un pan duro*. 1946.
 12. Elgueta Vallejos, Eduardo. *La noche y las palabras*. 1946.

Critical Appraisals of Nicomedes Guzmán

A[renas], B[raulio]. "El taller de escritores." *Atenea*, 394 (1961), pp. 133–37.

Belmar, Daniel. "Presencia de Nicomedes Guzmán." *El Siglo*, July 19, 1964.

Cabrera Leyva, Orlando. "Nicomedes Guzmán: 'Se nace escribiendo porque sí . . .'" *Zig-Zag* (Santiago), April 10, 1964, pp. 14–15.

Chapman, Arnold. "Perspectiva de la novela de la ciudad en Chile." In Arturo Torres-Ríoseco, ed., *La novela iberoamericana*. Albuquerque: University of New Mexico Press, 1952.

Cultura: Revista de educación, 96 (1964). Special number dedicated to Nicomedes Guzmán. Articles by Homero Bascuñán, Francisco Coloane, Edmundo Concha, Francisco Javier Fuentes, Julio César Jobet, Enrique Lafourcade, Ricardo A. Latcham, Carmen Muñoz, Luis Sánchez Latorre, Marcial Tamayo, Oscar Vásquez Salazar, and Fernando Duran V. "Impresiones," shorter notes or anecdotes, by Gonzalo Drago, Daniel Belmar, Orlando Cabrera Leyva, Mario Garfias, Baltazar Castro, Raúl Morales Alvarez, Irma Astorga. Four sections by Guzmán: "Algo de su autobiografía," "Plan de una novela: *Los trece meses del año*," an unpublished chapter from that novel, and an iconography of nineteen photographs.

[Díaz Arrieta, Hernán.] "Alone." "*Los hombres obscuros*." *El Mercurio* (Santiago), August 27, 1939.

———. "*La sangre y la esperanza*, novela, por Nicomedes Guzmán (Orbe)." *El Mercurio*, January 9, 1944.

———. *La luz viene del mar*, novela, por Nicomedes Guzmán (Aconcagua)." *El Mercurio*, March 9, 1952.

Drago, Gonzalo. "*La luz viene del mar*, de Nicomedes Guzmán." *Atenea*, 333 (March 1953).

Dyson, John P. "Los cuentos de Nicomedes Guzmán." *Atenea*, 404 (1964), 228–49.

Espinosa, Januario. "Nicomedes Guzmán y su libro *Los hombres obscuros*." *Atenea*, 172 (1939), 109–14.

Ferrero, Mario. "Cincuenta años y un día." *La Nación* (Santiago), July 11, 1965.

Goić, Cedomil. "*La luz viene del mar*, novela, por Nicomedes Guzmán." *Atenea*, 324 (June 1952), 536–38.

González Zenteno, Luis. "Nicomedes Guzmán, figura representativa de la generación del 38." *Atenea*, 392 (1961), 116–27.

Koenenkampf, Guillermo, "*Los hombres obscuros*." *Atenea*, 170 (August 1939), 337–39.

Latcham, Ricardo A. "Crónica literaria: Dos novelas santiaguinas, *Los hombres obscuros* por Nicomedes Guzmán, y *Muerte en el valle* por Bernardo Kordon . . ." *La Nación*, Sunday, April or July 25, 1943.

———. "Crónica literaria: *La sangre y la esperanza* (Barrio Mapocho)." *La Nación*, January 9, 1944. This review article was subsequently published in Latcham's *Doce ensayos* (Santiago, 1944). It has also appeared as the preface to every edition of *La sangre y la esperanza* beginning with the third.

————. "Crónica literaria: *Donde nace el alba,* por Nicomedes Guzmán." *La Nación,* Sunday, December [10], 1944.

————. "Crónica literaria: *La carne iluminada,* por Nicomedes Guzmán," *La Nación,* February 17, 1946.

————. "Nicomedes Guzmán," *La Nación,* July 5, 1964. Reprinted in its entirety (except for an error in the original which had given Guzmán's birthplace as Antofagasta) as "El escritor en su universo," *Cultura,* 96 (1964), 24–28.

Lomboy, Reinaldo. "El hombre y la palabra: Nicomedes Guzmán y el claroscuro," *Zig-Zag,* September 15, 1956.

Meléndez, Luis. "*La sangre y la esperanza,* novela de Nicomedes Guzmán." *El Mercurio,* February 23, 1944.

Melfi Demarco, Domingo. "Los libros: Dos novelas chilenas." *Atenea,* 170 (August 1939), 328–29.

[————.] "Alfa." "El viaje literario (De la cartera de apuntes de un crítico): Nicomedes Guzmán." *Atenea,* 223 (January 1944), 102–7.

Mondaca, Julio. "Nicomedes Guzmán, un escrito en la línea de la sangre." *Vistazo,* October 29, 1963.

Osses, Mario. "*La sangre y la esperanza,* de Nicomedes Guzmán," *Atenea,* 228–29 (June–July 1944), 319–23.

————. "Crítica literaria: *La luz viene del mar.*" *La Nación,* Sunday, July [3], 1953.

Plath, Oreste. "Quién es quién en la literatura chilena: Nicomedes Guzmán." *La Nación,* August 6, 1939.

Promis Ojeda, José. "El sentido de la existencia en *La sangre y la esperanza* de Nicomedes Guzmán," *Anales de la Universidad de Chile,* 145 (March 1968), 58–68.

Rossel, Milton. "*Hombres obscuros,* por Nicomedes Guzmán, Editorial Yunque, Santiago de Chile, 1939." *Atenea,* 180 (June 1940), 443–45.

S[ánchez] L[atorre], L[uis]. "Filebo." "Nicomaco." *Revista de los Sábados, Las Últimas Noticias,* June 26, 1971.

Santana, Francisco. "*La sangre y la esperanza,* por Nicomedes Guzmán, Editorial Orbe, Santiago, 1943." *Atenea,* 225 (March 1944), 282–86.

Silva Castro, Raúl. "Crónica de letras: *La sangre y la esperanza.*" *La Segunda de las Últimas Noticias,* January 17, 1944.

Tamayo, Marcial. "Nicomedes Guzmán y su herencia literaria," *El Siglo,* June 26, 1971.

Uriarte, Fernando. "*La sangre y la esperanza* (Orbe), por Nicomedes Guzmán." *Atenea,* 223 (1944), 90–92. The next page of *Atenea,* anonymous, entitled "Notas del mes," also includes comments on Guzmán's success.

Vásquez Salazar, Oscar. "Y me has dejado tu sangre y tu esperanza en mi hombro, Padre." *Cultura,* 96 (1964), 41.

————. "¡Así era mi padre! Aniversario de Nicomedes Guzmán," *El Siglo* (Santiago), June 26, 1966.

————. "La antigua calle Besa, Quinta Normal abajo y . . . 'Mi abuelo Nicomedes, el heladero ambulante.' " *El Siglo*, May 21, 1967.

————. "Niñez y adolescencia de un gran novelista." *El Siglo*, July 9, 1967; reprinted as "Niñez y adolescencia de Nicomedes Guzmán." *PLAN: Política Latinoamericana Nueva*, July 31, 1969.

Yankas, Lautaro. "Los libros: Dos libros chilenos." *Atenea*, 173 (November 1939), 242–48.

————. "*Donde nace el alba*, de Nicomedes Guzmán." *Atenea*, 238 (1945), 75–77.

Critical Appraisals of Nicomedes Guzmán and the Generation of 1938

Alegría Fernando. "Resolución de medio siglo." *Atenea*, 380–81 (1958), 141–48.

————. "Nuevos prosistas chilenos (Notas para integrar las generaciones de 40 y de 50)." *Asomante*, 16, No. 4 (1960), 20–26.

————. *Las fronteras del realismo: Literatura chilena del siglo XX.* Santiago: Empresa Editora Zig-Zag, 1962; 2d ed., 1967; 3d ed., 1970.

————. "Historia de un taller de escritores." *Nueva Narrativa Hispanoamericana*, 1 (1971), 7–16.

Atenea, 279–80 (1948), 1–574. A thousand copies of this anthology and collection of articles on the Chilean short story were printed separately under the title of *El cuento chileno* (Santiago: Editorial Nascimento, 1948).

————. 380–81 (April–September 1958). Special issue dedicated to the Encuentros de Escritores Chilenos. This volume includes photographs, biographies, essays, and poetry. Important articles by the following writers have not been listed separately: Braulio Arenas, Guillermo Atías, Paulo de Carvalho-Neto, Armando Cassígoli, Alfonso Echeverría, Mario Espinosa, Claudio Giaconi, Enrique Lafourcade, Herbert Müller, Mario Osses, Luis Oyarzún, Nicanor Parra, Gonzalo Rojas, Claudio Solar, David Stitchkin Branover, Volodia Teitelboim, and José Manuel Vergara.

Ferrero, Mario. "La prosa chilena del medio siglo." *Atenea*, 385 (July–September 1959), 97–124, and 386 (October–December 1959), 137–57.

Goić, Cedomil. "La novela chilena actual: Tendencias y generaciones." *Anales de la Universidad de Chile*, 119 (1960), 250–58. Reprinted in *Estudios de lengua y literatura como humanidades: Homenaje a Juan Uribe Echevarría*, pp. 37–45. Santiago: Universidad de Chile, 1960.

Guerrero, Leoncio. "La novela reciente en Chile." *Journal of Inter-American Studies*, 5 (January 1963), 379–95.

Lafourcade, Enrique. "La nueva literatura chilena," *Cuadernos Americanos*, 123 (1962), 229–56.

––––––. "Sobre el cuento y la literatura chilenos." In *Antología del cuento chileno*. Barcelona: Ediciones Acervo, 1969. Vol. I, pp. 24–39.

Latcham, Ricardo A. "New Currents in Chilean Fiction," *Americas*, 1 (October 1949), 39–41.

Lyon, Thomas Edgar, Jr. *Juan Godoy*. New York: Twayne Publishers, 1972.

Merino Reyes, Luis. "La generación del 38." *Portal* (Santiago), 3 (July 1966), 14.

Ramírez, Adolf. "The Chilean Novel of Social Protest." Ph.D. dissertation, University of Wisconsin, Madison, 1956.

Sánchez Latorre, Luis. *Los expedientes de Filebo*. Santiago: Empresa Editora Zig-Zag, 1965.

Santana, Francisco. "La nueva generación de cuentistas." *Atenea*, 279–80 (1948), 99–125, and 286 (1949), 62–92. Both articles were later incorporated into *La nueva generación de prosistas chilenos* (Santiago: Editorial Nascimento, 1949).

Serrano, Miguel. *Antología del verdadero cuento en Chile*. Santiago: Gutenberg, 1938.

––––––. *Ni por mar, ni por tierra . . . (Historia de una generación)*. Santiago: Editorial Nascimento, 1950.

Torres-Ríoseco, Arturo. "El nuevo estilo en la novela," *Revista Iberoamericana*, 3, No. 5 (1941), 75–83.

––––––. "Nuevas consideraciones sobre la novela chilena." *Papeles de Son Armandans*, 97 (April 1964), 7–16.

Uriarte, Fernando. "La novela chilena y la vida intrahistórica." *Atenea*, 389 (1960), 231–39.

Valenzuela, Víctor M. "A New Generation of Chilean Novelists and Short Story Writers." *Hispania*, 37 (1954), 440–42.

General References

Aaron, Daniel. *Writers on the Left*. New York: Avon Books, 1965.

Alegría, Fernando, "Una clasificación de la novela hispanoamericana contemporánea." In Arturo Torres-Ríoseco, ed., *La novela iberoamericana*, pp. 59–75. Albuquerque: University of New Mexico Press, 1952.

Bondy, François. "The Engaged and the Enraged," translated by Jean Steinberg. *Dissent*, 15 (1969), 49–58.

Booth, Wayne C. *The Rhetoric of Fiction*. Chicago: University of Chicago Press, 1961.

Brown, Edward James. *Russian Literature Since the Revolution*. London: Collier Books, 1969.

Carter, Paul J. *Waldo Frank*. New York: Twayne Publishers, 1967.

Castillo, Homero. *El criollismo en la novelística chilena: Huellas, modalidades y perfiles*. Mexico City: Ediciones de Andrea, 1962.

Dahlberg, Edward. *Bottom Dogs.* San Francisco: City Lights Books, 1961. Spanish translation, *Los perros de abajo* (Santiago: Ercilla, 1940).

Dahlström, Carl E. W. L. "The Analysis of Literary Situation," *PMLA*, 51 (1936), 872–89.

Ditsky, John M. "Faulkner's Carousel: Point of View in *As I Lay Dying*," *Laurel Review*, 10 (1970), 74–85.

Edwards Bello, Joaquín, *El roto.* Santiago: Editorial Nascimento, 1927.

Ellison, Herbert J. *History of Russia.* New York: Holt, Rinehart and Winston, 1964.

Empson, William. "Proletarian Literature." In *Some Versions of Pastoral,* pp. 3–23. New York: New Directions Paperbooks, 1968.

Farrell, James T. *Studs Lonigan,* Vol. I, *Young Lonigan.* New York: Signet Books, 1965. Spanish translation by Inés Cane Fontecilla, *El Chico Lonigan: Una niñez en las calles de Chicago* (Santiago: Ercilla, 1940).

Faulkner, William. *The Sound and the Fury* and *As I Lay Dying.* Modern Library. New York: Random House, 1946.

Fink, Georg. *Thirty-One Families Under Heaven,* trans. by Lillie G. Hummel. New York: Liveright Publishing Corp., 1931. Translation of *Mich Hungert* (Berlin: B. Cassirer, 1930). Spanish translation, *Tengo hambre* (Santiago: Ercilla, 1937).

Franco, Jean. *An Introduction to Spanish-American Literature.* Cambridge: Cambridge University Press, 1969.

Friedman, Norman. "Point of View in Fiction: The Development of a Critical Concept," *PMLA*, 70 (1955), 1160–84.

Frye, Northrop. *Anatomy of Criticism.* New York: Atheneum Publishers, 1967.

Godoy Gallardo, Eduardo. "Diálogo con Enrique Lafourcade," *Mundo Nuevo,* 54 (December 1970), 65–70.

Godoy, Juan. *Angurrientos. Novela.* Santiago: Editorial Nascimento, 1959.

Gold, Michael. *Jews Without Money.* New York: Avon Books, 1968.

González, Manuel Pedro. *Trayectoria de la novela en México.* Mexico City: Botas, 1951.

González Vera, José Santos. *Vidas mínimas. Novelas.* 7th ed. Santiago: Editorial Nascimento, 1970.

Hart, Henry, ed. *The American Writers' Congress.* New York: International Publishers, 1935.

Lafourcade, Enrique. *Antología del nuevo cuento chileno.* Santiago: Empresa Editora Zig-Zag, 1954.

Latcham, Ricardo A. "Perspectivas de la literatura hispanoamericana," *Atenea,* 380–81 (1958), 305–36.

Lukács, Georg. *Studies in European Realism.* New York: Grosset & Dunlap, 1964.

Melfi Demarco, Domingo. "Notas e imágenes del Congreso de Escritores," *Atenea,* 135 (September 1936), 321–58.

Mendilow, A[dam] A[braham]. *Time and the Novel.* New York: Humanities Press, 1965.

Meyerhoff, Hans. *Time in Literature*. Berkeley and Los Angeles: University of California Press, 1968.

Montes, Hugo, and Orlandi, Julio. *Historia y antología de la literatura chilena*. 7th ed. Santiago: Editorial del Pacífico, 1965.

Moretić, Yerko, and Orellana, Carlos. *El nuevo cuento realista chileno. Antología*. Santiago: Editorial Universitaria, 1962; includes Moretić's extensive essay, "El realismo y el relato chileno," pp. 13–81.

Muir, Edwin. *The Structure of the Novel*. London: Hogarth Press, 1938. New York: Harcourt, Brace and World, 1970.

Neruda, Pablo. *El habitante y su esperanza*. In *Obras completas*. 2 vols. Buenos Aires: Losada, 1968.

Perrine, Laurence. *Structure, Sound and Sense*. New York: Harcourt, Brace and World, 1970.

Prado, Pedro. *Alsino*. Santiago: Editorial Nascimento, 1959.

Rideout, Walter B. *The Radical Novel in the United States: 1900–1954. Some Interrelations of Literature and Society*. New York: Hill and Wang, 1966.

Romberg, Bertil. *Studies in the Narrative Technique of the First-Person Novel*. Trans. by Michael Taylor and Harold H. Borland. Stockholm: Almqvist and Wiksell, 1962.

Romero, Alberto. *La viuda del conventillo*. Buenos Aires: Santiago Rueda, 1952.

———. *La mala estrella de Perucho González*. Santiago: Ercilla, 1935.

Salmon, Russell Owen. "The *Roto* in Chilean Prose Fiction." Ph.D. dissertation, Columbia University, 1969.

Sánchez, Luis Alberto. *Proceso y contenido de la novela hispanoamericana*. 2d ed. Madrid: Gredos, 1968.

Santamaría, Francisco J. *Diccionario general de americanismos*. 3 vols. México: Robredo, 1942.

Sepúlveda Leyton, Carlos. *Hijuna. Novela*. Linares, Chile: Editorial Ciencias y Artes, 1934. Santiago: Editora Austral, 1962 (uncensored edition).

———. *La fábrica*. Santiago: Ercilla, 1935.

———. *Camarada. Novela*. Santiago: Editorial Nascimento, 1938.

Shideler, Mary McDermott. "The Ways of the Images." In *The Theology of Romantic Love: A Study in the Writings of Charles Williams*, pp. 11–28. Grand Rapids, Mich.: William B. Eerdmans Publishing Co., 1966.

Silva Castro, Raúl. *Panorama literario de Chile*. Santiago: Editorial Universitaria, 1961.

Silva, Víctor Domingo. *Palomilla brava (Papelucho)*. Santiago: Editorial Nascimento, 1923.

———. *El cachorro*. Santiago: Editorial Nascimento, 1937.

[Siniavskii, Andrei Donatevich] "Abram Tertz." *On Socialist Realism*. Introduction by Czeslaw Milosz. Trans. by George Dennis. New York: Pantheon Books, 1960.

Stevenson, John Reese. *The Chilean Popular Front*. Philadelphia: University of Pennsylvania Press, 1942.

Thrall, William Flint, and Hibbard, Addison. *A Handbook to Literature*. New York: Odyssey Press, 1960.

Trotsky, Leon. *Literature and Revolution*. Ann Arbor: University of Michigan Press, 1960.

Uriarte, Fernando. "La novela proletaria en Chile." *Mapocho*, 4 (1965), 91–103.

Voz de América, 1 (May 1944).

Yankas, Lautaro. "Literatura chilena de contenido social," *Atenea*, 188 (1941), 114–32. Revised as *La literatura chilena de contenido social* (Cochamba, Bolivia: Imprenta Universitaria, 1953). Notes of a lecture given at the Universidad Mayor de San Simón.

Zamorano, Manuel. *Crimen y literatura*. Santiago: Universidad de Chile, 1967.

Index